WE BOTH READ™

Parent's Introduction

We Both Read Books are delightful stories which **both** a parent **and** a child can participate in reading aloud. Developed in conjunction with early reading specialists, the books invite parents to read the more sophisticated text on the left-hand pages, while children are encouraged to read the right-hand pages, which have been specially written for beginning readers. The parent's text is preceded by a "talking parent" icon: ; the children's text is preceded by a "talking child" icon: .

Educators know that nothing helps children learn to read more than by reading aloud with their parents. However, the concentration necessary for reading is often difficult for young children. That is why *We Both Read Books* offer short periods of reading by the child, alternating with periods of being read to by their parent. The result is a much more enjoyable and enriching experience for both!

Most of the words used in the child's text should be familiar to them. Others can easily be sounded out. An occasional difficult word will often be first introduced in the parent's text, distinguished with **bold lettering**. Pointing out these words, as you read them, will help familiarize them to your child. You may also find it helpful to read the entire book to your child the first time, then invite them to participate on the second reading.

We hope that both you and your children enjoy the *We Both Read Books* and that they will help start your children off on a lifetime of reading enjoyment!

We Both Read: The Frog Prince

––––––––––––––––––––––––––––––––––

We Both Read® is a trademark of Treasure Bay, Inc.

Published by Treasure Bay, Inc.
17 Parkgrove Drive
South San Francisco, CA 94080 USA

PRINTED IN SINGAPORE

Library of Congress Catalog Card Number: 97-62025

Hardcover ISBN: 1-891327-02-X
Paperback ISBN: 1-891327-29-1

FIRST EDITION

We Both Read® Books
Patent No. 5,957,693

Visit us online at:
www.webothread.com

WE BOTH READ ™

The
Frog Prince

Adapted by Sindy McKay

From the stories by the Brothers Grimm

Illustrated by George Ulrich

TREASURE BAY

Long ago in a distant land lived a young Princess who was so beautiful that the sun beamed whenever it saw her.

This it did despite her often yelling at it to "stop being so hot!" For while the Princess was usually very polite, she could sometimes be very demanding.

One day the King gave her a new ball.

It was a golden ball.

She loved the golden ball.

She played with the golden ball every day.

The Princess was usually very good — but not always.

So one warm afternoon, though she'd promised never to do it, the Princess took her golden ball and wandered into the nearby forest.

There she began to play, tossing her golden ball into the air and catching it in her **hand**.

The ball went up into the air.

The ball came down into her hand.

Up into the air. Down into her hand.

Over and over.

The **Princess** continued her game, enjoying herself immensely. Until suddenly … she missed.

Plunk! The ball fell to the ground.
Splash! It rolled into a nearby **spring**.
Glug! It sank into the cold, deep water.

The Princess ran to the spring.

She looked into the water.

She did not see her golden ball.

The golden ball was gone.

The Princess began to cry. Louder and louder she wailed, until the noise was truly remarkable!

Suddenly a raspy voice called out, "Excuse me, Princess. Is something wrong?"

The Princess looked. And there in the spring, with his thick **head** stretching out of the water and his spindly **arms** reaching over the rim, was a **Frog**.

The Princess jumped back.

She did not like big heads.

She did not like thin arms.

She did not like frogs.

"Did you lose your golden ball?" the Frog asked the distraught Princess.

The Princess nodded and mumbled through her tears, "Yes, I did."

The Frog stretched his neck even further out of the water and politely asked, "Would you like me to find it for you?"

The Princess still did not like frogs.

But maybe this frog was not so bad.

Maybe this frog could get her golden ball back.

"Can you really find my ball?" the Princess asked hopefully.

"I can indeed," the Frog replied. "But then would you do a favor for me?"

The Princess did not want to do **anything** for the slimy creature. But she did want her ball back and so she inquired, "What do you wish?"

To this the Frog replied:

"I want to play with you.

I want to eat with you.

I want to sleep on your pillow.

I want to be your friend."

The Princess was not at all interested in being **friends** with a Frog. But she did want her ball back. And so she promised to do whatever the Frog wished.

But to herself the Princess thought:

"A Frog does not play games.

A Frog eats bugs.

A Frog sleeps near the water.

A Frog could **never** be my friend."

The Frog was deliriously happy!

He could not know that, while a **promise** is a **promise**, *this* Princess sometimes made promises she did not keep.

So it was with a joyful heart that he dove back into the spring and disappeared.

Down, down, down he went.

Down to the bottom of the spring.

Up, up, up he came.

Up to the top again.

And the golden ball came up with him.

With a bounding leap, the Frog emerged from the spring and graciously dropped the ball at the feet of the Princess.

Thrilled to see her toy once more, she scooped it up and skipped away, never even thinking to thank the Frog.

And certainly never intending to be his friend.

The Frog told her to wait!

He told her to slow down!

He told her to stop!

But she would not.

So the sad Frog jumped back into the spring.

The next evening, while dining with the King, the Princess heard an odd noise — plitch, plotch, plitch, plotch.

Something was climbing up the palace stairs.

Reaching the top, the "something" called out in a raspy voice, "Excuse me, Princess! Please **open** the **door**! You promised to be my friend!"

The Princess did not want to open the door.

But her father wanted to see who was there.

So the Princess opened the door.

And who do you think was there?

The Frog.

Quickly the Princess slammed the door shut again, her heart beating loud and fast.

The King could see that she was frightened. "My child, what is it? A **giant** who wishes to carry you away? A **monster** who longs to eat you? A **goblin** anxious to keep you from your sleep?"

Breathlessly, the Princess replied:

 "It is not a giant.

It is not a monster.

It is not a goblin.

It is only a silly Frog."

The King was somewhat perplexed by the appearance of a Frog at the castle door.

So the Princess was obliged to explain how the Frog had retrieved her golden ball and how she, in exchange, had made him a promise.

And when the King demanded to know what kind of promise she had made, the Princess begrudgingly replied:

"I said I would let him be my friend.

I said I would let him eat with me.

I said I would let him sleep on my pillow.

But I will not!"

At this the King was quite dismayed! "You will not keep your promise, Daughter?"

The Princess firmly shook her head. "I will not keep my promise, Father."

The King gave his daughter a disapproving eye. "A promise is a promise. And this one you must keep."

So, with a sigh, the Princess opened the door and reluctantly allowed the Frog to hop in.

The Frog asked to sit with the Princess.

He asked to eat from her plate.

He asked to sleep on her pillow.

He asked to be her friend.

The Princess was filled with dread. How could she let the cold, clammy Frog sit beside her and eat from her plate with his big, sticky tongue?

How could she allow the damp, goggle-eyed creature to sleep upon her pillow tonight?

How could she ever let a Frog be her friend!?

She would not do it!

She could not do it!

This Frog would **never** be her friend!

But then her father sternly reminded her, "A promise is a promise. And this one you must keep."

The Princess pouted. But she knew her father was right.

So she let the Frog eat from her plate.

She let him sleep on her pillow.

The Frog was nice and polite.

But the Princess did not like it at all.

Early the next morning, when the dark was graying into daylight, the Princess heard the Frog jump down from her bed and hop away.

She hoped he would never come back again.

But he did come back, the very next night.

So again she let the Frog eat from her plate.

Again she let him sleep on her pillow.

Again the Frog was nice and polite.

And this time the Princess did not hate
it so much.

Early the next morning, when the dark was graying into daylight, the Princess again heard the Frog jump down from her bed and hop away.

She wondered if he would come back again.

He did come back, the very next night.

So again she let the Frog eat from her plate.

Again she let him sleep on her pillow.

Again the Frog was very nice and polite.

And this time she almost liked it.

Early the next morning, when the dark was graying into daylight, the Princess waited to hear the Frog jump down from her bed and hop away once more.

The Frog jumped down from her bed.

But this time the Frog did not hop away.

This time was different. This time was magic. For the moment his webbed feet touched the floor, the Frog was transformed into a handsome young Prince!

Now she was glad she had let the Frog eat from her plate.

She was glad she had let him sleep on her pillow.

She was glad the Frog was nice and polite.

She was glad she had kept her promise.

"Now will you be my friend?" said the Frog-turned-Prince.

At this the Princess laughed, and they both ran out to play with her golden ball.

The Frog Prince and the Princess became the best of friends. And they **promised** to marry someday and live happily ever after.

Which they did.

After all, a promise is a promise.

And this one the Princess was happy to keep.

**If you liked
The Frog Prince, here are two other
We Both Read™ Books you are sure to enjoy!**

In this delightfully funny retelling of the classic story, the emperor hires two tailors to make him an elegant new set of clothes. The tailors say the clothes are magical and that some people will think the clothes are invisible. Can you guess what happens when the emperor wears his new clothes?

FLIGHT FROM NATCHEZ

BY FRANK G. SLAUGHTER

Flight

From Natchez

DOUBLEDAY & COMPANY, INC.

GARDEN CITY, NEW YORK

With the exception of actual historical personages, the characters are entirely the product of the author's imagination and have no relation to any person in real life.

CONTENTS

28059

FLIGHT FROM NATCHEZ

Pensacola

Once again, John noted, the woman had entered the courtroom unattended. Moving as gracefully as a butterfly in a cave, she had settled in the midst of the rough, polyglot crowd, to listen attentively as the court-martial droned on.

He had felt her eyes brush his when she appeared, and sensed that there was more of pity than censure in the glance. He could hardly stare back. As an officer of His Britannic Majesty, on trial for theft before his peers, Surgeon Captain John Powers dared not turn away from the concerted glare of the seven-man court. Still, he could not quite resist the hope that she had come for his sake alone.

It was the third time he had glimpsed her. Each glimpse had been tantalizing, and brief to the point of frustration.

He had seen her first from the battlements of the fort, the day he had been confined to quarters pending his trial. Pacing out his rage on the terreplein, he had paused at a gunport when he heard the rumble of anchor chains in the harbor. He was in time to see her step into a longboat at the gangway of the merchant-man and glide toward Barrancas Wharf. The mere sight of that poised figure (shaded by a saucy parasol, and flanked by the dress coats of brother officers) had been enough to blunt the edge of his despair.

The second glimpse had come in court, when his trial was two days old. Like today, there had been time for only a glance before she moved beyond his line of vision—but he could have described her gown to the last flounce. The gleam of sunlight on her ash-blond hair (demurely parted, and gathered at her slender nuque) had been more real, at that instant, than Surgeon Captain Powers' hope of heaven.

So far, he had made no attempt to learn the stranger's name; he preferred to grant her that aura of mystery. Nor had he wondered if she was as lovely as she seemed; at the moment, he had more immediate concerns. But he was profoundly grateful for the flash of pity in the woman's eyes when she settled in her place today.

As lives went, John reflected, his had been harried enough; neither pity nor love had been among its attributes. Tom Paine, that firebrand of a five-year-old colonial rebellion, had written that these were times to try men's souls. The soul of Surgeon Captain John Powers had been tested for more years than he cared to number. It had been torn by divided loyalties, twisted by the strictures of a world John Powers had never made. . . . Always, he had seemed to fight his way toward salvation alone—and the guerdon had eluded him. Yet he felt friendless no longer. Incredible as it seemed, his loneliness had left him, now that this blond unknown was in the courtroom again.

He blessed her silently for that bit of magic, even as he reminded himself that only a madman would thank a woman he could not name—or hope that the thanks might be repeated in person. But then John Powers had always considered himself a trifle mad. Today was only the culmination of his madness.

2

With an effort of will, he forced his mind to return to the trial.

Captain Thaddeus Fanning had been summing up for the prosecution ever since the court had sat that morning; now he was about to launch into his peroration. Much as John disliked Fanning, he granted that the handsome young officer was conducting a workmanlike case.

Colonel Montfort, who sat by the geometrical center of the green felt table, had always proceeded by the book. The scarlet dress coats of the officers, with their vast gold froggings and cream-white revers, encased their wearers as stiffly as mail. Knee-length boots gleamed with high lights below thighs that seemed about to burst through doeskin tights. Wigs all but sparkled with fresh powder, a trifle dampened by the sweating, close-shaven scalps beneath. The most industrious batman in the world could not disguise the fact that the colonel's braid was a bit tarnished. The brass shell of the sword that lay before him was more green than yellow. But such tarnish had been come by honestly. So far, the regiment had had no chance to write its name in the annals of this hobbledehoy war. Until now, its tours of duty had centered in the West Indies.

Even today (John reflected, as Fanning's well-modulated voice boomed on) their position in history was remote indeed from the vanguard. This fort in Pensacola, a grubby seaport town in the province of West Florida, was but an isolated command post, separated by a vast wilderness from the Atlantic seaboard, where the self-styled American revolt was now in full cry. True, there was an excellent chance that Montfort's men would soon smell powder —now that Spain had permitted her overseas garrisons to take a cautious hand. A force from New Orleans had already occupied Mobile, and it was rumored that Pensacola itself would soon be under siege. For all these rumbles on the horizon, it was hard to believe that the regiment would shake off its barracks fever. Or that the present court-martial, and the bitterness it had stirred, was more than a fantastic dream, from which its victim would soon waken.

John stole a glance at his counsel, and received a nervous grin in return, before Lieutenant Andrew Merrick's eyes returned to the notes he was amassing. The choice of Andy as a lawyer for the defense had fitted the situation neatly. John and Andy were the only two colonials in this very British regiment—and they would be regarded as colonials until the last trump.

Andy was a Scotch Loyalist from the Carolinas, John was a Philadelphian. Both could claim pedigrees as pure as their colonel's. Both had joined the colors in England; by all the rules, they were entitled to equal footing on the iron parade ground of tradition. Yet their brother officers had accepted them only to a point. Toleration had been all they could hope for—and that hope had gone glimmering, once the scandal of the paymaster's cashbox had broken.

Andy had labored mightily in John's behalf; but they had both soon realized that this trial was only a formality, conducted before closed minds. Now, as Captain Fanning warmed to his final argument, he made no attempt to conceal his certainty of the predetermined guilt of the accused.

"And in conclusion, gentlemen of the court, I submit that but one decision may be handed down——"

John felt his jaw harden, more at the manner than the words. The fact that Fanning had been chosen as his prosecutor was the crowning irony.

It was well known in the regiment that they were enemies— both at the card table, and in the backstairs amours at the Royal George which served to relieve the tedium of garrison duty. If John had outwitted the dashing (but somewhat dull-witted) captain in both fields, he could not reproach himself. A dozen others had beaten Fanning at piquet, or outbid him for the favors of Sally and Inez, the two serving wenches at the inn. Why, when he had only followed an accepted pattern, had he stirred Fanning's hatred so deeply? Was it because a mere colonial (or an American, as the term was now used) had dared to best an Englishman at gambling and love?

"You have no choice, gentlemen of the court," said Fanning. "You must accept the charge as proven—that Surgeon Captain John Powers did betray the trust placed in him by his commanding officer and His Majesty, the King. The facts have proved, beyond a doubt, that the said surgeon captain, in his position as paymaster, did take, purloin, and use for his own purposes sums entrusted to his care——"

There was more, but John had heard it many times before. He looked up only when the prosecutor clicked his heels in a smart salute to the court and sat down at his table. A low murmur rose from the spectators' benches—a sound that Montfort gaveled into silence with a single blow of his knuckles.

No word had been said of the defense Andy had offered in John's behalf; Fanning had evidently considered it too puny to deserve a rebuttal. For his own part, John was sure that his case had been impaired by his statement, under oath, that the money had been taken by his assistant—one Lieutenant Innes, a wastrel who was sober only on parade, yet seemed always in funds. More than once, he had been on the point of filing a complaint—but he had not wished to brand Innes until he could trap the man red-handed. Unfortunately, he had still been without proof a week ago, when the young rakehell had died under the hoofs of his own horse, when returning from a drinking bout in town.

No one but Innes could have borrowed so lavishly from the cashbox. But it had been a mistake to accuse the dead: by one of those strange quirks of fate, the boy had been one of the most popular officers in his mess. Fanning had made this part of his attack. When he had finished his skillful word picture, John had emerged as a scoundrel heartless enough to transfer his own guilt to one who could no longer defend himself.

Silence continued to press down on the room while Montfort conferred with the judges. John used the interval to study each of his inquisitors in turn, and read nothing but his own doom in the stony faces before him. Only one of those seven chairs held a glimmer of hope. The man who occupied it would have caught the eye at any gathering, even had his garb been identical with the lobster-red coats around him.

This judge was none other than Alexander McGillivray, often called the king of the Creek nation (though he held no patent of royalty), and one of Britain's stanchest allies. During the trial, John had studiously avoided McGillivray's eyes. If he stared at him now, it was only to gather what crumbs of courage he could. The man had been his friend in the past: he could not believe that he shared the others' desire to brand him guilty.

McGillivray wore snow-white buckskins today; the bandoliers that crossed his breast were heavy with new-minted bullets, and a hunting knife with a jeweled hilt hung between them. The hat that lay on the table in lieu of the usual sword or pistol was plumed with ibis and egret feathers. McGillivray's swarthy profile (handsome as some copper medallion) and his coal-black hair advertised his mixed blood: his father had been a Scotch pioneer, his mother the famous French-Indian beauty, Sehoy Marchand.

It was a commanding visage, John reflected, the face of a born leader. Since rebellion had rumbled into war on the Atlantic seaboard, McGillivray had steered his people on the rocky path of neutrality—between the Georgians to the east, the Spaniards in New Orleans, to say nothing of Loyalist pressures in the Floridas. Technically, the Creek nation owed allegiance to England; McGillivray himself was said to be an ardent monarchist. But he had managed the fortunes of the Creeks so shrewdly the horrors of war had scarcely touched them. That he had kept the respect of three governments in that process was his crowning achievement.

All this John knew only by hearsay. But the Creek leader had honored him with personal attention on his frequent visits to Pensacola: he felt sure that McGillivray respected him, both as a doctor and a man. He did not let his mind venture beyond that established fact as the court rose with Montfort.

On their feet, with swords under arm, these representatives of Britain's glory seemed even more majestic; with the simple gesture of rising, the colonel had assumed authority, as naturally as Caesar himself might have tossed the royal purple across a shoulder. The silence in the court was convincing evidence that the authority was still absolute; it seemed treasonable to admit (even in one's secret thoughts) that such power might be snuffed out tomorrow, so far as West Florida was concerned. Or to reflect that events were moving fast in these early months of 1781—that what had begun as a ridiculous, even slightly impertinent, attempt at secession here in North America was now a full-fledged conflict, involving traditional European rivals as well as rebellious colonials.

John just escaped smiling at his vagrant fancies. It was quite in character that he should be debating the imponderables of world politics at this time. Of all Montfort's officers, only he would dare to admit that the British flag might dip in surrender.

There was a sharp click, as the colonel adjusted the buckle of his saber. "This court," he said, "will now retire to reach its verdict."

No one stirred in the crowded benches as the judges filed from the room. This, to John, was the most damning cut so far: even the spectators (dazed though they were by Fanning's rocket bursts of rhetoric) seemed convinced that the verdict was already determined. When he turned at last to survey the courtroom, he saw that the lady of mystery had vanished by the side entrance —and he felt a cold hand compress his heart.

Like the others, this woman without a name, this presence that had made the whole farce bearable, had anticipated the finale. At least she had withdrawn in time, rather than witness his humiliation.

3

Side by side, Surgeon Captain Powers and his counsel paced the parade ground; across the way, Captain Thaddeus Fanning patrolled the terreplein in lonely grandeur while the recess lasted. If their brother officers ignored them at this moment, John was glad to observe that Fanning was also shunned. The pros-

ecutor had never been a favorite, and his furies in defeat were a
standing joke in the regiment.

"I could do with a drink," said Andy Merrick.

John kept his grin, though it was already hurting his lips. "So
could I," he said. "It would hardly be proper to drink the King's
health, while his court-martial is deciding to convict me."

"How often have I advised you to let the court make up its
own mind?"

"Only it hasn't a mind, Andy—if you count out McGillivray. All
it's doing right now is rearranging its prejudices."

"You needn't be so gloomy about it," muttered Andy—who
looked much the more downcast of the two.

"I'm not gloomy in the least. Shall I prove it by having a word
with Fanning?"

"Speaking of propriety, John——"

"Damnation to propriety. I've sweated in that courtroom. Why
shouldn't he sweat a little now?"

"Fanning hasn't sweated in his life," said Andy. "He has vinegar
in his veins."

"Perhaps I'll find his boiling point today." John was moving toward the parapet before he finished speaking. It was the first sense
of release he had known in days, and he made the most of it. He
could even enjoy the stares that followed him while he charged
down upon his enemy.

They were alone on the parapet; the sentries patrolling the catwalk were beyond earshot. Now that they were face to face, John
admitted he had chosen the moment of collision deliberately. His
encounters with Fanning had always been public; invariably, the
London-bred officer had drawn the mantle of caste about him and
refused to cross swords, verbal or otherwise. Today, John could not
keep down a bitter grimace as Fanning lifted his arm, as though
to ward off an unclean presence.

"A word, if you please, Fanning?"

"You've had your word in court."

"This is a personal question. When did you first decide to convict me?"

"You've heard the evidence, Powers."

"The evidence—not the truth."

"You should have told it, sir."

"I confess to no crime I've not committed. You and Innes were cronies. Perhaps I should have called *you* as a witness."

But Fanning had recovered his glacial poise, now that he had placed a carronade between them. His close-set, rather beady eyes were fixed firmly upon John. Only a slight flush betrayed his anger.

"Say what you mean, man."

"We all know your passion for cards. Surely you've observed that Innes enjoyed gambling—especially in his cups?"

"Are you accusing me of cheating?"

"I'm stating a fact you must have recognized, each time you sat down at piquet. A two-handed game—which you always played without witnesses."

"I'll hear no underhand accusation, Powers."

John placed one foot across the carronade. He held his ground as the color mounted from Fanning's collar, until his jowls seemed red as his tunic. "For the past month, you've rented a special room at the George: Sally told me as much, the day Innes died. Do you deny that you won large sums there? More than the seventy pounds missing from the cashbox?"

"You'll retract those words, sir!"

"Not until you've answered. If Innes were alive, he'd bear me out."

"Wasn't it enough to accuse the dead in court?" Fanning's ferret-like eyes were darting wildly now. "Would you seek to drag me down as well?"

"All I ask is the truth," said John. "I can see it's too late for evidence."

"I've nothing more to say."

"Then I'll take silence as my answer." Now that he had read

the guilt in Fanning's face, John felt only a vast weariness. The fact he had been used as a scapegoat could never be proved. If he meant to revenge himself, he would need more direct means.

"Let me pass, sir!"

"Willingly. But it's a poor revenge you're taking." With a thin smile, John drew aside. It was quite like Fanning to avoid physical contact to the end.

Andy was beside him now. Together, they watched the irate prosecutor stalk down the catwalk.

"You've stung him badly, John," said the counsel for the defense. "What goad did you use?"

"Something our friend Fanning has never faced—the truth about himself."

Andy gave a low whistle, when John had repeated the gist of his accusation. "Shall we move for a mistrial?"

"How can we? Either Sally or Inez would swear that Fanning and Innes were cronies, but that proves nothing. The man's a scoundrel, and he deserves a scoundrel's punishment. I'll see he gets it—when I'm out of this uniform."

"What do you propose, John?"

"Let Montfort pass sentence. We can't stop that. I'll take my revenge later."

"Fanning will never meet you on the field."

"I'm talking of fists, not swords. It's true I'm city-born, but I've seen frontier service. I can use mine well enough to give him a souvenir of this business."

"Just so long as you don't take an eye," said Andy. "It's some time since we've had a gouging on the post."

"This meeting won't be on post. Will you help arrange it?"

"Gladly, John. If you like, I'll call him out myself."

"That won't be necessary. When this courtroom farce is over, I'm moving on to the west——" John paused in some astonishment, as he heard his voice form a plan of sorts. So far, he had not dared to think beyond the trial.

"Montfort may still acquit you."

"I'll be in buckskins tomorrow: you know that as well as I. The moment I'm a free agent, I intend to force a meeting. A room in the Royal George will do."

"Fanning will refuse to come."

"Not if Inez sends him a note. He's been panting for a rendez-vous."

"You mean to thrash him there?"

"As thoroughly as possible. Will you see that the note is delivered?"

"You needn't use a note," said Andy. "Fanning dines at the inn with his sister. Inez can invite him upstairs herself."

"Did you say his *sister?*"

John listened in silence as Andy spoke of the lady who had arrived two days ago, via a ship from East Florida. Her visit would be brief, since she was soon returning to her husband. In fact, she was now awaiting the arrival of a neutral vessel to transport her. . . . For the moment, he was too numbed to curse his romantic vision, or to wonder how he could have strayed into so grotesque an error. In a community like Pensacola, it was impossible to doubt that the blond beauty who had arrived at Barrancas Wharf and Fanning's blood relative were one and the same. Naturally, she had attended court to hear her brother present his case.

"Why should she visit him in this God-forsaken corner?"

Andy shrugged. "Women have always had bad taste in men. Apparently, she's fond of her brother."

"Is the affection returned?"

"So it seems," said the other. "Not that we've heard much at mess. Fanning has kept the lady a mystery."

John turned with a sigh of relief as a sergeant major saluted from the catwalk. "If you'll follow me, gentlemen——?"

"Is the verdict in?"

"The court is sitting now."

John heard his fate with all the poise of a marionette. Guilty as charged, he knew he would be brought before his regiment at tomorrow's dress parade; his commission would be publicly destroyed while he was stripped of all rank and insignia, and he would be ordered to leave Pensacola forthwith, never to show his face there again under penalty of imprisonment. The sentence was lighter than the offense warranted: he suspected clemency on Montfort's part, toward an officer whose record was otherwise excellent. Now that it had been pronounced, he felt no new emotion, beyond a sense of relief.

It shocked him to discover that he could recall the woman about whom he had built a card castle of dreams with no feeling whatever. The fact that she was Fanning's sister was established when she took the prosecutor's arm outside the council hall. With a set smile, he watched them cross the parade together. *As romances go*, he thought, *mine is among the shortest in the records.*

And then—despite the emptiness of his heart—he felt a belated pang. It was a crushing discovery that Fanning's sister, like Fanning himself, must now be numbered among his enemies.

4

Late the next afternoon, standing at the window of the barracks room he shared with Andy Merrick, John looked down at that same parade ground with the same fixed smile.

On the table between the two camp beds, Andy's chronometer hung on the stroke of five: in a few moments more, the regiment would be forming ranks on that sun-bitten field. Already, John could hear the stamp of booted feet on Officers' Row, the twang of ramrods in the soldiers' cabins as anxious recruits made sure that muskets would be clean and shining against a possible inspection. Judged by any angle, he reflected, this was a crisis in his career. He should be trembling with rage, while his mind seethed with plots for retribution. . . . Actually, he continued to feel nothing, beyond that persistent, dull relief.

He could even rejoice (in the same muted fashion) that his

mother was two years dead, and unable to hear of his disgrace. His father (who had joined Howe in the first months of the rebellion and had fallen at Bunker Hill) would never add his note of mild but biting censure.

It was curious that he could hardly believe those two parents had once existed: try as he might, he could no longer summon a coherent picture of their years together. They seemed more remote today than the ghostly company they had joined—as unreal as his two younger brothers, who were serving at this moment under Marion, in the fens of Carolina.

These, of course, were facts he had never shared with Andy Merrick. He was sure that the apostasy of Clint and Ted Powers had hastened their mother's demise. By the same token, two shining facts had sustained Martha Powers in the early years of the rebellion—the hero's death of her husband, and the news, however sparse, of an eldest son who was serving in a British regiment of the line.

John had given her such comfort as he could—writing from the various fever holes of the Indies where Montfort and his men had chafed in barracks, knowing that few if any of his letters would reach Philadelphia. Even then, her world was crumbling fast, though he continued to picture it in its heyday—a squarish, red-brick mansion in Germantown, a solid advertisement that the folk who dwelt behind those shutters bore a name more ancient than Philadelphia's founder. . . . Sometimes he wondered how much of those walls was still standing. Or if such rubble could be fused into another shape tomorrow—a pattern that Martha Powers and her husband had never visioned, even in nightmares.

Surgeon Captain Powers studied himself briefly in the cheval glass, the only item of luxury these rude quarters afforded. His dress uniform was beyond reproach today: the face above that tight red tunic was impassive enough. He could only pray that the revealing flush of anger would not rise to spoil the performance he would soon be giving. Whatever their faults, the men of the

Powers clan had always taken the blows of fate without flinching. . . .

The family had come to Philadelphia when John's grandfather (who was also a doctor) had moved north from Virginia. It was a tradition that the eldest son should study abroad. Since young John had shown an aptitude with mortar and pestle (demonstrating, at the age of twelve, that he could set a broken bone), it was decided that he should prepare for an army career, after medical studies in Edinburgh.

True, his brothers had lured him from his grandfather's consulting room more than once in those early days, to go adventuring with the Rangers. When Ted was barely fifteen, the three of them had voyaged down the Ohio by flatboat to risk their lives in the Kentucky wilds. Looking back on those excursions now, John realized that his mother had suffered exquisitely at his absence. Being a lady, she had suffered in silence, convinced that the destiny of her eldest was written in the stars.

When he had visited the backlands of West Florida with a Creek brave as his guide—or enjoyed a short furlough in the duck-haunted sloughs of Santa Rosa—John had recalled those adventures as the time when his manhood had been forged. His picture of those lush Edens was greener than his memories of Scotland, or the year he had spent in London. As dream pictures went, they were clear enough to this day—bivouacs in cathedral-like glades deep in the virgin forest, the spine-tingling moment when he had nested in a tree above a chocolate-dark stream while a war party (naked as so many copper Adams) had ghosted beneath in a dugout. . . . Such memories were a special torment now. Though he reveled in them, they had made the walls of the present seem higher than ever, the taboos of military life that much harder to endure.

Now that he was escaping at last, he realized that a career in the British Army (a prize most young men would have seized avidly) was not for him. He would have remained a misfit to the end, even without the present scandal. It would be a blessed release to don those well-worn buckskins and follow another wilderness trail. Yet how could a man return to his first youth, with no tree blazes to guide his steps, and no real goal in mind?

Thanks to his father's wealth, and the friends who had opened doors in London, it had been easy to purchase his commission. No one had anticipated the fact that he would join his regiment the same year a group of patriots met in Philadelphia to make their treason official. Or that the life of a military surgeon could insulate him from civilian concerns, as completely as though he inhabited another universe. Only a tenuous family tie remained when he heard the news of his father's death. The last strand that linked him to that red-brick mansion in Philadelphia had been severed when he learned that his brothers had chosen the other side.

The news that the mansion itself had been burned by a looting mob, intent on revenge against Loyalist families after the British withdrawal from Pennsylvania, had been only a logical anticlimax. John Powers had long since resigned himself to the fact that he was an orphan in a world he had never chosen.

Now that his banishment from that world was certain, he was facing the future without a definite plan—beyond the punishment he would soon be inflicting on one Thaddeus Fanning. Even that thrashing, for which his fists had itched since yesterday, seemed a trifle absurd at this moment—the impetuous act of the youth he had long outgrown.

With something like relief, he turned from the window at the sound of feet on the stair.

"Come in, Sergeant. I'm quite ready."

But it was not Sergeant Simmons who waited in the corridor. Instead, John found himself facing Chris Martin, a Pensacola sutler who was a familiar at the fort—where his reputation for sharp dealing was matched by his generosity in such contraband as Cuban rum and other items that have always solaced bachelors in barracks. John had distrusted Chris from their first meeting. Yet, as was inevitable in army life, they had become intimates of a sort.

"I haven't much time, Chris," he said shortly.

"We've five minutes, Doc. Simmons isn't even on parade."

"What can I do for you?"

"Put it the other way. Can I do *you* any favors?" Chris bit the cork from the brandy, and poured himself a generous tot. As always, his eyes did not quite meet John's.

A broad-shouldered, leonine backwoodsman, Chris wore his homespuns with a certain dash: his dark hair shone with bear's grease, and his broad, moon-shaped face was handsome in a mongrel way. John had seen him break a man's jaw with a single blow; he knew that Chris Martin would knife a friend as casually as a competitor, if that friend threatened his prospects. In his way, the sutler was an epitome of a restless frontier town that was nominally an English garrison—though it had known the troops of France and Spain, and kept its own counsel in the shifting fortunes of war.

"At this late date," said John deliberately, "I can hardly believe I've something you can use."

"Easy, Doc," said Chris. "I happen to know you're friends with McGillivray—and they say he voted to acquit you at the trial. Could we strike a bargain on that?"

"What sort of bargain?"

The sutler's eyes went to the buckskins on the bed. "From the looks of things, your nose is pointed for Indian country. God knows McGillivray could use a good pill-pounder at Talassee."

It was not the first time that Chris had picked up rumors from upcountry ahead of the fort. Talassee was a Creek town on the Koosah, northwest of Pensacola. On some charts, it was listed as the capital of the nation. Was it possible that McGillivray intended to offer some white physician a post there, as doctor to the Indians?

"I haven't turned squaw man yet," said John.

"Suppose he does sign you on. Why can't you and I do business, same as before?"

The sly question brought Chris Martin's motive into focus. As one of the procurement officers for the garrison, John had dealt often at the sutler's store. It was natural that the connection would be continued, should he cast his lot with the Creeks; since his Indian trade had always been extensive, it was equally logical that Chris should hasten to establish a contact in advance.

"McGillivray's a stickler for rules," said Chris. "He'll stay clear, until you're out of that uniform. Mark my words, you won't leave Pensacola until he's made his offer."

"Have it your way," said John with a shrug. "I'd still refuse him."

"I could make it worth your while, if you'd act as my factor in Talassee."

"I'm sure you could. Probably we'd get rich together. I'd still advise you to clear out before the sergeant arrives. It wouldn't look well, to be found here with a guilty man."

"Who says you're guilty, Doc? *I* don't."

"You might have offered yourself as a character witness," said John dryly.

"Didn't I tell you to report Innes weeks ago? Didn't I say that Fanning would knife you, once he had his winnings?"

John could hardly deny the taunt. He remembered the whispered advice Chris had offered in the taproom—or across the counter of the untidy warehouse that served as his headquarters. At the time, he had disdained such interference.

"It's a bit late to argue over the verdict," he said.

"Much too late," said Chris, with a grin John had learned to suspect long ago. "Just the same, I'd like to see us partners."

"In crime?"

"Call it what you like, Doc. We could work together."

John's eyes were fixed on the window frame. Below him, the dust was rising in lazy spirals, a sign that Montfort's regiment had begun to wheel into position by companies. He saw that the gates of the fort had been flung wide to admit the citizens of Pensacola

—and that most of the town had taken advantage of the invitation. Life was dull enough here, and the pomp of the weekly dress parade made a welcome spot of color in the drabness. Today, of course, there was the added fillip of a cashiering to bring out the crowd.

"I think you've argued enough, Chris," he said—and was startled to find himself alone in the room when he turned. For a man with so huge a frame, the sutler could be light on his feet. Now that he had planted his message, he had lost no time in departing, a scant minute before the arrival of the guard.

For such an event as execution by hanging, the troops would have formed the traditional hollow square. Today, they were drawn up at parade rest, with a tight row of staffers in front, and Montfort himself, waiting like a scarlet silhouette of doom to the right of center. To approach this formidable grouping, the prisoner's guard was obliged to march past the main gate of the fort, where the townsfolk had gathered.

It was a situation that demanded decorum, but John could not avoid a quick glance at those faces. Many of them he knew by name, since he had cared for them in sickness during this tour of duty; he knew in advance that he would search in vain for a friendly glance. Then, with a little stir of anticipation, the group parted, and he found himself briefly face to face with the woman he now knew as Thaddeus Fanning's sister.

He had fully expected her to be present, and he made no attempt to mask a derisive smile as he stopped dead in the dust and raised his hand in a salute that was half mockery, half homage. She was all in white today, with a tiptilted straw bonnet and a parasol hardly large enough to shade a doll. For the first time, he saw that her eyes were a deep sea-blue, that her rich, full lips were made for laughter. Today, they seemed on the brink of speech as she sensed the meaning of his salute, and the distress in her face seemed genuine. That look of concern enraged him all the more. Somehow, he had expected her to meet his mockery with the icy glance of scorn.

"*Ave atque vale*," he murmured. "*Morituri te salutamus.*"

He moved on quickly before a bayonet could prick him into a resumption of his march. As he entered the parade, he roiled the dust deliberately. A moment ago, he had wished to go to his disgrace immaculate. Now, with those eyes upon him, he was strangely eager to begin his humiliation.

Colonel Montfort had witnessed the incident: his face seemed ready to burst into flame as the first command was barked.

"Prisoner, halt!"

John snapped to rigid attention, and met the commander's stare. A second order wheeled the guard into a swift about-face, leaving the culprit alone in the center of the parade. Montfort moved forward; a correct three steps behind him, Thaddeus Fanning, in the capacity of provost, bawled out the next command, snapping the whole regiment into a precise order arms.

Montfort had already drawn a paper from his sword belt. As the last gun butt slapped hard against the last British boot, he began to read, in measured tones.

"Surgeon Captain John Powers is, under an order dated this day, hereby removed from duty with this regiment. Having been convicted of a crime by a duly constituted court-martial, he no longer holds a commission as an officer in the armies of his King. He shall be bereft of all insignia of rank——"

The regimental drums had started their ominous rolling as the colonel proceeded. Now they began a furious crescendo, above which the next order was literally shouted.

"Captain Fanning, you will proceed!"

Fanning saluted his colonel and stalked forward. Thanks to his great, shaggy shako and his cliff-like epaulettes, he seemed larger than life as he stood eye to eye with John. There was a pause that seemed hours long, unbroken save for the mounting roll of the drums. Out of all the watchers, only John could read the hate in the provost's eyes, or catch the thin, sneering smile.

A white-gloved fist, knotting viciously in an epaulette, wrenched that emblem from John's shoulder, with enough force to rip the fabric beneath. The crown buttons of the tunic followed, one by one; next came the broad sash across the surgeon captain's chest. This Fanning claimed so violently that it seemed a mere silken fragment in his hand, as he knotted it into a ball and flung it contemptuously into John's face.

As a final act, the dress sword (already ripped from its sheath) was smashed down upon John's head so shrewdly that the blade snapped in two: the spectators at the gate, unaware that the steel had already been filed, gasped in genuine surprise. Unstirring beneath what he assumed to be the last assault, John held his ground as Fanning stepped backward. He had not noticed that the provost's orderly had broken ranks—until the soldier's boot, applied with numbing force to his backside, lifted him clear of the parade and dumped him in the dust at Fanning's feet.

Choking in the dirt, he was aware of a bray of laughter from the crowd. This, after all, was the last act in the age-old ritual of cashiering in the British Army. Seldom ordered in this enlightened age, the booting was entirely legal; only Fanning would have dared to use it at such a moment. Long before he could scramble to his feet, John realized that he had no possible recourse on the parade. It would be a different matter when he faced the provost at the Royal George.

Despite that impending revenge, he could not conquer the red burst of rage that lighted his brain: he watched his body brace itself, saw his fists cock as he started for Fanning, still calm as Jove in the dust. As he had expected, a pair of crossed bayonets barred his path.

The cursing died in his throat—and he came to attention for the last time. The final words of his sentence were still to be pronounced: Montfort's bellow rose above the penultimate roll of drums.

"It is further ordered that John Powers, if found within the limits of the town of Pensacola twenty-four hours from this moment, shall be arrested and punished accordingly——"

Montfort's voice seemed to trail off at the end, as though he had wearied of his task. It rose to its full volume as he addressed the provost.

"Captain Fanning, you may take command!"

The colonel stalked from the field without a backward glance; the troops wheeled into line of march when Fanning barked his order. The drums still rolled at fever pitch; the gates of the fort swung shut, forcing the spectators to give ground. In a few moments more, John Powers stood alone in his tattered uniform, steeped to the eyes in disgrace.

It was only when the dust had settled that he permitted his muscles to relax. But his chin was still high as he walked toward his quarters. Now that the pain of the ordeal had subsided, he felt only a cold contempt for Fanning. An hour ago, he had expected to leave the dress parade a ruined man. Now (for no reason he could name) he was quitting the British Army with a sense of release that just escaped elation.

So far, he had not the remotest idea of his goal, or of the steps he must take to achieve it. But he could not escape the conviction that the journey would be well worth making.

5

The bridal suite at the Royal George (as it was facetiously called) was actually no more than the upstairs parlor of the inn, plus a somewhat battered couch in an alcove. Since Pensacola had become a garrison town, it had served as a place of assignation for officers who could afford it—to say nothing of the favors of the ladies with whom they made rendezvous. That evening, as John Powers tossed his knapsack and rifle into a corner, he saw that Inez had already set the stage.

Hurricane lamps on the mantel cast a grateful light that softened the room's essential bareness. The wine cooler beside the round marble table (though it lacked ice in this subtropic climate) supplied an air of bogus elegance. John grinned broadly as he read the label of a superior Bordeaux: Fanning's love for high living had always been a regimental joke.

John had approached this meeting with care. Dressed for the trail, he had stabled his horse and slipped upstairs via the kitchen. At his urging, Inez had long since promised Fanning a few hours of her company in the bridal suite; it had been agreed that they should meet here, the moment he finished dinner with his sister, in the respectability of the inn parlor below. Inez, who had always rather disliked the captain, had entered the conspiracy with zest; only a moment ago, she had delivered the key of the suite to John, and accepted his sovereign and a goodbye kiss as her just reward. It had amused her greatly to know that Fanning would find two hard male fists awaiting him here, rather than the conquest he had pursued so ardently.

John's heart did not miss a beat as he paused to study his brand-new image in the mirror. It had been one of his mother's fondest beliefs that a gentleman never changes, regardless of garb or setting—but the tall, somewhat lanky figure with a powder horn at one armpit and an ancient palm-thatch hat aslant on one brow, seemed a backwoodsman in the manner born. Only the clean-shaven cheeks, and the ramrod-like alertness of those square shoulders betrayed the soldier-surgeon underneath. Perhaps the gentleman and the pioneer have more in common than most ladies think, he told himself, with another sidelong grin at his image. Perhaps it takes only a few whiskers and a little wood smoke to make the whole world kin.

He glanced over the room again, moved the marble table out of harm's way, and dimmed down the lamps until the whole slightly raffish parlor was deep in evening shadow. Fanning had paid well for this rendezvous. It seemed only fair to grant him a romantic snatch of chiaroscuro before his chin stopped the first blow.

Apparently he had set the stage with no time to spare. As he swung back to face the doorframe, he heard a step in the hallway, followed by a discreet tap on the door itself. Suppressing an impulse to mimic Inez's contralto Spanish, John flung the portal wide, taking care to use the door as a shield.

"Are you there, Dr. Powers?"

He closed the door softly as Fanning's sister entered. In the half-light, she seemed more phantom than woman.

"Am I interrupting a rendezvous, Doctor? This needn't take long."

He managed a bow of sorts. "I'm in no hurry—now."

"You don't know my name, of course——"

"I know you're Fanning's sister," he said bluntly. "I won't attempt to guess why you're here."

"I'm not quite sure I know myself," she said quietly—and permitted him to offer her the one armchair the room boasted.

Once he had seated her, John stood his ground. He made no effort to question her further; he had learned that it is best to hold one's tongue when a situation defies the give-and-take of ordinary discourse.

"My brother was called to the fort," she said. "Naturally, when I heard you were under the same roof——"

"Who told you I was here?"

"Have you forgotten that Inez serves as waitress?" Fanning's sister, John observed, had a smile as disarming as her candor. "It seemed a golden opportunity to—make your acquaintance."

"Perhaps it would be less trying if you introduced yourself."

"I'm Stella Wright. My husband is Dr. Evan Wright, a physician of Natchez."

"You're a long ways from home, Mrs. Wright."

"So are you, Dr. Powers."

"Perhaps I have no home at all. I might even be searching for one now."

"Would it surprise you if I confessed that I'm aware of that lack?"

"You'll find me difficult to surprise," he said.

"Perhaps I should also confess that I had a long talk with Lieutenant Merrick today."

This meeting, John told himself, was growing more bizarre by the moment. He had adjusted to the fact that Fanning (and a revenge that now seemed crude indeed) had escaped him. He could accept the intrusion of Fanning's sister—but the motive for that intrusion was still a mystery. If only to gain time, he brought both hurricane lamps to the table: with the light full upon her, he could study her at leisure, while remaining in the thick dusk that now filled the room.

"Andy Merrick is my friend," he said. "I trust he gave you a good report?"

"What he told me, Dr. Powers, was all I needed to convince me of your innocence." Stella Wright's eyes had strayed to the wine cooler, and her lips parted in a smile. "I can hardly blame you if you—celebrate your departure from Pensacola. And I won't intrude for long. But I felt I must tell you that, at least."

John found he was returning her smile with interest. The story that Inez had invented, it seemed, had been simplicity itself— once she had realized there was no chance of bagging Fanning.

"Perhaps I'm luckier than I know," said Stella Wright. "As Thad's sister, I could hardly seek you at the fort. The most I could do was attend the court-martial—and hope for a chance to speak when it was over."

"It's clear you want something," he said. "Will you give it a name?"

"Until yesterday, I wanted justice, though I saw it was a forlorn hope. Now I'd like to make what amends I can."

"I'm in no need of help, Mrs. Wright. Nor am I sure I want your pity."

"When you deserve it so deeply?"

"Does your brother know you're visiting me?"

"Of course he doesn't." Her hand closed briefly on his arm—and there was a pleading pressure in her finger tips that seemed as ardent as her words. Though he was fighting her with all his senses, John could not doubt her sincerity.

"I *had* to see you for a moment, Doctor. I couldn't let you go with this bitterness in your heart."

"Perhaps I'm not bitter at all. I may even welcome my release."

"You can't mean that. Not after what you suffered today."

"If a man's conscience is clear, he can endure a few kicks."

"What of your reputation?"

"I've no longer a family to disgrace. Only a pair of brothers who have disowned me, because I called myself a Loyalist."

"And are you a Loyalist still?"

The shades of the hurricane lamps kept John's face in shadow —which was perhaps as well, for the smile on his lips was hardly fit for a lady's eyes. "I was born and raised a subject of the King," he told her. "Why should I change, because justice miscarried?"

"Yet you're going west—to New Orleans."

"So I told Andy. To be honest, I've no real plans."

"You could be taken for a spy, before you got past Mobile."

"Not in these buckskins—and calling myself a citizen of the back country eager to see the world."

"How far do you intend to explore, Doctor?"

"As far as my wits will take me, Mrs. Wright."

"Would you think me quite mad if I offered you passage—at least as far as Natchez?"

"I'm not sure." Startled though he was, he kept his voice even. "Would you care to explain?"

Stella Wright had colored faintly, but her eyes did not waver. "I know I'm saying this badly—but I'll do my best to sound sane. For the past month, I've been in East Florida, settling land grants in my husband's name. I think I should tell you that he has a large practice in Natchez. The Wrights are an old family, Doctor. Our roots go deep."

"How does your husband's pedigree affect my prospects?"

"Be patient, Dr. Powers. You'll understand me in another moment." She spoke slowly now, with emphasis on every word. "Ours is a pioneer community, but we've a future ahead. A great future——"

"I'll grant you that. Why should I be part of it?"

Stella Wright ignored the interruption. "I needn't tell you that most of us are devoted to the English cause. My husband believes that victory will be ours, if we have the faith to persevere."

"Forgive me if I seem to contradict you again," said John. "But aren't you at the mercy of Spain at present?"

"Perhaps—and perhaps not. That will depend on events elsewhere. So far, the Spaniards occupy only a fort on the fringe of Natchez. They've made no effort to force their rule upon us."

What she had said, John reflected, was accurate enough. Bernardo de Gálvez, the able Governor of Louisiana, had not neglected his vulnerable position in New Orleans when he had begun his offensive in West Florida. Fort Panmure (the bastion of which Stella Wright had spoken) had been invested some time ago, to protect the river approach to the larger city downstream. But de Gálvez had respected the Loyalist sympathy of Natchez itself— and had wisely refrained from further moves which might incite the inhabitants to open revolt.

John continued to regard Stella narrowly, as these facts rushed helter-skelter through his mind. Already, he had begun to guess what lay behind her offer. "You've summed up the situation perfectly," he said. "What comes next?"

"Spain has played the coward's part in this war. I won't deny that de Gálvez can take Pensacola, if he wishes. But he can be defeated in the end, if Natchez stands firm against him."

"May I finish your story, Mrs. Wright?"

"If you like, Doctor."

"First of all, it was more than sisterly affection that brought you to Pensacola."

The wide blue eyes were unwavering. "I came here to ask help for Natchez. They can hardly send troops, with a siege impending. I'd have been content with a few trained officers. Even a single man——"

"Did you hope your brother would be that man?"

"Yes, I did."

"I gather he's refused you."

"The colonel can't spare him."

"May I ask why you conducted this recruiting instead of your husband?"

"His health has been poor of late: I was glad to come in his place. As I've said, most of us are loyal in Natchez." She had bent forward as she spoke: the ardor in her voice was so intense, he might well have misread it for another emotion. For that instant, at least, he had the absurd conviction that he had only to lean forward in turn to claim the full red lips with his own.

"So the story ends with me," he said. "Since you can't get an officer of the line, you'll settle for a cashiered pill-roller."

"That isn't true, Doctor."

"What would my first task be? To drill the Natchez Volunteers? Or to storm Fort Panmure?"

"How can you misjudge me so badly?"

"You still mean to use me. Can you deny it?"

"I came here tonight to ask you to become my husband's assistant. No more than that." Again, her fingers closed on his sleeve; she seemed to offer her whole heart with her pleading smile. "Heaven knows I don't expect you to win the battle for Natchez between you. My husband is no military strategist—but he's an excellent doctor. His practice is too large for a well man to handle. When England wins the war, it could be the start of a prosperous future."

"And what if England loses?"

"England *can't* lose, Dr. Powers."

"Does your husband know you planned to make this offer?"

"He asked me to bring home a doctor. He trusts my judgment."

"And how do you know I'm to be trusted?"

"I believe in your innocence. Now that we've met face to face, I think you're one of us. Will you prove I'm right?"

This time, when she offered her hand, he took it in his own and kissed it. "I'm honored by your confidence, Mrs. Wright," he said slowly. "But I must decline the offer."

"It'll be open tomorrow, if you change your mind."

"I'll remember that," he said. "For your own sake, isn't it high time you left this room?"

Stella Wright inclined her head gravely, then moved to the doorframe. "I sail in the morning for New Orleans," she said. "On the Danish ship that's unloading now at Barrancas Wharf."

"May I wish you a safe journey?"

"Governor de Gálvez would give us both a *laissez-passer*, if I introduced you as my husband's colleague."

"The prospect is enticing," he said. "But I must decline again. I've decided to see a bit of the world before I settle down. Understand me, that doesn't mean I won't appear on your doorstep in time."

She turned on that, so eagerly that he could have sworn she had rehearsed the move. "I don't think I've seen the last of you," she said.

"May I endorse that sentiment, Mrs. Wright?"

With only a cursory glance to make sure the hall was empty, she left the room; though it cost him an effort, he made no move to detain her. It was only when he was alone that he expelled his pent-up jubilation in a long whistle, and settled in the chair she had just vacated, to pour himself a glass of claret.

He could afford this moment of repose, he told himself—to say nothing of his satisfaction at his own restraint. Considering the fact that Stella Wright had burst into his ken without warning, he had handled himself well enough.

Now that she was gone, he could not question the purity of her motives; he could even admit that he had been touched by her words—to say nothing of her pity. At the same time, he could not put down the conviction that those full, red lips were his for the asking—if he accepted an offer that was still conveniently open.

Obviously, he had been wise to decline that offer tonight; he would need time while he plotted ways and means. Twirling the wineglass, he poured again from Captain Fanning's expensive bottle. In a little while, he would get to his feet, shoulder that long-barreled rifle, and begin his journey. It was good to loll here a moment more, while he considered that journey's end.

It was quite true that he had missed a chance to thrash Fanning tonight. A far more subtle revenge awaited him on the Mississippi.

6

An hour later, riding at a slow trot down the corduroy road that snaked through the outskirts of Pensacola, he noted a gleam of light at the shutter of Chris Martin's warehouse, and almost reined in at the sutler's porch. Then, recalling the reference Chris had made to Alexander McGillivray, he yielded to a second impulse and turned down a sandy path leading to the pine grove (perhaps a mile beyond the last house) where visiting Indians from the friendly tribes to the north had made camp for generations. The king of the Creeks, as McGillivray was often called, might hold a colonelcy in the British Army—but he camped with his people, and John was reasonably certain he would find him here tonight.

The hour was still early, and a number of cook fires burned before the high-stilted, palm-thatch huts that stood in a semicircle about the council ground; in the Gulf Coast region, the Indians favored these airy sleeping platforms above the conventional wattled lodge. It seemed quite natural to find McGillivray seated in the place of honor, brooding in solitary majesty upon the sweep of barrens to the east—where a huge lemon-yellow moon had just freed itself from a skein of cypress, to bathe the palmettos in cold radiance.

The Creek chieftain lifted one hand in the traditional gesture of peace. Tonight, he was wearing satin knee breeches, high-heeled shoes with silver buckles, and a claw-hammer coat brilliant with lace; the tricorne hat beside him and the evening dress wig might have come straight from London. Assuming that he had dined at the fort, it was quite like McGillivray to sit thus, permitting his subjects a discreet glimpse of the white world's splendors.

"Welcome, Dr. Powers. I was expecting you."

John mounted the platform and sat down facing his host. With a slight inclination of the head, he accepted a calabash, a replica of the monster pipe McGillivray himself was smoking. Tamping the bowl with Havana shag, he lit it from the pot of coals that stood between them, and took a few deep puffs. This, too, was part of the ritual when one visited the camp, even when the call was in no way ceremonial.

"Did you meet Charley on the road?"

John smiled to himself. Charley Emathla was the Creek king's sense-bearer to the Seminoles, whenever McGillivray found it necessary to hold council with that offshoot to his nation. Here in Pensacola, Charley's chief task was to keep track of braves who showed too great a fondness for the illegal strong waters dispensed at the rear entrance of the Royal George, or at Chris Martin's store. Thanks to his own training as a hunter, John had been aware of Charley's shadow on his trail, ever since he had quitted the fort.

"Did I miss a message, sir?"

"By no means. If you called here willingly, Charley was to do no more than follow. If you seemed about to leave Pensacola without seeing me, he was to request you to do so."

John nodded above the smoke from the calabash. As one white man to another, McGillivray might have requested an interview with a British officer freshly convicted of thievery. As head of the Creek nation, it was more seemly to wait—on the chance that same officer might pay his respects voluntarily. John was thankful now for the impulse that had caused him to enter the camp. He was in no mood for the persuasion of Charley Emathla's knife—even if the point did no more than prick his backbone.

"I dined with Colonel Montfort tonight," said McGillivray. "Various matters were discussed—including chances of survival when Governor de Gálvez drops his first cannon shot on Pensacola."

"You expect an attack?"

"I'm surprised it hasn't come sooner. If you ask my opinion, Doctor, you've left the British Army just in time."

Again, the two men puffed away for a moment of silence. Though he could guess the offer he was about to receive, John knew it must not be hastened.

"We also discussed your trial," said McGillivray. "You heard, didn't you, that I voted for your acquittal?"

"I hoped you had, sir."

"I might add that I was outnumbered six to one. The British are a clannish people. As a Scot, I understand them well enough; as a Creek, I can see their underside, as it were. Like the Indians, it is all-important that they walk with pride. Today, they needed a scapegoat and found one. It would never do to admit that one of their own kind was a common pilferer."

"Do you believe Innes guilty?"

"Of course he was guilty," said McGillivray calmly. "And I'm equally certain that Fanning fleeced him. It's something you'll never prove. I'd advise you to forget it."

"Would you forget, in my place?"

"I'd have cut out Fanning's heart and roasted it. You will only be signing your death warrant, if you take such revenge."

"Is that why you put Charley on my trail?"

"Yes, Doctor. He watched Fanning, too. If you showed signs of meeting, he had orders to step between."

"You can set your mind to rest on that point," said John. "I'm now on my way to Mobile."

"With the town in Spanish hands?"

"As you see, I'm no longer in uniform. They'll naturally call me an American."

"There's a certain chance they won't."

"I'm aware of that, sir. But I'm in the mood for travel."

McGillivray studied him for a while—so intently that John was sure he was reading his thoughts. "Revenge can take many forms," he said at last. "It's a poor compass to guide one's future."

"You may be right, sir."

"Would you consider coming north with me?"

"For what purpose?"

"My people have adopted many of the white man's ways, but they have no white physician. They would welcome you."

Three offers in a single day, thought John, are more than a reasonable man could expect. He had refused Chris Martin's by instinct; he had deferred Stella Wright's, until he could attack on that front with his own weapons. For an instant, he was tempted to accept McGillivray's.

In Talassee, he might find the peace that had escaped him so far. With patience, he might even forget the need to even the score with Fanning. But he put the temptation aside, with no real effort. His goal was still Natchez on the Mississippi—and the home of an unknown physician whom he proposed to cuckold thoroughly. He must approach that goal in his own fashion, with no outside commitments.

"I've business in Natchez," he said. "It can't wait."

The Creek king shrugged. Apparently, he had expected his suggestion to be rejected.

"Perhaps I am being presumptuous, Doctor. But isn't it necessary that you earn your bread?"

"Highly necessary, sir."

"You propose to seek your living as an American?"

"I'll not have much choice, while I'm in Spanish territory."

"But Natchez is still Loyalist."

"So I've been told."

"The people in that area intend to remain English in thought and deed. There's even talk of a separate peace, to hold the east bank of the river. In such an event, would you remember your oath to serve your King?"

John frowned behind the screen of tobacco smoke. McGillivray had put his finger on a problem that still tormented him, whenever he dared to face it squarely.

"To be honest," he said, "I hadn't thought that far."

"At least you can see both sides."

"I'm not sure I can see either clearly. By birth, I'm a colonial; by training, I'm English. My only home has been the British Army. Certainly I've no hankering to change sides. Yet I owe nothing to England. After today, I feel she's betrayed me."

"There are many in the colonies in your situation. Can you afford to remain neutral?"

"I can try."

"Neutrality is always an expensive luxury, Doctor. I've preserved mine, simply because I'm boxed in by the wilderness. Yet I can see your dilemma clearly. Don't forget I was educated in Charleston, in the heart of rebel country—yet I am a Tory by inclination. I could see the storm coming, years before it exploded. So could you—if you'd been allowed to stay at home."

McGillivray puffed for a long moment. "Not every revolution is a holy cause," he said. "It's hard to judge this one fairly, while it's still raging. Surely it's too soon to be positive it will succeed. If it does, there will be a thousand historians—and ten times that many spellbinders—ready to insist it was both just and inevitable."

"They may be right, sir."

"I disagree. There was nothing inevitable about the secession of thirteen colonies from their mother country. Nothing a little enlightened diplomacy couldn't have settled, to the benefit of all. The whole business was started—as most revolutions are—by hotheads with special axes to grind. The heroes took over later, when the breach was too wide to heal."

"Most thinking men would argue that point, sir."

"Give the poets time to work on it," said McGillivray. "Secession from lawful authority will become a crusade against despotism —but only if the secession is a complete success. Meanwhile, the bitterest enemies on this continent are not the Continentals and the redcoats. They are the King's men—and the men who would destroy the King's power here for all time. At the moment, the odds favor the destroyers. One rousing defeat would swing the balance to the King again."

"Do you hope for such an event?"

"My sentiments are on record," said the Creek chieftain. "Officially, I mean to remain neutral to the end. But I can't help feeling that this land could still know greatness under English rule."

"And I find it impossible to cheer either side," said John.

"If you truly wish to remain neutral, Dr. Powers, come with me."

"Perhaps I can pretend to belong to both camps, and join neither."

"Some men could play that part, and relish it. Take my word, it will end by destroying you."

John got to his feet. Again, he raised his right palm in the Indian gesture of peace. "Thank you for your offer, sir—and your advice. I must still go to Natchez, and play my part."

"Without even knowing how the curtain rings down on the play?"

"Isn't it sound dramatics to make the most of suspense?"

"It's your own life, Doctor. I won't advise you how to spend it. But if you wish my help in the future, I'll be at Talassee until the summer's end."

"I'll remember that, too, sir."

A moment later, wheeling his mount beside the council fire, John lifted his rifle to McGillivray in a final gesture of farewell. As he rode toward Mobile in the white bath of moonlight, he laughed softly at a joke all his own. It was strange that the king of the Creeks should now represent security—perhaps the only security he had ever known.

Mobile

Though he was familiar with most forms of dicing, craps was a new game to John. In Pensacola, he had played it at the Royal George, where it seemed well known among the natives. Tonight, as he flourished the dice above the felt-lined trough in another ordinary, he felt his heart lift with the gesture; tonight, it was John Powers against the whole world, and John was winning handily.

"Seven!"

"Seven it is, sir."

For the past quarter-hour, thanks to the rum he had downed, he had seemed to float a slight distance above the floor. He had not quite reached the point where a man is no longer accountable for his actions. Fifteen straight passes were something of a record: should he throw again? He felt his fingers close round the dice—and lifted his fist one more time, in another ritual salute to the gods of chance.

"Seven—eleven!"

"Eleven it is."

The shoal of gold and silver that lay before him was larger than his hands could scoop. He balanced the dice on his palm, looked round the circle of intent faces, and decided against another throw. Resigning his turn to the man on his left, he stalked from the game as abruptly as he had entered it.

His winnings tugged agreeably at his pockets when he moved to the bar and ordered another rum. Tonight, he told himself, it's the only medicine to blot out loneliness.

"Would you offer me a libation, sir—to console me for my losses?"

It was the same soft voice that had confirmed his points at the dice trough. Standing with an elbow on the bar, John studied the elderly dandy through eyes that still managed to focus.

"The pleasure is mine, sir. The name is John Tarbell. May I ask yours?"

"Beauvais, Mr. Tarbell. Henri Beauvais. Your servant."

The pewter noggins clinked as the two men continued to measure one another. Beauvais, John estimated, was as French as his name and his lisping, faintly melancholy accent. The white mane that fell to his shoulders was unpowdered and gathered in an eelskin. But the satin coat and the buff-colored stock were a striking contrast to the homespuns that filled the taproom of the Bird and Bottle, the most elegant caravanserai in Mobile.

"You are from this region, monsieur?"

"A visitor from abroad, by way of Havana," said Beauvais. "I'm booked for New Orleans tomorrow. Or rather, I *was* booked to sail —until we met." The Frenchman's shrug was a well-bred dismissal. "Now, I fear, I must set foot in the New World only to return."

"Were your losses that extensive?"

"It seems you are an amateur gambler, Mr. Tarbell. Just as I am a professional. It was I, and I alone, who covered your last eight throws."

John knew he was smiling no longer: the statement had been too abrupt for that. Clouded as they were by alcohol, his first impressions of Mobile were none too sharp. He could hardly permit this wiry adversary (who had come into his ken so abruptly) to assume an importance beyond his size.

"Count your winnings," said Beauvais. "You'll find they come to more than a hundred pounds—most of which was mine. Enough to finance my winter in New Orleans, before I return to Paris. Would you give me an even chance to get it back?"

"What are you suggesting?"

"I've a cabin on the *Hirondelle*. Anyone will tell you it's worth five pounds. I've also a room upstairs, for which I've already paid.

Will you cut me for both, against one of those ten-pound notes in your pocket?"

2

John sipped cautiously from his noggin, and continued to study the Frenchman with cautious eyes. So far, he reflected, his journey into the unknown had been much like tonight—a kaleidoscope where nothing stood out clearly, varied by a few lightning-sharp vignettes. If he hesitated now, it was only to assure himself that Henri Beauvais was real.

Memory brought back the first lap of that journey as he continued to ponder the gambler's dare—the bone-weary torture of a ride by moonlight, when each shadow on the Camino Real had seemed a Spanish patrol, and the screech of an owl in the next hammock had been a signal for that same patrol to close in upon another hapless traveler. He had slept until sundown in a palmetto thicket, resuming his journey only when darkness had fallen. Somehow, it was logical for a man whose name was in shadow to travel thus. . . . On the second day, when he saw that the track calling itself the King's Highway was unpoliced (and largely untraveled, save for solitary horsemen like himself, who showed the same eagerness to be left alone), he had pushed on, to reach his goal before daylight ended.

Mobile, when he entered it at last, had a nightmarish resemblance to the settlement he had just quitted. The old French fort was a brick rectangle, as compared to its star-shaped counterpart in Pensacola. Mobile Bay was larger, and alive with shipping—in itself, a bleak proof that the Spanish star was in the ascendant. But the same air of sleepy unconcern prevailed in the town itself. The raffish houses that lined the sandy streets might have been transported bodily from Pensacola, to the last whitewashed patio. The soldiers he met in the byways seemed part of that easy repose.

Did it matter that their uniforms were a dirty green-white instead of scarlet? Or that they spoke a guttural Latin tongue, instead of the cockney of the London stews?

Even the inn where he sold his horse had a surface kinship with the Royal George. Both were rambling structures, their taprooms roaring with games of chance and the explosions of male cursing. Both seemed to bustle upstairs and down with swirling petticoats. However, the Bird and Bottle—save for its public rooms—seemed more on the decorous side. It all but straddled the long, spider-legged dock that walked across the mudflats of the bay, permitting contact with the ships at anchor in blue water to the south.

John had chosen the inn for this reason, since he intended to invest part of his funds in a cabin to New Orleans. Now that he had come this far unmolested, it seemed vital to arrive at the Mississippi port in style—though it would have been quicker (and less costly) to take passage on one of the sloops that skimmed the back bayous, to approach the town from the east. Instinct had advised him to assume the disguise of an upcountry farmer for this stage of his journey. Once he was safely aboard a French merchantman, he could discard his pseudonym, and blossom into finery of another sort.

So far, he had made no attempt to implement these half-formed plans. He could not escape the fear that he was an object of suspicion, though he had been challenged just once—at the city's edge, by a sleepy sentry who had accepted both his Spanish accent and his shilling tip, and had waved him on his way. It was evident that the troops of de Gálvez (wary of Loyalist sentiment in the country behind Mobile) were making no real effort to police the town. Confident that Pensacola must surrender at the first real show of strength, they were holding Mobile on a live-and-let-live basis. The implied contempt in this attitude was chilling enough. Yet it was reassuring to discover that he was in no immediate danger of hanging as a spy.

At the Bird and Bottle, the boniface had advised him to repair to the ordinary for a while, on the chance that a room might be vacated later. Trade was roaring now that Mobile Bay was crowded with the freight of Mars. John had already marked the *Hirondelle* as his transport, if he could bribe his way aboard. He had looked forward to a bed, even if it was only a shared mattress under the rafters.

Now, prompt as some djinn from Araby, Henri Beauvais had appeared to offer the solution to his present problems, on the turn of a card.

The gambler's mask was benign as ever as he produced a brand-new deck, broke the seals, and fanned the cards across the bar. John could feel silence clamp down on the taproom: the argument (if one could call it that) had attracted the company's attention, almost to the last man. Staring arrogantly into the faces that had clustered about the bar, John slapped the rum-soaked planking, and called for another dram.

"Ten pounds for both, monsieur," he said in French.

Beauvais drew a paper from his coat sleeve. John read it through to the last word: fuddled though he was, he saw that this was an authentic receipt for passage, aboard the barkentine *Hirondelle*, to the river port of New Orleans. With a similar flourish, the gambler tossed a room key on the bar. John matched it with a ten-pound note—and held out his hand for the cards.

Common sense warned him that the deck was marked, though his surgeon's fingers could detect no pinpricks or other signs that might aid the Frenchman. At play, of course, it would have been folly to accept his adversary's cards. Here, with the deck face down on the bar, he was willing to match his tactile skill against the other's. After all (he told himself, with the drunkard's logic), he was risking a small sum on the cut. Better to lose that sum out of hand than to risk a brawl with this bantam—which might expose his identity to the Spanish commandant in Mobile.

"Ten pounds, against a night's lodging—and transport to the Mississippi," said Beauvais, in his odd, lisping English. He repeated the words in both French and Spanish, as his eyes swept the bar. "The wager is heard—and understood?"

The gambler chuckled, as a murmur of assent filled the room. John disliked that chuckle as much as his adversary—to say nothing of the fact that the sentiment in the taproom seemed on the side of the loser. Already, he could feel that there was something contrived in this meeting—an element of *diablerie* that went beyond mere chance.

"Will the winner cut first?"

"As you like," he said. His hand was clammy with sweat, but he forced them to steady as he split the deck, and exposed a six.

Beauvais accepted the deck with delicate fingers: his free hand thrust back the lace of one cuff, as though to demonstrate that he was relying on his luck, with no help from the sharper's arts. Certain that he would be overcut, John had pushed the cash toward his opponent when he heard a concerted sigh from the crowd. His vision cleared as the Frenchman, with a grimace, exposed a four.

"I trust you'll be half so lucky in love, monsieur," he said quietly.

"Will you cut again?"

"Thank you, no. Clearly, this is no time for me to tempt chance further."

"If I can help——"

The Frenchman squared his shoulders. "The fortunes of war, my friend. Since I am not quite destitute, I will take ship for Havana."

He was gone with that pronouncement, so quietly that John found himself staring blankly at the spot his opponent had just occupied at the bar. Now that it was over, he was certain that it had all happened much too quickly. Beauvais had forced the wager for some reason of his own. So far, John had no way of knowing who had really emerged the victor.

"Will you go to your room, sir?"

He found himself facing the innkeeper; he knew that he was staggering as he turned from the bar. Prudence dictated that he accept help on a stairway that had begun to heave beneath his feet. The eagerness of the man to remove a good customer from the taproom was another puzzling item. John tucked it away for resolution later.

The fact that he was being transported (so lightly that he seemed to fly rather than walk) to the first bedroom he had occupied in three nights was enough to soothe his senses. Drunk though he was, he was still in possession of his faculties. He could even remember to smooth out his cabin receipt, and study it solemnly, while his boniface turned the key in his bedroom lock.

"Sleep well, sir. The *Hirondelle* won't sail before noon."

John produced his best parade-ground scowl. "I always rise at six, and drink a cup of tea before breakfast."

"Tea, sir? I'm afraid that Tory drink's hard to come by in Mobile."

"Then look sharp, man. See it's sent up with my shaving water."

"As you wish, sir. Is there anything else you require?"

The question was put so artfully that John steadied a moment more in the doorway. "Thank you, no."

"Not even a nightshirt?"

"I sleep in my skin. Don't desert your guests. I'll manage nicely."

"I'm sure you will, sir," said the innkeeper, as he whisked down the stair.

The doorsill had receded alarmingly, John found, when he sought to cross it. He just escaped tripping when he pitched into the room, and stood swaying in the moonlight. Carefully he stepped from his boots and moved in stocking feet to bolt the door. His hands followed a familiar, drunken ritual thereafter—stripping off his long-skirted coat, rolling it into a tight ball, and placing it precisely in the center of the carpet to serve as his pillow. He had slept thus more than once, when the precise location of a bed had eluded him.

The breeze from Mobile Bay fell on his skin when he unlaced the waistband of his breeches. Just in time, he remembered the pistol, and settled on the carpet to examine the priming. The ladder of moonlight at the wide-open window bathed him in its radiance as his fingers (practiced even in this final stage of intoxication) assured him that the lock was dry and the charge rammed home.

He had located the bed at last—a huge four-poster in an alcove that resembled an argosy with furled sails, now that its curtains were drawn. For an instant, he half rose on hands and knees in a futile effort to reach it, knowing in advance that such an enterprise was too much for his spinning brain; though that argosy was his for the asking, it would never waft him to the safe harbor of repose.

He remembered to rest his head on the coat as his limbs relaxed on the carpet. One arm embraced the patch pocket that held his winnings: his right fist was closed firmly on the pistol butt. With no conscious sense of change, he plummeted into a slumber too deep for dreams.

3

The dreams came later, when the first promise of daylight invaded the room. For a space, his private world seemed dove-colored as the morning: the dream took fire only when the first splinter of sunlight broke against his eyelids.

He was reveling in Stella Wright's arms, in a sea of eiderdown. Rapture choked his throat in a strangled cry as the image faded —and he was staring wide awake, with his coat clutched in both arms. Every bone and sinew ached from the pressure of the floor boards beneath him; and yet, though his head was far from clear, he had endured worse morning afters.

While his mind fumbled for orientation, he stared resentfully at the bed that he had just missed reaching. A light tap sounded on the door while he was scrambling to his feet. He could have sworn that he saw the bed curtains stir, though the breeze from Mobile Bay had died, and the water beyond his window resembled a burnished copper mirror. Knuckling his eyes to remove the last trace of fog, he swayed gently toward sanity as the knock on the door repeated.

"Shavin' water outside, sir," drawled a back-country voice. "Will you take cawfee 'stead of tea?"

He shouted the slavey away and flung the bed curtains wide. Backed by a nest of pillows, the girl stared at him across the barrel of a cocked pistol—a girl whose russet hair was still tumbled by sleep, though her blazing green eyes were completely awake.

Despite that first shock of discovery, he had time to note details—the golden-brown arm thrust clear of the sheet bunched in her free hand, the nightshirt at the bed's foot, which told him that both he and the lady had slept in their pelts. John felt his fingers unlatch slowly, as he gave up all hope of reaching for the pistol in his waistband. The murder he read in the girl's eyes was real enough.

"What are you doing here?"

Like the voice in the hall, her tone held all the music of the South, without the drawl. A wildcat cornered in her lair could not have snarled more lustily.

"I might ask that same question," he said, blinking at her warily. "Last midnight, the landlord handed me the key himself."

"How could he? I've been here since sundown."

His hand, extended to grasp the bedpost, froze in mid-air when he saw her finger tighten under the trigger guard. "Last midnight, they assured me the chamber was empty."

"Go on," she said. "Just keep your distance—and tell me who you are."

"John Tarbell," he said, with an unsteady bow: he had no desire to take his eyes from that gun barrel. "To whom should I apologize for this intrusion?"

"The name is Gordon," she said. "*Miss* Faith Gordon. Are you asking me to believe a landlord would rent a room twice?"

"It's been done before, I'm afraid," he said. "At least I didn't spoil your rest."

He could have sworn that a smile softened her lips momentarily.

Like the full oval of her face, they needed no rouge pot to bring out their savor. He wondered if this auburn beauty could be one of the coast Creoles, nested here for an unmistakable purpose. Then he realized that those cheeks (like the strong young arm that held the sheet) were as deep-tanned as his own skin. Faith Gordon, whatever her virtues, was simply a back-country girl; her outdoor complexion (so frowned on by the fashion of the time) had been earned in the open fields.

"How long have you been here, Mr. Tarbell?"

"Since last midnight, as I said."

"Where did you sleep?"

"Where I belonged. At your feet."

"When you'd paid in advance for this bed?"

"It's fantastic, I'll admit. But it's quite true."

John launched into an account of his encounter at the dice board and his wager with Beauvais. With no attempt to minimize the aftermath of last night's potations, he explained just how he had invaded the room. She heard him in silence: he could read nothing but simple interest in her eyes.

"Henri Beauvais is my uncle," she said. "I hardly think he'd wager my bedchamber against a ten-pound note."

"Nor do I, now I've visited it."

"Never mind the compliments, Mr. Tarbell. Will you swear on the Book that you've told me the truth?"

"How else would I be standing here?"

Faith Gordon lowered the derringer at last, and used both hands to gather the sheet about her nudity. "Fantastic is the exact word for your story," she said, "but I'll accept it. What comes next?"

John shrugged: though he was still groping, he could sense a pattern in this adventure. "We can hardly ask your uncle, Miss Gordon."

"You said he'd taken ship for Havana. I'll verify that part of your story first."

"May I suggest you clothe yourself before we investigate Henri Beauvais?"

He had expected her to blush—but Faith Gordon only laughed. "Will you turn your head?"

Facing the open windows, he forced himself to keep his eyes on Mobile Bay when the creak of the mattress sling told him she had stepped from her bed. When she called permission, he saw that she had retired to the closet behind the four-poster, leaving the door ajar.

"We can talk while I dress," she said. "Will you send for my uncle now?"

"How can I, when he's at sea?"

The voice from the dressing room was tranquil as ever. "There's been some mistake. I don't understand all this—but you've no right to say he's deserted me."

John saw that she had left the pistol on the bed. He took the precaution of pocketing it before he spoke again. "May I ask how you came to the Bird and Bottle?"

"My uncle fetched me here. From my family's place on the Perdido."

The picture was clearer now, but he held his tongue. He knew the Perdido River well—a place of pine barren and savanna, spaced by bottom lands along a stream that debouched into the Gulf, between Pensacola and Mobile. If the girl belonged to a farming family in this region, her life had been hardscrabble enough. Regardless of her relation to Beauvais, he could hardly blame her for escaping by the most convenient means.

"My uncle is a planter in Haiti," Faith explained.

"Indeed?"

"I've been an orphan for almost a year, living as best I could. Uncle Henri was sent for when my mother died—but the letter was late."

"I see," John murmured. Already, he saw all too well.

"The land deed to our homestead was in order. Thanks to my uncle, we were able to sell on good terms." The girl could not have spoken more casually, had John been the family lawyer. Some-

how, her air of confidence distressed him far more than her early
suspicions.

"And why did Beauvais bring you to Mobile?"

"We're sailing this noon for New Orleans. He's taking me to
France later, to complete my education."

The pattern was now shockingly complete. Beauvais, it seemed,
had not cheated his ward entirely, once her inheritance was neatly
tucked away in his purse. Instead, he had played a more heartless
game. Bringing her to the very threshold of the bright future he
had promised her, he had set last night's trap with care. The
cabin receipt for the *Hirondelle* was proof enough of that. So was
the artful dodge that had brought John to within a few yards of
Faith Gordon's bed. . . . Like all cynics, Beauvais had been willing to believe the worst of everyone—his niece included. The losses
he had taken at dice, the final losing cut of the cards, were the
sops he had allowed his conscience for abandoning her.

John considered the situation while he waited for the girl to
emerge from the dressing closet. It was one thing to convince himself that Beauvais was both thief and conniver. How could he explain that conviction to Faith, without destroying her belief in
God and man? A half-formed inspiration had suddenly begun to
flower in his mind, but he knew he must go slowly. A single mis-
placed word, at this point, might nip it in the bud.

"Tell me this," he said, "did your uncle name the vessel that
would take him up the Mississippi?"

"The *Hirondelle*. You can see her mooring from the window."

4

Faith emerged from the closet as she spoke. John found
he was staring incredulously—as though a brand-new woman had
burst into the room without warning.

He had expected a backwoods jenny, whose traveling dress and petticoats would match that nut-brown tan—whose toes, trained from childhood to hug the earth, would look tortured in shoes. The woman who faced him might have stepped from a Paris salon. The redingote that covered her whaleboned frock was quite in fashion. So, he observed, were the ringlets framed in the calash bonnet, the knitted gloves folded above the reticule she carried on one wrist.

Only the tight pressure of her fingers on the handle of this carryall betrayed her anxiety. Her smile was as confident as her manner—hiding the scared young girl beneath to anyone but an acute observer.

"*Now*, Mr. Tarbell! Let us summon my uncle and explain this mystery."

"You may write him in Havana, if you wish," John said now, with calculated brutality. "Or in Port-au-Prince—if he really lives in Haiti. I'm afraid your letters will go unanswered, though. You see, Mistress Gordon, he's had all he wants of you."

He saw the flash of anger in her eyes, and held up his hand before she could speak. "I'd break this to you gently, but there's no way. Beauvais has decamped—and your inheritance has gone with him. I'll take odds you'll never lay him by the heels in these troubled times. And don't ring for the landlord, I beg of you. It's known below that I spent the night in this room. Since we can't recover your money, we must do what we can to protect your name."

Moved by compassion for her as he watched the color drain from her cheeks, John put out a hand and patted Faith's shoulder gently. He made no effort to console her further: words were futile, until the facts had sunk home. When she settled on the windowsill with a choked cry, he moved quietly to sit beside her. Side by side, they looked down at the harbor (still bright with the gold of sunrise) and the silhouette of the *Hirondelle*, a cable's length beyond the pilings of the dock.

"Tell me how it happened," she said at last. "I've the right to know everything."

John rehearsed the story a second time, taking care to under-line Beauvais' shoddy motives, item by item. The plan had now fully burgeoned in his mind, but he still hesitated to offer it for approval.

"Believe me, the old rip schemed well," he said. "From the mo-ment he laid hands on your homestead, he meant to rid himself of you. Curse him all you like—he's earned it. But admit he's cut and run with éclat."

At the moment, he was speaking more to clear his own mind than to comfort the girl beside him. He looked up in some surprise when Faith answered with a toss of her head and the faint be-ginnings of a smile.

"Now you mention it," she said, "éclat is Uncle Henri's stock in trade. And you needn't look so startled, Mr. Tarbell, just be-cause I understand French. My father was a schoolmaster before he turned to farming: he believed that women have brains. Un-fortunately, his instruction didn't include the life history of my relatives."

John rose from the windowsill. That half-smile did much to make up his mind. Though her life had been boxed by poverty and piney woods, Faith Gordon was no country primitive. She had suffered a hard blow today, and come up all the stronger. It took a thoroughbred to do that.

"May I offer my sympathy?" he asked. "And what help I can?"

"I could use help today," she admitted, with lowered eyes. "But I've no right to ask for yours."

"Perhaps we can help each other."

He saw her color rise: it was natural that she should misunder-stand, especially at this stage. Before she could speak, he took the cabin receipt from his pocket, and offered it to her.

"It's true I won this at cards," he said. "But it's yours as much as mine."

"Either I don't follow you at all, Mr. Tarbell. Or I follow you too well."

John breathed deep; once the next words were out, there could be no retreating. "I'm offering to take your uncle's place as best I can," he explained. "I can't promise you Paris. But I'll see you to New Orleans, if you'll permit me."

"The cabin's yours," she said. "You won it fairly."

"Quite fairly," he assured her. "So fairly, in fact, that I'll introduce myself properly. Tarbell is only my temporary alias while I'm in Mobile. My real name is Powers. Surgeon Captain John Powers, British Army. I've just been cashiered from my Pensacola regiment. And I've no desire to be hanged by the Spaniards."

"Why do you tell me this?"

"I've said I need your help. More, perhaps, than you'll require mine. I'm traveling to Natchez, where I have friends. It's easier to go by way of New Orleans. And it will be easier still if I arrive on my wedding trip. Spies seldom appear with brides on their arm."

Faith Gordon seemed to draw in her breath as the import of his offer struck home. Then, with a flick of her traveling skirt, she rose to face him. Standing eye to eye with her, he was startled to find her almost as tall as he. At that instant of appraisal, she seemed just as determined.

"Do you think me desperate enough to marry a man I've just met, Doctor?"

"The marriage need be in name only. We can dissolve it in Natchez—or New Orleans."

"Are you asking me to share your bed?"

"Only the cabin on the *Hirondelle*. Naturally, we must play our part before the world. I've already proved I can keep my distance."

"So you have," she said. "Would you be as circumspect tomorrow?"

"After all, Miss Gordon, one must take some risks if one hopes to see the world."

He watched her chin lift, and knew that he had been weighed in the scales, though he had no idea of the result. "Could I really help you?"

"I have a position waiting in Natchez," he said formally. "A chance to be partner to a doctor with a large practice. It seems a chance worth taking. You needn't share it, of course, if you'd prefer to stop in New Orleans."

"Don't take my consent for granted," she warned. "I can still find work in Mobile."

"That gown was never meant for Mobile. Shall I order a wedding breakfast for two, while you pack your bags?"

"Do you always get your way, Doctor?"

"Call me John, Faith," he said. "We've both been betrayed by others. We can start as equals. How many marriages can boast so happy a beginning?"

"We aren't quite even," said Faith. "You know my reason for being here. I haven't heard yours."

He met the question squarely: it was fair enough. "I was tried by a court-martial, and convicted of stealing. Once I was drummed out of my regiment, I had no choice but to move on."

"Were you guilty?"

"Would I be this frank if I were?"

Faith pondered the forthright answer. "You're running away," she said at last, "from something more than the British Army."

"Say I've joined the greater army of the homeless. Or call me an adventurer who won't put down roots—and needs a companion for his wanderings."

"You've troubles enough. Why burden yourself with mine?"

"I've money in my purse, Faith, enough to take us to Natchez and beyond. I'm fancy-free—with a future waiting, if I wish it. What man could ask for more?"

"You'll travel faster alone."

"No man travels faster alone. It's one of the falsest proverbs ever coined."

"You're making it hard for me to refuse."

"You've no plans for tomorrow," he reminded her gently. "No more have I. Why shouldn't we travel together—until we've found where we're going?"

He broke off on that and turned away, a little startled by the depth of his feeling. He had blundered into this insane offer as casually as he had staggered into Faith Gordon's bedchamber. Yet he did not regret a word of it.

"Will you order our wedding breakfast, John?"

He turned to find her seated demurely in the window frame, with her hands folded and her reticule beside her. The light that poured in from the harbor made a halo for her innocence. Come what may, he told himself sternly, it's an innocence you must respect. Then his mood melted as she giggled suddenly, like a little girl. They were laughing together as he touched the bell rope at last—in a shared camaraderie that would have seemed impossible a moment ago.

New Orleans

All that night, rain had covered the Mississippi. Coming with the dark, it had swallowed the sunset in a whirling white cloak. It had blotted canebrake and cypress slough, the mudsill shacks at the mouth of the next bayou. It had hidden the shoal water the *Hirondelle* had skirted so painfully in her long, hard wallow upstream.

In the uncertain dawn, there was no slackening in the downpour. Captain Etienne Dufour had ordered anchors down in the half-hour before absolute darkness descended. Now he stared upstream from his quarter-deck, and swore a round Norman oath while he tried to mark the channel.

"*Mille pardons, M. le Docteur.* I trust your lady understands no French."

Dufour's two favored passengers were huddled beneath a shared poncho at the rail. Dr. John Powers of Philadelphia (the taller of the two by a fraction) drew his bride even closer before he answered, in the Frenchman's own tongue.

"She understands quite well, Captain—and echoes your sentiments."

"Coffee and cognac are ready in my cabin. Won't you go in out of this rain?"

John looked to Faith for an answer, but the girl only moved closer.

"You'll catch cold, my dear——"

"I've waited a long time to see New Orleans," said Faith. "Don't cheat me of my view, John."

"We must make sail again and set a course. It may take hours."

"*C'est vrai, madame,*" said Dufour. "With the best of luck, we cannot reach the city before noon."

John lifted Faith to her feet. They ran to the companionway, holding the poncho over their heads. "We'll take coffee with you later, Captain," he promised. "Thanks for the invitation."

Hand in hand, the pretended newlyweds descended to the waist of the barkentine, and followed the sheltered passage to their cabin. Our performance, thought John, is now letter-perfect. Dufour can hardly doubt that this marriage is genuine. Only brand-new lovers would rise in a rainy dawn, to glimpse the town they had chosen for their honeymoon.

2

It had been an exasperating voyage from Mobile. Bad luck had dogged the *Hirondelle's* course, from the moment she entered the green-brown apron of silt that advertised the nearness of the Mississippi Delta. Dufour's charts were the best available —but the ship had gone aground twice in the entrance they had chosen. Long before the river had become a tan-colored entity between its drowned banks, it had been necessary to man the kedging lines and fight toward the first of their overnight moorings.

When the rain fell, it came in sheets, with a keening wind behind it. Thanks to shifts in the channel, Dufour had proceeded under shortened sail, lest his vessel rip her bottom among the cypress knees. When the sun shone, the wind had a trick of dropping, forcing the kedgers to strain for sweat-soaked hours at their oars. . . . Days after they had fought their way beyond the delta, it was difficult to tell where river ended and spongy land began. Sometimes, to John's untutored eye, a bayou resembled the true channel—and he could only marvel at the captain's skill in holding his course.

During those first skirmishes, both river and land had seemed as deserted as on the day Hernando de Soto first came to what the Spanish had then called Florida. It was hard for John to grasp the need of swivel guns at each rail, or the reason these compact batteries were constantly manned. He understood well enough when a fleet of pirogues and outrigger canoes, flashing their patchwork sails in a watery maze to larboard, seemed about to surround the barkentine. A full-throated salvo from the cannon, plus a show of pikes and muskets at the rail, had been enough to send these river pirates back to their lair.

Word had evidently gone upriver that the *Hirondelle* was equipped to repel boarders, for there had been no further threats from the bayous. But they had seen few signs of civilization as they fought their way northward in the oxbows—only an occasional fish seine, or a few weeping acres of farmland, clinging to a patch of higher ground. New Orleans itself remained elusive as a mirage.

"Actually, the levee is a hundred miles upstream from the delta," said John. He tossed the poncho aside, and closed their cabin door. "I suppose ours has been an average passage."

Stretching full length on the settee that had served as his bed since they left Mobile, he watched Faith through lazy-lidded eyes. She moved serenely about the cabin—checking the strap on a portmanteau, pausing at the glass to make sure that the bonnet she had chosen for going ashore was set at the proper angle. For the hundredth time, he marveled at her assurance. He could not quite put down the suspicion that she had relished this game from the start—for all its explosive potential.

"Dufour assures me that the city's around the next bend," he said. "Or the next but one. We may not get another chance to—discuss the future."

"What else have we done but talk?"

"Don't think I'm complaining," he said. "You've been a wonderful confidante. But you must admit our talk has been mostly of the past."

It was true enough. He had told his story from the start—including the ruin the war had brought upon his family and his own bleak prospects. He had spoken of the Wrights, and the offer that might recoup his fortunes in Natchez—omitting the motives that drew him toward Stella, as inevitably as the barkentine was fighting her way to the New Orleans levee. . . . Faith, for her part, had spoken quite as calmly of her own starved youth as a schoolmaster's child in Georgia. She had told him of her father's urge to break free of that mold, of his homesteading foray to the Perdido —and, finally, of the fever that had claimed both parents' lives, when that homestead had just become a reality.

Neither had sought the other's pity in these recitals. So far, their talks together had been leisurely appraisals. If John felt something akin to panic this morning, as he attempted to vision Faith's prospects, he was careful to conceal his misgivings.

"Let's say we've proved that fate was on our side in Mobile," he told her. "I'm still wondering about tomorrow."

"I've no complaints so far. Have you?"

He did not stir from the settee while she lifted a night robe from the pillow on her bunk and folded it into a second portmanteau, along with her quilted peignoir. Had we been wedded for twenty years, he thought, she could not make these moves more casually.

"We'll go through customs as man and wife," he said. "That's our bargain. Dufour tells me the Ecu d'Or is the best inn. Once I've settled you there, I can go upriver to arrange my affairs in Natchez——"

"Surely you aren't leaving a new wife so soon?"

"It will save your face if I pretend I'll send for you later," he said patiently. "Surely it'll be simpler if we say our goodbyes now."

"You had other plans in Mobile, Doctor."

It was part of her defensive ritual to use his Christian name when they were on deck—and to reserve this formality for their cabin. From the first, he had understood her strategy well enough —and applauded it. Today, for no real reason, the usage irritated him.

"I'd be happy to transport you to Natchez," he said. "The Wrights would welcome my bride, I'm sure. But it's a rough journey north. Besides, I'm afraid you'd find the country a replica of the wilderness you've just escaped."

"Natchez is still an outpost town," said Faith, as tranquilly as though she were reciting a lesson. "But it's far from uncivilized. Some say it can outstrip New Orleans, once the war is over."

John frowned in earnest; this was not the first time the schoolmaster's daughter had corrected his mistakes in North American geography. "Are you thinking of settling there?" he asked. "Growing up with the town?"

"We could do worse," said Faith. "Not that I'm considering my comfort, Doctor. If it will really help you, I'll push on to the Pacific. You've no idea what a good traveler I can be."

He decided to shift his attack. "Whither thou goest, I will go also? Are you comparing us to Ruth and Boaz?"

"*That* speech was to Naomi," said Faith, with the same detachment. "But I needn't remind you how the story ended."

"You aren't my wife, so far."

"Dufour believes I am. I've heard the French were hard to deceive in such matters."

"That's what troubles me," he confessed. "I think we should end this play-acting before either of us is hurt."

"How have I hurt you, Doctor?" she asked demurely.

"Damnation take you," he cried. "My name is John."

"So it is, my dear. Is this to be our first quarrel?"

"You understand me well enough," he said. "No woman under heaven could be that innocent."

"Of course I understand," said Faith. "May I compliment you on your forbearance?"

"I don't deserve your compliments," he said. "I'd deserve them far less if I continued to want you—without taking what I want."

"Is this a proposal—or a proposition? Should I be shocked or flattered?"

"Use your woman's instinct," he snapped. "Remain in New Orleans."

"In Mobile, you said you'd need me in Natchez. Now you're inventing this argument to get rid of me."

"I'm only trying to be fair. A bargain's still a bargain. This cabin was bought and paid for. I agreed to share it with you—if you'd help me past the New Orleans custom shed. Once I'm on Spanish soil, I'm my own man——"

"And I'm my own woman. I don't know what you're seeking, John Powers. But I'll help you find it, if it's in me."

Thrown back to his last line of defenses, he had no choice but to attack.

"Suppose I said my goal is before me now?"

"That just isn't true. It isn't *me* you want——"

"What man could help wanting you?"

"I might be a diversion for a while," she said. "But your search —or your flight—would begin again. Sometimes, I can't be sure which is more important."

Astonished though he was by her penetration, he found that he could hold his tongue no longer. "You're right," he said. "I wasn't being altogether frank. You *could* help me in Natchez—if you dared to come that far."

"How, John?"

"I can't tell you now. But I'll say this—it may be a bargain you'll regret."

"Say you still need me. That's all I care about."

"I need you, Faith. And I'll welcome your company, if you'll take the risk."

"I'll take the risk, John."

They were still eye to eye, there in the shuttered cabin. Neither of them stirred for a moment, when the long-drawn hail reached their ears from the crow's nest. The lookout's cry had come to them clearly: standing aside to let Faith pass, John realized that the drum of the downpour had long since ceased.

"So the first lap of our journey is ending," he said, as they went on deck together. "Let's hope the others will be as stimulating."

Sunlight smote their eyelids when they reached the starboard rail of the barkentine. Dead ahead, the river had widened in a long and lazy curve. He caught a glimpse of steep-pitched rooftops shining with rain, a massed pattern of buildings white and blue and golden in the radiance that poured down from the clearing sky. New Orleans lay before them at last, precise as an architect's drawing behind the humped shoulders of its levees.

3

The matter of his identity had been debated in some detail on the voyage from Mobile. In the end, he had decided to be himself again.

His army papers had been destroyed in Pensacola. But his wallet still contained a valid passport, identifying him as Dr. John Powers, a physician with a Philadelphia domicile and no visible leanings toward the English cause. The story he had rehearsed with Faith was simple enough. Having stopped at Mobile to acquire a bride, he was en route to the upriver country to inspect family land. Whether or not he would settle there depended on the outcome of the rebellion.

Now that he had shed his buckskins for the wardrobe of a gentleman, it seemed impossible that his story would be questioned. True, there was a certain risk in the use of his own name, especially if news of the court-martial should follow him. It seemed far less dangerous than using an alias, without even a forged document to back him.

Dufour's estimate had been correct. Though they had sighted the town in early morning, it was afternoon before the barkentine could be warped into the New Orleans levee. John and Faith did not leave the deck during that last fight against the current. Each fresh view had charmed them more—from the maze of flatboats before the levee (that served as a kind of floating market) to the gray thrust of the cathedral behind the Place d'Armes. This square, John observed, was both a parade ground and a public park, and served as a focal point for the *carré* that Bienville had designed on this river crescent more than a half-century ago. Today, it was bright with gaudy flowers that bloomed here in all seasons—to say nothing of the chromatic garb of the Negro vendors, endlessly hawking their wares in a patois that seemed a blend of many tongues.

The chant of these dusky merchants (who carried their goods in headbaskets larger than tables) established the essential rhythm. The palisade that fenced the town on three sides and the gun platforms along the levee were serious reminders that war still rumbled beyond the horizon. New Orleans herself seemed able to take such rumors in stride. Here was a core of civilization, set down to ripen in a green wilderness. Pensacola and Mobile had been mere log-cabin bastions compared to this city in miniature.

As John had hoped, the Spanish officers in the custom shed gave his passport no more than a cursory glance. They seemed far more interested in ogling Faith while they descended the landward slope of the levee and threaded an open-market square that opened, in turn, to the central plaza. Behind them a Negro wheeled their luggage in a hand barrow. Across the square was the Ecu d'Or, a deep-walled tavern built around a courtyard, with a gigantic gold piece set in its central arch.

"Well, my dear—is it all you pictured?"

Faith's eyes sparkled as they took in the bright scene before them. "Couldn't you hang out a shingle here and forget Natchez?"

"The temptation is great," he said. "But I'm afraid I must surmount it. If I can engage the right boatman, and grease the proper palms, we'll be on the water again tomorrow."

The banner of Spain, he noted, flew above the Cabildo, the squat government house that stood beside the weather-worn cathedral; another red and golden standard whipped smartly in the river breeze, where the gun mounts frowned across the levee. Spanish soldiers were present in great numbers, their green-white uniforms making a vivid contrast to the butternut-yellow homespuns of boatmen from such distant spots as Nashville or Detroit. Yet the twang of the American backlands and the lisp of Castilian could never drown the dominant note of New Orleans, which was French to the last haunting overtone.

Most of the buildings forming their geometrical pattern around the Place d'Armes were single-story—with long, sloping eaves that made a perfect shelter for the latticed sidewalks, or banquettes. Now and again, John saw a grillwork before a patio entrance, or an iron cobweb on an upstairs gallery, which advertised the hand of a Spanish artisan. But the buildings, like the inhabitants, were dominantly French. Some of them (like the steep-roofed Ursuline convent, muffled to the eaves in palms) might have been lifted from Provence stone by stone.

Even the Ecu d'Or, with its marble-topped café tables and its click of billiard balls, suggested Paris rather than Madrid. So did the aproned maître d'hôtel who rushed forth to welcome them, and bowed them upstairs to the bridal suite.

Their parlor, airy with latticed windows, opened to a gallery that commanded a sweep of rooftops to the north. Far down the levee, John picked out a line of rafts bobbing in the tug of the current. This, Dufour had said, was Bayou St. Jacques, a rendezvous point for Mississippi boatmen. It was here that rafts were broken up for their logs, after disgorging their wealth from upriver.

This particular bayou, said Dufour, was a clearing house for rivermen of all sorts. He had recommended one *voyageur* in particular, an Afro-Indian named Yulee who had bought his freedom years ago. If Yulee was unengaged, he would be an ideal pilot for the trip to Natchez.

John returned from the gallery with something like reluctance.

After their near-quarrel aboard the *Hirondelle,* he hesitated to face Faith alone. But his alleged bride, bustling happily about the suite, seemed oblivious of his slight awkwardness as he came into the parlor.

"I've no time for food," he said. "Have you enough French to order *déjeuner* for yourself?"

"More than enough, John. Go engage your boatman, by all means. I've things to do right here."

"Surely it isn't necessary to unpack. Not if we're leaving tomorrow."

"You might change your mind."

"Speak for yourself, Faith. You still have a choice, you know."

"Not if you meant what you said this morning."

"I meant every word—including the risks you'll be taking."

"May I be the judge of that?"

"I'm not sure I deserve such loyalty."

"Whether you do or not, I'm still grateful," she said firmly. "So grateful, I won't let you make this journey alone—if you're positive it must be made."

He went out on that; the problem of Faith's devotion was something he could hardly solve today. It was harrowing enough to admit that the ties already binding them could only grow stronger with each hour they passed together.

Curiously enough, the fact that he had yet to hold her in his arms seemed of small import, when measured against the pleasure he took in her company. Thanks to her own easy candor, he realized that his pleasure was shared. And yet, if she was a little in love with him now (or even imagined herself in love), nothing but heartbreak would await her in Natchez.

In the garden of the inn, he paused for his last indecision of the day. It would be a simple matter to leave half his funds in the landlord's care and depart alone. Faith could live here for months, with such a sum at her disposal. . . . His mind admitted as much, even as his heart counseled otherwise. Since man's heart has guided his footsteps from the beginning, he found himself in the Place d'Armes again, en route to Bayou St. Jacques.

Faith was his partner now, for better or worse: they had crossed their special Rubicon in their cabin on the *Hirondelle*. Though they might continue to argue details, they were already bound for Natchez.

4

At the boatyard, he found Yulee busy with the light-draft sloop he used to transport passengers upstream. As John had hoped, the riverman was at liberty—and willing to take a pair of travelers to Natchez. Departure on the morrow, he said, was by no means impossible.

Thanks to the armed emergency in New Orleans, it would be necessary to procure a clearance before the sloop could proceed. That, too, was part of the boatman's routine. For a price (said Yulee) a *laissez-passer* could be procured at the Cabildo. He would collect that vital document personally, and deliver it at the Ecu d'Or.

The half-breed was both stumpy and wiry—yet there was a grace about the man that suggested his Indian blood, even if one ignored the bold hooked nose and snapping eyes. Yulee's skin was the color of strong tea: one needed another glance to make sure the blood of African tribesmen was mingled with the oldest American heritage. There was no sign of remembered servitude in Yulee. John could see that the man's pride extended to his boat, now rubbing gunwales with a dozen of its kind in the bayou. It seemed likely that Yulee could be trusted.

John had not expected his exit from New Orleans to open so easily. The town still drew him with a hundred lures while he followed Royal Street again, to the remembered turning into the Place d'Armes. It would be a simple matter indeed to surrender to that love song. The Queen City (a Creole belle all too conscious of her charms) was only waiting to be conquered. . . . Tonight, it seemed a simple thing to turn his back on Stella Wright—and the challenge she had offered in Pensacola.

He entered the archway of his inn with the thought still before him. The sunset still blessed the courtyard; the fountain made its own music in its framework of jasmine and oleander. This, he thought, was a new world in the making, powered by all the remembered wisdom of the old. As Faith had said, a man might hang out his shingle here and prosper, regardless of his past. Had Faith been sent like an omen, to recall him to his role as healer?

As though in answer to that question, a man rose from a bench in the patio, and touched his arm as he was about to mount the stairway to his suite. John saw that his visitor was wearing one of the many rebel uniforms—in this case, the white surcoat, bright-blue weskit, and buff-colored smallclothes of the Continental Dragoons. It was the first American uniform he had been near enough to touch. He knew he was staring hard: he had not expected to encounter the enemy so abruptly, in the heart of New Orleans.

"Dr. Powers?"

"Your servant, sir."

"Captain Charles Shaw, Continental Army. Will you attend an emergency case at Mr. Oliver Pollock's establishment on Bourbon Street?"

John could feel himself recoil from the request, though it was one he could hardly refuse. Oliver Pollock was a Philadelphia merchant who had settled in New Orleans some years ago; it was common knowledge that he served as paymaster for the American cause. Now that Spain was openly at war with England, it seemed that he boasted a military aide.

"Who told you I was here, Captain?"

"Your name was on the passenger list of the *Hirondelle*," Shaw told him blandly. "Mr. Pollock would hesitate to trouble you, but his own doctor is away."

John considered swiftly. On the surface, the request seemed natural. "I'll come at once," he said. "Will you wait until I fetch my kit?"

It was assurance of a sort to find that the dragoon made no attempt to follow when he dashed upstairs and snatched his surgical bag from the armoire. He could hear Faith humming in the bedroom. Walking on careful tiptoe, he paused just long enough to place his wallet in plain view on the table. If this was a prelude to his arrest as a British spy, she, at least, would be provided for.

On the gallery, he stifled the impulse to break for freedom, and rejoined Shaw in the courtyard. "What is the nature of Mr. Pollock's illness?"

"Mr. Pollock is well enough," said the dragoon. Already, they were hurrying down an alley that made a short cut to St. Ann Street. "It's one of his freedmen—a factor he values highly. The fellow was hurt in a market brawl. Stab wound, in the right breast. How are you on stabbings, Doctor?"

The query seemed innocent enough, but John answered warily, "If it's a chest wound, the chances are poor."

"That's what Mr. Pollock feared. All he asks is that you do what you can."

Bourbon Street was only a short walk from the inn. The Philadelphian's establishment, John saw, was a square white bastion, with a dozen doorways opening flush with the banquette. A gold-lettered sign, extending the length of this emporium, informed the passer-by (in both French and Spanish) that Oliver Pollock dealt in flour, meats, and provender of all kinds. Despite the hour, the shutters were closed down the building's length. This, as John recalled from Pensacola, was in deference to the long siesta—a sensible pause in Creole communities, which usually prolonged itself from midday to the cool of evening.

John found his patient on a table, in what was evidently Pollock's countinghouse. A half-dozen flour sacks served as effective pillows: the man's only attendant was a white-haired Negress whom John assumed to be a native midwife. He nodded to this outlandish nurse as he shucked his coat. Despite their fondness for amulets and love philters, he had found such assistants effective enough.

There was no sign of Pollock himself. He was relieved at the merchant's absence: it was still possible that this would be only a routine emergency case.

"I'll help, if you like," said Shaw. "I've done my stint as surgeon's mate."

"Fair enough, Captain. I may need you."

The Negro on the table, a handsome fellow just past his prime, offered them a heartbroken smile as the examination began. It was evident that he considered himself beyond hope—though he was resting comfortably enough, between his labored attempts to draw breath. The pulse, John found, was strong but racing; the sheet beneath the patient was stained with blood, but he seemed in no danger at the moment.

The stab wound was a neat, deep puncture in the right rib cage. A red froth, welling from its depths with each tortured exhalation, was ample proof that the lung had been pierced. John had ministered to a hundred such wounds. The fact that this one was not yet fatal was proof that no major vessel had been damaged in the lung beneath.

He opened his bag and took out the instruments he had brought from Pensacola—forceps, a pair of scalpels, a few small lancets. There were several vials of medications in the case. He selected a bottle of laudanum, and poured a liberal dose into the glass the black midwife offered. Mixed with wine, it would dull the factor's pain while he decided upon a course of action.

When the patient had downed this potion, John beckoned the dragoon captain aside. In his student days at Edinburgh, when he had treated such cases under a teacher's guidance, it had been deemed prudent to wait—in the hope that the straining, sponge-like mass of the lung would compress the laceration with its own tensile strength, before the labor of breathing grew too heavy to be borne. Usually, of course, congestion increased until the patient drowned from lack of air, thanks to the steady seeping.

"It's a deep stab, but a clean one," he said. "Was it made by a stiletto, or a regular knife?"

"A stiletto, I believe."

"Then we've a fair chance to save him. Will you bring me that quill from the inkpot?"

Shaw watched as John stripped the quill of its feathers, slashed it neatly near its end, and again at the nib. With two scalpel strokes, he had created a somewhat flexible tube, perhaps five inches in length; its circumference, at first glance, seemed only a trifle smaller than the puncture bubbling between the patient's ribs.

"Will you take his shoulders, Captain?"

Shaw's broad hands, anchored on the Negro's triceps, were ample assurance that the patient would not flinch. The man's lips were taking on a bluish tinge, a sure sign of impending trouble. No risk, however great, seemed unjustified if air could be restored to that heaving lung cage.

With a pledget of cotton, John wiped away the froth of blood and studied the wound with care. A slight enlargement was all he needed to correct the retraction of skin tissue. As he worked, he could feel a crackling beneath his fingers, as though he were pressing on finely crumbled eggshells, another indication that air was escaping into the fascia of the chest wall.

The quill slid easily into the wound. John explored the tissue beneath, seeking the opening where the blade had done its damage. At the first try, the resistance he encountered seemed too stubborn to conquer. Then, just as he had resigned himself to forcing an entrance, the quill sank into the wound a good inch, as it found the path the knife had carved.

He felt the midwife's eyes upon him, and read the same question in Shaw's glance. "This is an emergency measure," he explained. "If it fails, the quill may rupture a major vessel in the lung, and drown him in a matter of moments. But he's suffocating without it. If we can reach the space around the lung itself, it should relieve pressure instantly."

Shaw nodded, though John could see that he only half understood. "Won't it let air in as well as out?"

"We'll cross that bridge when we reach it. Steady now."

Twice more, he probed deeply with the quill, and twice he chose the pathway of the knife. On the third try, the tube found the puncture in the pleura itself, and glided into the space around the lung. The result was dramatic, filling the empty counting-house with a shrill whistling, as though a teakettle had materialized from thin air. Blood dripped from the exposed end of the quill as John stepped back. The patient, snoring under the heavy opiate, had already relaxed visibly, thanks to the relief of this crude but effective safety valve.

Stopping the tube with his thumb before the Negro's next inhalation, John nodded his satisfaction to Shaw. "May I trouble you for a glove, Captain? Meanwhile, you might stop this with your thumb when he takes breath."

It was a simple matter to cut a rectangle from the dragoon's glove, at one of the finger ends. Once this rudimentary valve had been fitted across the quill, it was no longer necessary to block the inhalations manually. The leather flap, anchored with a strand of whipcord, performed exactly as the valve on a blacksmith's bellows—permitting the air exhaled from the lungs to issue forth unimpeded, and closing snugly each time the patient inhaled. The whole procedure had consumed less than ten minutes' time.

"The nurse can attend him until morning," John told the American officer. "There's nothing more we can do now."

Shaw gave an appreciative chuckle. "I was sent to fetch a doctor —but I never thought I'd return with a magician."

"The trick worked today," said John. "It might fail tomorrow. It's still possible that Mr. Pollock will lose his factor, but I'll lay odds on his recovery. Give that lung a fortnight, and it should be as good as before."

"Mr. Pollock will regret he can't thank you in person," Shaw told him. "Just after he sent for you, he was summoned by the Governor."

"Is de Gálvez in New Orleans?" John asked—startled, for once, out of his pretended calm.

"He returned only yesterday from an inspection trip to Mobile. Did you know that the siege of Pensacola has been ordered?"

Now that his show of surprise was behind him—safely, he hoped —John could smile after all. "Do you discuss military matters this readily with everyone, Captain?"

"No one keeps a secret long in New Orleans," said the dragoon. "The siege will be common gossip tomorrow. Would you care to wager on its duration? My guess is the lobsterbacks can't last a fortnight."

"This war has already divided my family," said John stiffly. "I've no wish to bet on its outcome."

If the brusque answer offended Shaw, he gave no sign. "That's your privilege, Doctor," he said affably. "Mr. Pollock will call tomorrow to thank you. In the meantime, I'll settle your fee."

"There's no fee, Captain; the pleasure was mine. And will you present my regrets to Mr. Pollock? I'll be headed upriver tomorrow, if my boatman can clear his craft."

"All good wishes on your voyage then, sir."

Though he had listened carefully, John detected no shadow of threat in Shaw's manner. As his boots raised echoes on the banquette of Bourbon Street, he was surprised to note that dusk was already here; in this river valley (which was, in effect, only an endless green table) sunset was abrupt, plunging the streets of New Orleans in a violet half-light that was not without a sinister charm.

Tonight, thanks to the fears Shaw's visit had raised, he found himself staring down each alley he passed. When a shadow came alive in the archway of the Ecu d'Or, he paused with one hand on his pistol—and moved forward only when he saw it was Yulee.

"Did I startle you, *jefe?*"

"My thoughts were elsewhere, Yulee. Did you get a clearance?"

"*No, por desgracia.* The clerk who attends to such matters had left his desk early. I could have insisted—but it seemed wiser to avoid argument."

It was a flat statement, with no hint of hidden meaning. Reading the gleam of intelligence in the half-breed's eyes, John felt that Yulee shared his eagerness to push upstream.

"Did you know that Governor de Gálvez had returned from Mobile?" he asked.

"The news has reached the cafés. They say that a great battle is joined in West Florida. Perhaps it is as well we travel north tomorrow."

"Aren't you comfortable in New Orleans, Yulee?"

"If that means, am I wanted by the *guardia civil?* the answer is no. But I am a man of nature, *jefe.* I prefer the forest to the city, and the water to the land. The Cabildo opens at an early hour. I will procure the clearance, and await you in the boatyard."

"Do you think Governor de Gálvez will close the Mississippi until Pensacola is taken?"

"Señor de Gálvez is an able governor and a genius at war," said Yulee. "But no Spaniard living can close this river. The Mississippi is stronger than the laws of men."

"He can stop us from sailing north."

"Not if your wish is strong enough. I will arrange everything. Bring your lady to the boatyard tomorrow: you will find me waiting."

"Go with God, Yulee."

"Go with God, *Señor Médico.*"

John opened the door to the parlor at the Ecu d'Or without knocking. Faith was standing on the balcony, with the last pale arrows of sunset lighting her russet hair. She was wearing a low-cut robe of China silk, with vast panniers; the shawl she had tossed about her golden-brown shoulders was as insubstantial as green mist. When she lifted her face to greet him with a smile, the illusion was complete. For that moment, at least, he had come home again, though it was only the parlor of a tavern they would be quitting tomorrow.

Just in time, he reminded himself that this was his wife in name only. He bent to kiss her hand, instead of the softly parted lips that smiled up at him so confidingly.

"Welcome back, John. Have you arranged our transport?"

"We sail in the morning. I hope you've ordered dinner."

"They're sending it up in a half-hour. You'll find rum on the sideboard, if you'd like a glass."

"If you don't mind, let's first rehearse our plans."

"I thought your plans were made."

"So they are," he told her. "I still want you *au courant*."

"I'm glad I'm included," she said. "For a while today, I was afraid you'd taken French leave. It was a most unflattering suspicion, John—will you forgive me?"

"Perhaps I should tell you how I spent my day," he said. "You'll see how valuable you are."

Faith listened attentively while he described the surgery he had just performed, and the comments of Captain Charles Shaw.

"Do you think they suspect you?"

"I can't be sure," he confessed. "The summons could have been a test—to make sure I'm really a doctor. There's bound to be a sequel, if we don't get clear tomorrow."

"You mean that they'd hold you as a Loyalist?"

John studied her from his perch on the gallery rail. "Would you welcome detention, Faith?"

"Only if it would stop you from doing something rash in Natchez."

"Let's forget Natchez, for the moment," he said. "Our present problem is to get out of New Orleans. Since I did come here with a wife, I'm afraid she must stay in the picture."

"This wife, as you know, is more than willing," said Faith. "Even if she doesn't quite grasp your point."

"It's simple enough, my dear. We can't take a chance on Mr. Oliver Pollock. Unfortunately, we're both Philadelphians. It's just possible that he'll remember my family. No Powers in good standing would bring a bride this far and leave her."

"You see, John? You *do* need your bride. I'm so glad you realize it."

"And you're still enjoying the fiction?"

Faith touched the green gossamer of her scarf. "So would you, if this were the first luxury you'd ever known. I can't tell you what it's meant to me, just ordering a dinner. And dressing for it, as though I'd been wearing silk and rouge forever——"

"Life is more than silk and rouge."

"Not if you've never worn them. Is that too much for a man to grasp?"

"On the contrary. I wish you could enjoy them forever. Unfortunately, reality must intrude tomorrow."

The straw-covered demijohn had already drawn his eye. He moved toward it now, dismissing a few realities of his own. "Shall we pretend this is our future home—just for tonight? And that our journey ends here, instead of in Natchez?"

Faith watched with glowing eyes as he poured out a bumper of rich, blackstrap rum. "May I have one too, John? If you're building air castles, I'd like to share them."

He looked at her with startled eyes, then laughed at his own surprise. Immersed as he had been in his role of *homme fatal*, he had forgotten that Faith Gordon, for all her China silks, was a child of nature. In the Pennsylvania backwoods (when he had gone surveying with the Rangers) the ladies of the house had drunk their cup of whiskey before meals as naturally as the men. The memory made it logical to pour a second dram tonight. Presenting it to Faith with a flourish, he could honestly feel that he stood with a foot in two worlds.

"To the illusion of tonight," he said. "Perdition take the reality of tomorrow."

5

A rich turtle broth had begun their repast. It was succeeded by a brace of canvasbacks stuffed with oranges and wild rice—a dish worthy of Paris itself, with a Creole flavor that defied analysis. Dry sherry had appeared with the soup, white Burgundy with the duck. Now, sipping *café brûlot* in the starlit gloom of the gallery, with Faith close beside him, Dr. John Powers admitted that his sense of belonging was complete.

Faith had matched him glass for glass while the wine was poured. He had offered no objection as the ducal meal proceeded. It had seemed just as natural that they should settle here on the wicker love seat, to listen to the soft, insistent poetry of a guitar, somewhere in the darkness of the courtyard.

Half-forgotten images of similar moments had begun to swim through his mind. There had been an *auberge* in Normandy years ago, sweet with the aroma of clover and the breath of the summer sea—an inn outside Auld Reekie itself, tangy with peat smoke— a bed-parlor above the taproom of a London pub, with the fog a discreet curtain at the windows. . . . Always a tavern setting, he thought sadly. The wenches who had shared those moments seemed much the same today, regardless of what language they had used to create the counterfeit of love.

Would Faith Gordon join that company, once she had served her purpose?

He put the accusing question aside as he felt her shoulder touch his. Instinct told him that she was pretending, too, as ardently as he—insisting, with pathetic stubbornness, that this corner of New Orleans was really home. Giving her every chance to resist, he bent to claim her lips for their first kiss.

For a dizzy moment as their mouths clung in the throbbing darkness, he told himself that vision and reality had merged, that this was indeed the end of his seeking. But the mood of ecstasy shattered, as abruptly as it had begun. Even before she broke from his arms (an explosion of energy that all but toppled him into the courtyard), he knew it was wine, not Faith, that had sponsored their embrace.

He saw that she was more frightened than angry as she stood poised in the doorway. And though she seemed about to take flight, he had the swift conviction that he could claim her lips again, merely by holding out his arms. If he hesitated, it was only because the ardor of her kiss had shocked his conscience wide awake. This after all, had been the response of innocence. He had made love in too many languages not to be sure of that.

"I won't ask you to forgive me," he said.

Faith did not answer him directly. When she spoke, she seemed to be thinking aloud.

"I'm afraid I *was* dreaming," she said. "A pleasant dream—while it lasted."

"Must you waken so soon?"

"Only a moment ago," she said, in that same lost tone, "I was floating between earth and heaven. Now I've touched ground."

"Was my kiss a disillusion?"

"No, John. On the contrary." But she held up a detaining palm when he moved to join her in the doorway. "Don't make me sound more a hussy than I am."

"I told you this morning that I wanted you. Now you can see why."

She laughed then, a little bitterly. "And I thought you were only making an excuse to leave me here."

"You know better now."

"Is this why you rescued me in Mobile?"

"Soon you'll be asking if I'm like all the others," he said. "The answer is yes—with reservations. To name just one, I've never taken so much as a kiss before, until it was offered freely. I don't choose to do so now."

"So I was on trial tonight," she said quietly. "Is that it?"

"What happened was inevitable, Faith," he told her. "As I've said, I can't apologize. I can promise you this much: it needn't happen again. And you can still come to Natchez, if you will."

"Would it be fair of me, John? To accept so much and give nothing?"

"Why not?" he asked lightly. "It's a game women have played for centuries."

"And what if I want you too? Had you thought of that?"

"Go on," he said, with a smile. "A good wife can confess anything to her husband."

"I did want you, just now," she admitted. "I wanted you so much nothing seemed to matter. But love is more than just wanting—it must be."

"I wouldn't know, Faith," he said quietly. "You see, I've never been in love. Nor have you. I could tell as much, the moment I took you in my arms."

"You don't love me now," she said accusingly. "Yet you would have——" Her voice broke as her eyes filled with tears.

"Perhaps I did think you'd help me forget my loneliness tonight," he said. "Just remember you're as lonely as I am; you could use that comfort too."

"Is that why you gave me the wine?" The note of accusation had deepened.

"I won't say you asked for it," he reminded her. "That would be really ungallant."

"I'll play the coquette no longer then," she told him, with an angry lift to her chin. "If you wish another kiss, you must claim it on your merits."

He knew the wine was speaking still, in both of them, and watching her vanish through the bedroom door, he felt his nails dig deep in his palms as he fought down an impulse to fling it wide. He listened for the sound of a turning key. Some of his frustration ebbed away when he realized that she had made no move to shut him out. It could mean that she still trusted him—or that she expected him to follow.

A discreet tap sounded on the hall door. He opened it upon the French innkeeper—and saw the man was a trifle breathless, as though he had run upstairs.

"Captain Shaw, Doctor. He requests your company."

John remembered to double-lock the outer portal, and thrust the key in his belt: he even remembered to turn the lock again, to make sure his wallet still reposed on the center table in the parlor. Hurrying downstairs in the landlord's wake, he rejoiced at that extra precaution; if Faith found herself alone on the morrow, she would read but one motive in his departure.

Shaw was seated on a bench in the patio, beneath an orange tree in full bloom: the spray of blossoms, milk-white in the dark, made a bizarre frame for that dashing warrior.

"This time I must really apologize," he said. "I knew you'd brought a wife to Orleans: I didn't realize she was also a bride."

"Is the patient worse?"

"The patient is sleeping like a child," said the dragoon. "Maman Tina tells me you've cured him with your magic. This time, I'm here on other business."

"And I'm still your servant, Captain."

"Governor de Gálvez requests an interview. I'm to escort you to his mansion."

John felt his heart sink as he identified the two silhouettes in the tavern archway. The Spanish infantrymen, in their white surcoats and matching bandoliers, lounging at ease on their muskets, were quite capable of pouncing as one man, if he balked at Shaw's soft-voiced invitation.

"Is this a request, or a command?"

"Don't be disturbed by the infantry, Doctor. The town's full of drunken boatmen tonight. It isn't safe to walk alone."

John found he could smile, if a trifle grimly. He had heard a great deal of General Bernardo de Gálvez. This summons was quite in character.

"Don't soften the blow," he said. "I'll come quietly."

6

The Governor's residence, one of the larger leftovers from the French regime, seemed ringed with sentries tonight, and pulsing with a separate heartbeat. The Governor's study, to which John was led, was an oasis of calm in this martial bustle. The book-lined room, with its deep leather armchairs and massive mahogany writing table, obviously belonged to a man of culture. Whatever de Gálvez might think of his motives, John felt sure now that he would be allowed to argue his case as an equal.

When the door opened, he knew it was not de Gálvez who entered: the newcomer's face suggested the map of Ireland rather than the peninsula of Iberia. His boots, deep-burnished as ebony mirrors, were handmade; the claw-hammer coat was a rich maroon, and the high velvet collar rose level with his ears, ambushed in a maze of fresh-curled hair, as precisely plastered as the lovelocks on a statue. The presence of an Irishman in the Governor's study was no cause for surprise. The Irish adventurer had fitted the pattern of Louisiana from the days of the blood-thirsty Don Alexander O'Reilly, who had first put His Hispanic Majesty's seal on New Orleans.

"Oliver Pollock, Doctor," said the newcomer pleasantly. "I am in your debt for saving my factor's life."

"I was glad to be of help, sir." John shook hands with Pollock heartily enough—and rejoiced to find he had no memory of having seen him in Philadelphia.

"The Governor will join us soon," said the merchant. "He's led a busy life since his return from Mobile." He settled in a facing armchair. "It's always pleasant to welcome a fellow American to New Orleans. Especially a fellow townsman."

John stiffened in his chair. Philadelphia, after all, was the largest city in North America. He could only pray that Pollock's knowledge of his family stopped at the threshold of their estate in Germantown.

"I'm afraid my home is a casualty of war," he said carefully.

"I can hardly claim to be a native," said the merchant. "Though I'm now an American citizen, I was born in the old country. Still, I called myself a Philadelphian for a while, before I got my start in commerce. Your father visited my emporium more than once, while you were getting your education in Scotland. A fine man, Doctor, and a generous one, even though we were poles apart politically. May I ask why his son has strayed so far from home?"

John weighed his answer carefully. Only a few brush strokes were needed to complete the Tory portrait Pollock had sketched with such a deft hand.

"I abandoned my father's politics long ago, sir," he said. "At present, I'm seeking a practice in the Mississippi country."

"So I gathered, from your declaration at customs," said the merchant. "If the miracle you worked today is an example of your skill, your success is assured. Of course, it will help if you'll give the Governor what assistance you can."

"I'm a stranger in a strange land, Mr. Pollock. But I'd be delighted to assist Señor de Gálvez. Does *he* have a servant who requires surgery?"

"The wound from which the Governor suffers is personal," Oliver Pollock said quietly. "Were I inclined to be poetic, I might call it a thorn in his side."

"I'm afraid I don't understand, sir."

"I refer to the English colony at Natchez."

"I know little of Natchez, beyond the fact it's in Loyalist hands."

"Perhaps we should let the Governor himself explain the situation."

A short, stocky man in a truly resplendent uniform had entered the room on silent feet and was glancing through a sheaf of papers on the desk. There was no denying the authority of Bernardo de Gálvez's presence. The swallow-tailed coat he wore was of pure white silk, without epaulettes: the general's rank was advertised only by the sash, embellished with three bands of gold embroidery, that crossed the pouter-pigeon chest. At first glance, the Governor of Louisiana seemed young for his rank. It was only when he looked again that John noted the circles under the drooping eyelids, the spatter of gray in the coal-black sideburns. He had heard enough of this remarkable Spaniard's exploits to have a healthy respect for his intelligence. He made no effort to break the silence, as de Gálvez continued to study the papers on his worktable.

The Governor spoke quietly—with his eyes on the dispatches. "You'll forgive my tardiness, Doctor? Mr. Pollock has already explained it, I trust."

"Adequately, sir," said John. Though he understood the strategy well enough, he could feel himself bristling.

"Pensacola was invested, as of today," said de Gálvez. "We hope to be masters of West Florida by May. Does that shock you, Dr. Powers?"

John stole a glance at Pollock, but the merchant had given the Governor the floor. "I've already said I'm above politics," he murmured. "Like many another, I'm choosing no side in this rebellion."

"What of the red coat you lost in Pensacola? And the oath you swore in England to defend King George?"

John felt his heart plummet, even while he stared back boldly at the Governor. Clearly it was too late to dissemble; if the Spaniard had already ticketed him as a spy, his case was desperate indeed. "A doctor takes no active part in a war, señor," he said. "Does it matter which army he serves?"

"You had the rank of surgeon captain. Surely that implies a certain loyalty."

John forced a smile, without too much effort. "It seems you know a great deal about me, Governor."

"But naturally. I've had agents working inside Pensacola for months. I know the details of your court-martial, and the exact circumstances of your departure."

De Gálvez was smiling as he spoke. When John saw that Pollock, too, was smiling, he permitted his guard to relax a trifle.

"I'm glad I used my right name at the custom shed," he told them. "It must have saved you time."

"Names seldom mean too much in Louisiana," said de Gálvez. "Many a man has begun a new life here, under another label. Intentions are a different matter. I'm afraid I must ask for yours."

"I assure you I've nothing to hide."

"Let us hope you mean that, Doctor. You'll admit that your court-martial *could* have been staged for a purpose. Officers have been cashiered before, so they could join the enemy as secret agents."

"Believe me, I came here on my own. You no doubt know I was ordered to leave Pensacola at once. It seemed only natural to travel west—out of British territory."

"Is it not also natural that I should question your reason for visiting New Orleans?"

De Gálvez spread his hands in a quick, explosive gesture. "Permit me to rehearse your actions after your trial. First, you confer with Señora Wright—a lady who might be described as more royalist than the King. Next, you proceed to Mobile—and acquire a charming companion you call your bride—although the alcalde has recorded no marriage. Finally, you hire a boatman to whisk you to Natchez, with the least delay. Can you blame me for being more puzzled than ever?"

John paused over his answer, though he sensed that hesitation could be fatal. The feel of a hempen collar at his throat—no more than a threat when he entered this room—was now far too real for comfort. De Gálvez had never been said to temper justice with mercy. John was sure he could be ruthless as Torquemada himself when he sensed a real threat to his power.

"I'll take your points in order, if I may," he said. "As to my interview with Mrs. Wright, the explanation is simple. The lady offered me a share in her husband's practice—in Dr. Wright's name."

"Why did you refuse the offer?"

So Inez, like the shameless baggage she was, had been listening at the keyhole, that night at the Royal George. John could not keep down a sardonic chuckle. "It seems your eavesdropping was thorough, señor. Apparently you understand my motives better than I do myself."

"I don't understand this one, Dr. Powers. If you intended to practice medicine among the English, why didn't you join Mrs. Wright on her return journey?"

"Frankly, I was in no mood to settle down at once. I'd worn a British tunic for a long time, and the memory still choked me. The offer was left open. I decided to adventure a bit on my own before I took it up."

"Your adventures, I take it, included the lady in Mobile?"

"The lady I won at cards," said John dryly. "She's a prize few men would surrender. Does that answer point two, General?"

"Fair enough, Doctor. Why must you go upriver tomorrow?"

"My reason seems logical to me. I needn't remind you that it's often easier to acquire a lady's friendship than to surrender it."

"Your point is well made."

"Call me a moralist, if you like—but I feel responsible for this lady's welfare. The nearer one is to the frontier, the fewer questions are asked about one's past."

De Gálvez shook his head—and his perplexity seemed genuine. "The Anglo-Saxon male is a strange animal, Doctor. I'm afraid I shall never understand him too well. Still, I'm disposed to accept your story—since it fits the known facts."

John breathed deep, though he kept his bland mask unchanged: it would never do to expose the profound relief he felt. "Does that mean we've your permission to proceed?"

"Of course. The necessary document will be ready in the morning. But I must ask a price for it."

Again, John glanced quickly at Pollock, but the merchant now seemed half asleep in his armchair. "I'm at your service," he said. "At this time, I could hardly be otherwise."

"The favor I ask is important to me, Doctor. You must do it willingly. Let me begin by saying that it concerns your friends the Wrights—both Señora Wright and her husband."

"I'm hardly intimate with either. In fact, I've yet to meet Dr. Wright."

"The lady trusts you," said the Governor. "We can assume her husband will do likewise. Will you convince them they are playing a dangerous game? That their lives may be forfeit if they continue?"

"I don't think I follow you," said John—who followed perfectly. Be as ruthless as you wish, he told the Governor silently. But I insist you show your hand.

"You're aware, of course, that Natchez has been a rallying point for Loyalists since the American Revolution began? That Dr. Evan Wright is the center of the Tory faction—with his wife a most spirited collaborator?"

"Of course."

"Naturally, we knew of her trip to Pensacola to seek military help. Since that mission was fruitless, we made no attempt to detain her when she passed through New Orleans." De Gálvez turned to Pollock, whose eyes were open now. "Señor Pollock, I might add, was in agreement with that decision."

"As a former horse-trader," said the merchant, "I've yet to tether a mare on a short rope. Especially a high-stepping filly like Stella Wright."

"Patriotism is a strange flower," said the Governor. "In this colonial war, it has bloomed on both dunghill and aristocrat's lawn. Señor Pollock tells us that its fruit will be something the world has not yet seen—but that is no concern of mine. I'm here to hold the river for Spain. I'm asking your help in that task."

"Let me make sure I understand," said John. "You're releasing me tonight on condition I persuade the Wrights to remain neutral. What argument can I use to convince them?"

"A simple one—live and let live. If England wins, the land is still theirs. If she loses, nothing can keep the Spanish standard out of Natchez. If the Wrights will mind their manners, they'll find me a generous conqueror."

"And if they don't?"

"Then I must strike back with all my force. Pensacola may be a hard nut to crack after all. I can't afford insurrection in my back yard while the siege is in progress. Dr. Wright is well aware of my dilemma. If he means to launch a war of his own in Natchez, now is the ideal time."

"You've a garrison at Fort Panmure."

"It is inadequate for offensive action. I will be even more candid: a determined assault on the fort might reduce it tomorrow. New Orleans itself might be the next victim of a Loyalist revolt in Natchez."

"Surely they'd never risk an attack on the city."

"Mr. Pollock will tell you that his rebels have been just as daring —and succeeded. The people of Natchez are the same men—with different views. Who am I to say what risks they'd take, in the flush of victory?"

The Governor sat down at last, and lifted exquisitely booted feet to his worktable. The appearance of repose hardly deceived John: like a coiled spring, de Gálvez was incapable of containing his expansive strength for long.

"No matter how great his triumph," said the Spaniard, "Evan Wright must understand it would be temporary. My sovereign's flag still flies above Fort Panmure. Let him fire a single musket against it, and I'll hang both him and his citizen army."

"I'm to convey *that* message, sir?"

"In so many words. Convince them it's no idle threat. Above all, insist I'm eager for their friendship. If they will curb their patriotism, there'll be no confiscations—and no punishments. Not even an oath of allegiance to Spain. Only the promise to obey our laws, when the east bank of the river is ours."

"Why choose me as your advocate? Why not Mr. Pollock?"

"Dr. Wright would consider me a special pleader," said the merchant. "A red-handed renegade in fact—of the same stripe as

John Hancock or Sam Adams. No, Dr. Powers: you're our candidate for dove of peace. You can never be accused of self-interest."

"Señor Pollock is right," said de Gálvez. "Naturally, there is no reason why you should refer to any reward I promised you."

"No reward was mentioned, besides your gratitude," said John. "Or should I include the happy fact that my own neck is still unstretched?"

"Frankly, Dr. Powers, I wished to secure your help before bringing so mundane a subject as money into our conference. But His Catholic Majesty is prepared to pay you liberally. If Natchez is still neutral when peace is signed, I'll present you with a thousand-acre land grant—and a substantial loan to put that land to work. You may choose your acres near either New Orleans or Natchez. Both cities have their greatest years before them."

John swallowed hard. The Governor was certainly not ungenerous.

"If you'd care to become a Spanish subject," de Gálvez added, "there's no real limit to your future. I'd be glad to appoint you as my personal physician. So, I'm sure, would Señor Pollock. You could become the richest doctor in the province."

"I'm afraid your offer is out of all proportion to any service I can render," said John—feeling the stiffness of his disclaimer even as he uttered it.

"By no means," said de Gálvez. "I shall put it in writing, and include it with the dossier I'll send you tomorrow. Memorize it, Doctor—and hold it before you as an incentive. It may give you some notion of your value to our cause."

7

There was more, but John remembered but little of it when he stood on the steps of the *palacio* and breathed deep of the humid night breeze from the levee. His brain was whirling with a dozen contrary impulses; when he glanced at his watch in the light spill from a sentry box, he was amazed to find that only an hour had passed since he left the tavern.

He had entered the Governor's mansion, certain that he would emerge in irons—if he emerged at all. Yet he had no real sense of freedom as he took the first turning to the Place d'Armes. He was his own man again—with a sloop to take him upriver and a clear path to Stella Wright. Why, when the most powerful man in Louisiana had lifted the last bar, did he feel an irrational urge to hold back?

On his way to the inn, he was aware that his white-uniformed bodyguard was still three paces in his rear. He heard the click of flintlocks as they passed a café, and knew that a brace of footpads, intent on trailing him to the darkness of the next crossing, had slunk back to the bar. Again, at the entrance to the inn, he saw one of the guards spring forward and deflect a great, hulking fellow at bayonet point, just as the man was about to envelop him in a bear hug he might never have survived.

The perils of the polyglot town held his attention but lightly. New Orleans was already behind him now, no less firmly than Mobile and Pensacola. His mind was riveted on a frontier outpost far upriver, and what awaited him there.

The two infantrymen presented arms smartly at the stairway to his suite. He watched them take up their vigil in the courtyard; it was only right that he should be under surveillance. Not that Bernardo de Gálvez feared he would break his promise. Those two long-legged soldiers (who resembled a pair of mournful wading birds as they paced the court) were his guard of honor.

A candle still burned in the parlor of the suite. He was a little startled to observe that the door to the bedroom was now open wide. The question answered itself when he picked up the square of note paper propped against the candlestick.

> *Dearest:*
>
> *I'll try to wait up for you.*

He read the note twice before he grasped its full import. Was it possible that Faith (suspecting that his departure was a prelude to serious trouble) was covering his tracks, in the event his rooms were searched in his absence? Or was that veiled invitation all it implied—a summons to make this wedding masquerade real?

Pondering this second possibility, he slowly burned the note in the candle flame. The hammer blows of his pulse sounded their own warning: once he stepped across that bedroom threshold, he might no longer be the master of his desire. Remembering the kiss they had shared, he could understand Faith's train of thought perfectly. An honest partner to the end, she had regretted her frightened withdrawal. Understanding his yearnings accurately enough, she was offering herself on his terms.

He sighed deeply: it was a sigh that came from the heart. Moving on tiptoe lest he waken her, he closed the bedroom door firmly, and sought the spartan comfort of the settee.

Natchez

*D*awn had broken behind the bluff on the river's eastern bank. On the western shore, where the sloop darted like a restless bird, the memory of night still lingered, along with the mist in the cypress hammock that fringed the bank. Standing in the bow with a grains-pole, testing the bottom as Yulee managed the tiller, John Powers continued his search for an observation point, now that another morning was about to spread across the Mississippi.

He turned to smile at Faith, poised with a foot on the gunwale, her fingers gripping the sheets. In doeskin breeches and shirt, a man's slouch hat level with her eyes, she could have passed for a boy in that uncertain light.

"Hard larboard, skipper! Dry land ahead!"

"Hard larboard it is, sir."

Yulee's answering shout, delivered in a clipped British accent, would not have disgraced the quarter-deck of an English man-of-war. The sloop, taking the easy water under the bank, continued to play the homing swallow, there in the shadow of the cypress. Then, as the bottom lands receded downstream, a high, deep-wooded point lifted from the mists ahead.

Faith dropped the mainsail instantly as John called a second order. Riding smoothly behind the tug of the jib, the vessel plunged straight for the land. Just in time, Yulee brought the bowsprit into the wind. The anchor dropped in shoal water, holding the sloop steady until John could complete the mooring by lashing the painter to the first convenient tree.

At that precise instant, the sun lifted above the bluff on the far shore. In a twinkling, the Mississippi changed from slate-gray to a rich golden-brown; the channel danced with a hundred white-caps, where the wind roiled its surface at the bend upstream. John shaded his eyes against the glare. He felt his spirits lift as he picked out the silhouette of the man-made palisade against the sunrise.

"Fort Panmure, Doctor," said Yulee. "The town itself lies under the bluff. You will see it plainly, once the sun has lifted."

The half-breed leaped ashore, and offered Faith his hand. The trio climbed the shore line, through a dense growth of dog fennel and water oak. Beyond, a knoll lifted cleanly above the leafy tangle. Yulee, John gathered, had chosen this mooring with care. Cautious to the end, he had brought his sloop upstream in the shadows of dawn, to a spot where they could study their destination in safety.

2

The precision of today's mooring was part of the routine that had featured their voyage. Veteran of a hundred similar journeys upstream, Yulee had timed the laps perfectly. They had made camp each sundown on a towhead, or an islet that was both dry and deserted. Shunning the bivouacs of the riverside trails, the half-breed had spared his passengers all contact with the ruffians who frequented such spots, ready to relieve unwary voyagers of purse and life.

Each night, Yulee had built a sapling framework as a foundation for their camp. Here, he spread an extra sailcloth to make a tent for Faith; he and John slept before the coals of the campfire, wrapped to the eyes in their blankets as a protection against the insect hordes. Each dawn, the half-breed had wakened them as he bustled over that same fire, where slabs of bacon broiled in the skillet, along with corn cakes and catfish fresh from the river.

John had hoped to find Faith adjusted to the rough-and-ready tempo of this voyage. Not even in his most sanguine dreams had he expected her to become part of the boat from the first day. When Yulee rested for an hour at midmorning, she had handled the tiller as easily as he. When they camped at sunset, she had hunted at John's side—and shown herself equally adept at bringing in a rabbit or a wild turkey for the skillet.

There had been a special enchantment in those sorties among the moss-draped oaks of some island—or into the woods beyond the bank, on the rare occasions when they camped on the mainland. It was a magic John had never dared to break with such intrusions as queries on their future. Here in the wilderness, with the river as their only adversary, it had been a simple matter to still the ghost of passion—and easier still to forget the note he had burned above the candle flame in New Orleans. If Faith had wondered at his withdrawal she did not betray her pique. Had she been, in truth, the slender boy she resembled, their voyage upriver could not have been more innocent.

As for Yulee, if he was puzzled by the fact that Faith slept alone in that canvas shelter, he made no mention of it. The courtesy he showed both passengers was a constant thing—and it seemed untroubled by curiosity. From the first day, he had been Faith's friend as well as John's. This, too, had seemed natural, once they had adjusted to the close quarters aboard the sloop. Yulee was both Negro and Indian—in a land where such breeds were generally regarded as inferior. Yet he was as free as the passengers he served with such quiet devotion; he had never presumed on the relationship, though both treated him as an equal.

Last night, they had camped on an island thick with willows. A light drizzle had tapered off at midnight, promising a clear dawn. As was their custom, they had broken camp before sunrise, taking to the river the moment there was light enough to mark the channel. Yulee had set his course along the western bank; thanks to the bend upstream, the current followed the bluffs on the other shore.

They had moved upstream rapidly in the sluggish shallows. Now, staring across the whitecaps on the Father of Waters, marking the exact shape of Natchez for the first time, John knew their arrival could not have been better planned. Sunrise was the proper moment to view a strange land. Any mystery, however deep, must inevitably seem clearer in the first flush of morning.

He saw that Fort Panmure was strategically placed. Known as Fort Rosalie in the days of the French occupation, rechristened when the British took over that bank of the Mississippi, it seemed ridiculously small at that distance. John could understand why de Gálvez had not troubled to change its name when a force of Spanish rangers had captured it, remounted its gun swivels, and settled behind its palisade to await the outcome of a war fought elsewhere.

He counted a half-dozen gunports on the riverside. Save for the snouts of the battery, there was no sign of human occupancy. The main gate (which opened direct to a rough corduroy road that snaked down the bluff to the river's edge) seemed to stand a trifle ajar. The flagstaff, thrust against the sunrise from a corner sentry box, was bare of its standard. Expecting the sound of a Spanish bugle at reveille, John wondered at the laxity of the commandant—then shrugged off the question as he turned to examine the town itself, clustered on the riverbank almost in the fort's shadow.

Founded no more than a generation ago by the French, drenched in blood after Indian raids, Natchez was more village than town. Most of the houses clustered thickly below the bluff, where a few jerry-built wharves thrust into the suck of the river. John could see that these dwellings were little more than four-square log cabins. Some of them were clay-chinked and white-washed; all were blank-walled save for loopholes beneath their eaves—self-contained bastions even today, though the threat of Indian reprisal had receded years ago.

Yet even in this straggling community, it was possible to read the future of Natchez as well as the past. Situated at a strategic

point, surrounded by the richest farmlands in all the Mississippi
Valley, the town could not help but prosper when the swords of
three hostile powers were sheathed. Here and there along the
bluff, vast stretches had already been cleared to make way for
plantations-to-be; while most of the land thus exposed was a
wilderness of stumps, other areas were green with fresh cotton.

Despite the early hour, John could pick out slave gangs at work
in these prosperous furrows. Farther back from the sharp-etched
silhouette of the bluff, he could see the roofs of houses that would
have ornamented the demesne of any Eastern squire. These, he
gathered, were the dwellings of Loyalists from the seaboard colonies; many had flocked here with their families at the outbreak of
the revolution.

Faith's voice broke his inventory. "Are you disappointed, John?"

"Not at all," he smiled. "Did you expect another New Orleans?"
He turned as Yulee, crouched in the fork of a tree behind them,
gave a sharp exclamation of surprise.

"Look again at the fort, Doctor. They are watching the boats
coming downriver—but they do not show themselves."

John swung his eyes upstream. Intent on the town and the
land above the bluff, he had forgotten the river that was the genesis of Natchez. A group of flatboats, rounding the mile-long bend
with the current behind them, were just drawing within gun range
of the fort. The muzzles of the cannon seemed to converge on the
little water caravan as stealthily as though the unseen gunners
were crouched in some monster duckblind.

"What do you make of it, Yulee?"

The half-breed stripped a handful of leaves from the nearest
wild grape, rolled them into a tight funnel, and handed it to John.
"The Indians use this when no spyglass is handy," he said. "See for
yourself, Doctor."

John turned his crude telescope on the flatboats; it was aston-
ishing how clearly the boatmen sprang into focus, now that
he could concentrate his vision on a single area. Even without
the sun-faded deerskins and biblical beards that muffled their

faces to the eyes, those lanky river rats bore the mark of Kentucky. The tarpaulin-lashed barrels amidships could contain nothing but salt meat for the New Orleans market. The cargo in the snug after-houses were pelts from backwoods trap lines, destined for sky-rocketing markets abroad.

"Study the fort again, Doctor," said Yulee.

His words were punctuated by the boom of a swivel gun. The cannon of Fort Panmure fired singly rather than in salvo. Round shot, falling in midstream, made a neat pattern of waterspouts, each a trifle closer to the flotilla. The meaning of the threat was unmistakable. Deep-loaded as they were, these clumsy log rafts had no choice but to run with the current, in the very shadow of the bluff. A second volley, dropped as precisely as the first, could send the entire flotilla to the bottom.

John watched as the boatmen scurried to raise a white flag. As though in response to this signal, a broad-shouldered figure leaped into view on the ramparts. A sword flashed in the morning sun, pointing imperiously to the docks below the rampart. One by one, the flatboats snubbed in at the bank, where a score of figures were already dancing in triumph.

The whole maneuver had had a ghostly quality, now that the boom of the cannon had died. A Louisiana heron, which had risen from its perch with a guttural scream, settled in the ambush of another treetop. As the first flatboat came to rest on the far bank, a flag whipped into view at last above the sentry box of the fort. It was the ensign of England, proud as a bugle call against the morning sky.

3

John returned to the realities of his own position when he felt Faith's hand on his arm.

"What's happening over there, John? Why are they firing on the boats?"

He passed her the spyglass. "It seems that Spain has lost the Battle of Natchez."

The broad-shouldered figure was capering wildly on the ramparts; even at that distance, there was something familiar about the man that John could not pin down. But the central situation was evident. The Loyalists of Natchez, by whatever stratagem, had already taken possession of Fort Panmure—and had just offered graphic proof that the guns of that tiny bastion could control the river below them.

When Faith returned the telescope, he swept the eastern bank more carefully. At least a score of flatboats and bateaux were already moored there, beside the most recent arrivals.

"I still don't understand," said Faith. "Is your mission over here before it began?"

"What else?"

The trio scrambled down from the knoll in sober silence. The sloop was still at its mooring, but a visitor had gone aboard—a long-legged visitor in butternut homespuns, with an even longer rifle cradled in one arm. John's hand closed on Yulee's wrist as the latter lifted his own rifle. It was essential to walk warily, until this situation was clarified.

Three other men emerged from a canebrake with rifles alert. Like the man on the sloop, they wore homemade trousers, butternut shirts, and snakeproof boots—the universal garb of the riverman. And yet, they had more than a semblance of military authority about them. All were obviously awaiting orders from the man on deck, whose lopsided grin seemed oddly friendly, when measured against those leveled guns.

"Just drop your fowling piece, mister," he called. "And tell your boy to do the same. That way, no one's likely to get hurt."

"Who are you?"

"I'll ask the questions. You're doing the visiting."

John spoke loudly enough for all four captors to hear. "I'm Dr.

John Powers. These are my wife and boatman. I'm en route to Natchez to call on Dr. Evan Wright."

"Are you, now? Is he expecting you?"

"Of course. May I ask your name?"

"Major Ned Beasley, Doc. Militia commander of the forces of King George."

"I thought the only troops here were Spanish."

"If you were spying from that knoll, you'll know different now."

John kept voice and temper level. "We ran upriver to approach with the current," he said. "We were taking a bearing on the town."

The lanky countryman shrugged. "Best tell that story to the colonel first. I'll send word to Dr. Wright that you've arrived safe and sound."

"As you like," said John. He stepped aboard the sloop, and gave his hand to Faith. "Come, my dear. We must satisfy the military that we're honest. Can we ferry you across, Major?"

"Sure can, Doc. The boys will follow us."

Yulee was already at the sheets without awaiting orders. They slipped from the mooring ahead of a freshening breeze, with Beasley nursing his musket in the bow. The militiamen followed at a short distance in their own craft—a dugout canoe, fitted with a crude sail, which had been nested in the canebrake. Running upstream in the slack water along the bank, Yulee took his vessel into a sharp tack, to enter the river channel at a point above the bluff. John felt the worst of his fears dissolve when the butternut major, stretching his legs, began to chat as easily as though they had been friends of long standing.

The fort had fallen to the English two days ago—just how, it seemed, was a military miracle not even the major had grasped too firmly. Their commanding officer had arrived but recently from Pensacola. He had taken a firm hand with the secretly armed forces in Natchez: with Dr. Wright's permission, he had driven the Spaniards from their bastion with only negligible casualties. Now, acting as representative of his King, this wily warrior was halting all flatboats at cannon point, with the hope of cutting off supplies to New Orleans from the upper valley.

Most of the American heartland, Beasley conceded, was now in Whig hands (this, as John knew, was the usual label for rebels in Tory areas). So far as Beasley was concerned, the enemy might consolidate his conquest and keep the Atlantic seaboard as well, providing the valley stayed English. Eventually, he felt sure, the forces of the rebel General Clark would give up all attempts to maintain a supply line to New Orleans. With the coming of peace, Natchez would be in a position to establish herself as a river queen without rival, including the upstart city to the south. . . .

Now and again, as this recital continued, John stole a glance at Faith. It was reassuring to find that the girl was listening with an interest that matched his own. He had suspected that she would face most emergencies with that same aplomb.

"Tell me this, Major," he said, "why were you on the west bank this morning?"

"Routine patrol. Some of these river rats drive their rafts aground when we challenge 'em. Our job's to make sure they're collared."

"What of the Spanish garrison at the fort? Did you make them prisoners too?"

John noted a gleam of caution in Beasley's eye. "Guess that's the colonel's story."

"And who is this paragon from Pensacola?"

Again, the major had the look of a solemn boy guarding a military secret. "I'll let him introduce himself, Doc."

On that note, Beasley composed himself in the bow and looked up proudly at the hill of Natchez—a two-hundred-foot bluff, shining with burgeoning wild grape and white bursts of dogwood. Already, this massif had begun to cast its shadow on the smooth flow of the river. At closer view, the tumbled roofs of the shacks along the water were even less imposing than they had seemed from the western bank; Natchez was revealed as an outsize village that had somehow managed to cling to this muddy lip of land, despite the threat of flood and tornado.

Save for the zigzag of corduroy that ascended to its summit, the bluff seemed untouched by human hand. It made a bizarre natural monument in the flatlands that surrounded it; from this angle, it was impossible to pick out the plantation rooftrees that had stood out so boldly at a distance. Only the frowning palisade of the fort was visible, and the black-nosed cannon waiting to challenge the next flatboat that swept into their sights.

Evidently their coming had been witnessed. John observed a corporal's guard awaiting them—a half-dozen men in homespuns whose discipline was in startling contrast to their garb. Beasley accepted their present arms with an acceptable salute and stepped up to the rickety pier he had selected as a mooring. With John in the van, and Faith clinging to his arm, the procession began the steep climb to the fort.

"Don't worry, Faith," he whispered. "These fellows must play hero until the novelty wears off. We've a straight story, and nothing to hide."

"Do I look afraid?"

"If I didn't know better, I'd say you were enjoying this."

Fort Panmure was a primitive bastion indeed. A palisade of pine and cedar logs, vaguely circular in shape, was buttressed by a terreplein for the gun mounts. The terreplein sloped to a constricted parade, flanked by barracks and the commandant's quarters. These were mere log cabins, cheerful with cook fires and the rough male laughter of farmer militia. Yet discipline seemed sharp, for all the horseplay. The sentries that patrolled the riverside were alert as hawks as they scanned the Mississippi for fresh plunder. The guards at the commandant's doorsill crossed muskets with a precision worthy of the London Horse Guards.

Major Beasley emerged in a moment with a beetle-browed aide in tow, and presented the latter with a flourish.

"Colonel Larkin, Doctor."

The newcomer was a humpbacked giant in a uniform that

strained at every button. Both the once bright tunic and its wearer had an air of costume about them. John suspected that Larkin was a relic of England's last long conflict with France: he was sure of it when the colonel addressed him in a parade-ground bellow grown rusty from disuse.

"You'll forgive us if this detention is unwarranted, Doctor—and my best compliments to your lady. But I needn't remind you that England's at war."

Larkin frowned but briefly at the passport John offered, though his eyebrows lifted as he noted the New Orleans custom stamp. Nor did he seem to listen with more than half an ear as John detailed the story of their upriver journey, and his intention to visit the Wrights.

"Stay a moment more—I'll see if our commandant can give you an audience," he said. "Ned, get the lady a chair."

Beasley had barely time to carry out this request when Larkin was back. Whatever had transpired inside the cabin was clearly in John's favor. Larkin all but swept the dust with his moldy tricorne as he stepped aside to let him enter.

"The commandant will talk to you now. Colonel Martin, may I present Dr. John Powers?"

4

Chris Martin sat behind a table loaded with maps and papers. He was wearing a new officer's coat with the double epaulettes of a colonel; even without this item of apparel, John would have recognized the man who had capered so gleefully on the ramparts. The coat was open to the last button, revealing the wearer's magnificent, bull-like chest—and the fact that he wore nothing beneath it, save a pair of farmer's breeches. But there was no escaping the former sutler's authority. The bark he offered

Larkin was enough to send that aged warrior scurrying, in his eagerness to leave the two men alone.

"Welcome to Natchez, Doc," said Chris. "I sort of figured you'd turn up here in time."

Ever since he had quitted Pensacola, John had forgotten the sutler's existence entirely—along with the sly offer he had made there. Now that they stood facing each other in Fort Panmure, he could still hardly believe what he saw.

"Don't tell me *you're* in command here," he managed at last.

"Complete with commission," said Chris genially. "Like to read it?"

John glanced at the sheet of foolscap the sutler tossed across the desk. He had examined a hundred such documents, and knew it was genuine enough. The Great Seal of Britain embossed the signature of Brigadier General Campbell, the representative of His Majesty in West Florida. With the usual rhetorical flourish, the paper informed all and sundry that Christopher Martin was hereby appointed colonel and leader of such volunteer inhabitants as he could procure to serve under his command.

"Did General Campbell send you here?"

"That he did. He figured a ruckus in de Gálvez's back yard was just what this war needed. I know the Creek country, so he made me his courier."

Chris had been sent from Pensacola, then (probably at the moment the town was put under siege), to deliver commissions to all those in Natchez loyal to King George. At least it explained Beasley's shambling but effective force, and Larkin's moth-eaten regimentals. It was possible that Campbell himself had signed the order elevating Chris to command—though it seemed far more likely that Chris had forged his own commission during his journey. But John kept this surmise to himself.

"You've done well as a soldier," he observed.

"Well enough," said the brand-new colonel. "If you were captured by Beasley, you'll have the story. He's gabby enough."

"I'd rather listen to your version, Chris. How did you reach Natchez?"

"Campbell sent me to the mouth of the Pearl River in a fast sloop. The Indians paddled me upstream to Red Bluff—and I cut across country from there."

John nodded. Such a journey, while hazardous, was feasible enough for a trained woodsman.

"I gather it's you who trained the militia?"

"I'll take most of the credit. Old Larkin helped. So did Doc Wright."

"Who persuaded the fort to surrender?"

"Who else but your humble servant? First off, I knew the dons had been chewing their cuds here—with the Wrights' militia getting meaner each day. Second, I had a piece of luck on the trail. Picked up a Choctaw chief I know—fellow named Red Shoes, with a fair-size hunting party, heading home for the Yazoo country. Persuaded 'em to camp under the bluff awhile, and make a powwow——"

Again, John found he was nodding in grudging admiration. "Don't tell me you used Indian allies?"

"Not all the way. Those powwow drums were enough. All that time, you understand, we were deploying around the fort, and bringing up fieldpieces. Two days ago, I figured we sounded mad enough. So I sent in a message, saying we'd tunneled through the bluff, and were ready to blow the palisade to hell—before I sent in two hundred braves with tomahawks."

"And they believed you?"

"They'd been penned in a long time—and they were really scared. All we'd traded so far were a few shots—but my boys had picked off a dozen of their sentries, neat as squirrels. A bit of cannonading from the woods finished the persuasion."

Chris chuckled at the picture he was drawing. " 'Course I turned generous when they asked for surrender terms. Let 'em march out with their colors, once they'd stacked their arms. I even gave 'em the first batch of flatboats we captured, so they could go cry on the Governor's shoulder."

The stratagem was complete now. In his mind's eye, John could see the defeated garrison slinking downstream in the dark; he could hear de Gálvez's bellow when he learned of the shabby but effective ruse that had forced his troops to surrender. As an item in the grand pattern of frontier war, such a defeat could prove decisive. It might even permit Campbell to strike at New Orleans, in conjunction with British forces already in Georgia and the Carolinas. Yet John's mind refused to admit such rosy possibilities; Fort Panmure, and the backwoods force that had seized it, were problems the Spanish Governor would settle later.

"You might congratulate me, Doc."

John came back to Chris Martin with a frown. The story of the Battle of Natchez was clear enough. But he could not yet believe the part the ex-sutler had played.

"One question more," he said. "What's your profit in this business?"

"Look over that parapet, Doc. Count the flatboats we've bagged. I've two warehouses splitting their sides with plunder, and more to come each day. So far, we're calling it the spoils of war. But don't tell me the citizens of Natchez won't vote me my cut."

"What happens when Pensacola falls?"

"Doc Wright is willing to take that gamble. Why shouldn't I go along?"

"Knowing you, I can see no reason at all."

"What d'you mean by that?" For the first time, the self-styled colonel's eyes had narrowed dangerously. John remembered, all too vividly, that Chris Martin was in absolute command here. Clearly (since Chris had the power to smash him beyond repair, with a single order) he could be goaded just so far.

"Keep your temper," he told the sutler. "I'm neither a spy nor an informer. I don't belittle your military genius for a moment. But I do happen to be fresh from New Orleans. My information's more complete than yours."

Chris listened in a kind of sullen aloofness while John told the story of his meeting with de Gálvez and the message he had brought.

"Sorry, Doc," he growled. "I don't scare that easy."

"Do you object to my delivering this threat to Dr. Wright?"

"Say what you like. You'll find him twice as brave as me. But I'd advise you to hold your tongue. You've a good reason for coming here. Keep your mouth shut, and you'll be sure of a welcome."

The sutler was still scowling, but John risked another prod. "Be honest, Chris. Do you think Natchez can hold out?"

"We can last until Pensacola falls. By that time, anything can happen. Clinton and Campbell may move in from the east. We could take New Orleans together."

"Perhaps you can sell that brand of opium to the Wrights. But you must know you can't wound a Spaniard in his pride and survive."

"What's that supposed to mean?"

"It's only a question of time before de Gálvez comes upriver for his revenge. When that happens, it'll be easy enough for you to fade from the picture. What happens to the Wrights—and the others who have roots here?"

"Damn it all, they *asked* me to take the fort. Doc Wright blessed the attack——"

"I'm not reproaching you. Just answer my question."

"Roots or no roots," said Chris, "they'd have to skedaddle fast."

"Then you do believe me?"

"'Course I do. I don't doubt de Gálvez will stage a lynching bee here, if he's able. He's well within his rights."

"And yet you picked off his sentries, and took the fort."

Chris shrugged. "All right, Doc," he said belligerently. "I'm here to line my pockets—and there's many another on both sides who'll do the same. But you needn't call me a coward; I'm taking my chances, too, along with this clutch of Britishers. And I'll tell you more. If the Governor does come calling, I'll lead 'em to safety. Can I say it fairer than that?"

There was something disarming about Chris Martin, even when the scoundrel was closest to the surface. "That'll do nicely, for now," John told him. "Do I have your permission to call on the Wrights?"

"My permission, Doc, and my blessing. Just don't upset the old man with too many cold facts. Remember he's a *real* patriot. The genuine article, if I make myself clear."

John could not avoid smiling, as he paused in the doorway. "And how would you define the genuine article, Colonel?"

"A man who won't let go till it thunders," said Chris. "A man who won't surrender, never mind the odds. In this war, you'll find most of that breed are Whigs. This one's a Tory, more's the pity."

5

The sandy Trace, winding north and east from the Natchez bluff, seemed more a prehistoric ditch than a formal road, though the light gig in which they were riding bounced easily along the ruts. Notched into the verdant forest that hemmed it, muffled in cascading masses of laurel and wild grapevine, it had a strange beauty of its own. John could almost believe that it had been carved here by some superhuman hand, for a purpose no mere mortal could divine.

Major Beasley (flicking a lazy whip as the gig eased downhill toward open farmland) was explaining that this portion of the Trace had once been a buffalo wallow, then an Indian trail. At present, it marked the beginning of the only well-marked path across the virgin wilderness. Its other terminus was Nashville, and the settlements on the Ohio. Generations of flatboatmen had used it as a practical, if highly dangerous, route for their homeward journey, once they had left their cargoes at Natchez or New Orleans.

Faith and John, seated beside their garrulous driver, were quite content to let his voice drone on. Yulee followed them in a buckboard, with their portmanteaux and other gear.

"You'll see Trail's End in a moment, Doc. It's a sight worth waiting for."

"Trail's End?" said Faith. "Surely that's a rather special name for a plantation house."

"Blame it on Mrs. Wright," said Beasley with a grin. "She's pretty special herself, if you ask me. 'Tisn't just because the Wrights' land marks the end of the Trace, more or less. She was hoping the doctor had seen the end of their own wanderings when they built here."

"How long have they lived in Natchez?"

"More than ten years now, if I remember rightly. Leastways, it was the year I brought my own brood out of Carolina. Larkin's been here almost that long; so have a few others you'll be meeting. *Those* are the nabobs—though it'd be fair to call 'em pioneers too, since they came in on the heels of the French. Most of 'em had land grants straight from London. All of 'em are rich enough to keep slaves."

John glanced at the plowmen working a strip of cleared land beside the Trace. To his surprise, they were white, to the last man—lanky fellows of Beasley's own cut, who raised a shout of greeting as the gig rolled by.

"Are they landowners too?"

"Yes and no. Some of 'em have a few acres. Mostly they're farmers who moved west ahead of the rebel armies. Those you just saw are 'croppers, breaking ground for the Wrights. The old doctor's given 'em asylum till the war's over."

"Dr. Wright sounds like a good Samaritan."

"He's that, all right," Beasley said heartily. "And a Croesus to boot, I might add. Enough in London to outlast any wind that blows. Land in East Florida, and land in the Old Dominion. 'Course the Whigs have taken most of *that*—but there's plenty left.

He's lived in all those spots I mentioned, until he couldn't stand the politics. They say he came here for his health."

With each turn of the wheels, the road was opening to bright vistas of cotton fields, foaming with the green of spring. At first glance, the Wrights' land seemed to sweep nearly to the horizon's rim. A second look told John that no more than a few acres had actually been cleared for planting; but it was apparent from the fire lanes in the encroaching forest that Evan Wright had staked out a vast preserve as his own. His home, rising on a hill in the very center of this domain, gave the scene its focus and its gracious meaning.

Trail's End, John saw, was a classic plantation house—redbrick, hip-roofed, with a two-story portico on its western face, framed in square white columns. Yet there was nothing formidable about this pleasant abode. Trail's End was simply a part of that landscape, like the camellia bushes that softened the long rectangle of its eastern wing, the massed scarlets of the azaleas along its driveway. The house belonged to these rich acres, as inevitably as the slaves in the rose garden that dropped in gentle terraces to a pond reflecting the bright blue of the Natchez sky.

Red brick was an almost unheard-of luxury three hundred river miles north of New Orleans—but Trail's End was built to endure. John had expected Evan Wright to plan boldly: his house was a visible proof of the enterprise that had put those fields to cotton, a crop that was only beginning to prove its value in the world market. Yet Trail's End was down-to-earth, for all its aura. As the gig rolled up the drive, John saw that each window was fitted with its iron shutter; behind the kitchen wing, the whitewashed quarters of the slaves were bricked as solidly as the main dwelling. Natchez (expanding in the sun like a confident giant) was still mindful of its last Indian attack—and stood ready to repel invaders.

Beasley's whip pointed to the forest-bound horizon. "Yonder's the Rodell chimneys—Alvin Rodell put down his foundations the year after the Wrights. And that's Poling Hall on the next rise.

You won't see many mansions, this far upriver: the war's slowed down building, but these folks will own the world, when Natchez comes into its own."

"Providing they've bet on the right side," said John.

"How's that again, Doc?"

"Did these neighbors join the attack on the fort?"

"That they didn't, now you mention it—and more's the pity. Both families boarded up solid, and took off for other parts." Beasley gave a short and bitter laugh. "If you ask me, they're lucky not to be burned to the ground."

John heard this news with no real surprise: from the oldest street in Boston to the farthest limits of the backwoods, the American rebellion had set brother against brother, clan against clan. Though Natchez was a Loyalist hotbed, he could well believe that there were dissenters here as well—malcontents who would gladly cheer any blow against British power, or plain do-nothings who refused to risk their whole future on a concept as nebulous as King George and England.

"Where are they now—stirring up trouble in New Orleans?"

"Not Alvin, Doc—he's too good a businessman to jump ahead of the cat. And Sam Poling's every bit as shrewd. My guess is they're holed up in some backwoods cabin—trusting de Gálvez will hear *they* weren't on hand when the fight started."

Though his manner was still cheerful, there was a furrow in the butternut major's brow when he tossed his reins to a house slave. "Reckon I'm giving you folks too many facts," he said. "You'll find the old doc's a better explainer. You can go straight through to the back gallery; he'll be waiting for you there."

Faith glanced down at her boyish garb, as though her surroundings had shocked her back to a sense of propriety. "If you don't mind, John," she said, "I'll face no more strangers until I've changed my clothes."

A black major-domo was already bowing them up to the portico. From the corner of his eye, John saw that a pair of house slaves, in the same canary-yellow livery, had come forward to help Yulee unload the portmanteaux.

"Don't tell me we're staying here, Major?"

Beasley laughed aloud. "The Wrights won't let you stay anywhere else. Your room's been ready, ever since I sent word from the fort."

"In that case," said Faith, "I'll go up and change. My husband will explain to Dr. Wright, I'm sure."

Even in her incongruous garb, she managed to look every inch the lady as she swept through the tall, plain-paneled doorway and ascended the spiral of stair well beyond. The Wrights' butler led the way with episcopal dignity; the house slaves followed with the baggage. John, since he had no choice, walked with Beasley down the long, sun-shot hallway that divided the formal rooms of Trail's End into two equal segments.

The proportions of the interior were designed to soothe both eye and spirit. A magnificent Adam mirror welcomed the visitor from an overmantel of fruited Italian marble. Ancestors, in ritual poses, looked down from cool wall panels. To the left, half-open doors permitted a glimpse of a baronial library. To the right, an archway opened to a double parlor with recessed window boxes and furniture that could have come only from Paris. John could picture the labor required to bring those mahogany pieces from the New Orleans levee after their Atlantic voyage, the bribes that had changed hands before that marble could leave its Italian hillside. It was evident that the Wrights felt the bribes well spent —if only to prove that civilization could plant its banner on the Natchez bluff.

He discovered his host on the rear gallery of the house. Evan Wright sat in an old-fashioned horsehair rocker, with his eyes on a cherry laurel that had just burst into bloom on the lawn. Viewed against that background, the master of Trail's End seemed secure as time: only the blanket that covered his knees and the cameo-sharp profile of the man himself suggested his frailty. John needed but a glance at his host's almost translucent skin, the spots of red on each cheekbone, to divine the nature of his illness.

Yet there was no overtone of death in that sun-warmed gallery, no hint of weakness in Evan Wright himself. The hand he offered John was firm with purpose. The eyes were bright with a spirit that transcended the fever within.

"This is a pleasure too long deferred, Dr. Powers. Won't you sit here beside me? Ned won't mind ringing for London."

Settled in an armchair, feeling the benison of the river breeze, John fought hard against an irrational conviction that this wisp of humanity was already a friend of long standing. *Evan Wright is like his wife,* he thought—*serene in his belief that most men are brothers, positive of his own essential rightness. A nabob and a gentleman, in short—rolled into one neat package. . . .* John smiled inwardly at the conceit. He had met his share of purse-proud aristocrats; he had known gentlemen in both rags and satin. This was his first encounter with wealth and humility, in the same person.

"I hope you've come to stay, Dr. Powers. My wife told me of your interview in Pensacola."

"I've yet to settle anywhere for long, Dr. Wright."

"Yet you've come to us, just as we hoped you would. With a bride on your arm, to make sure you'll put down roots."

London (the major-domo who had admitted them) had already appeared with brandy and Madeira, and a cedar box fragrant with Havana segars—a luxury John had first sampled on his arrival in West Florida. A draught from a decanter, joined to the aroma of the well-cured leaf, helped to bring his situation into perspective—including the picture of Natchez, which his host continued to paint in glowing colors.

"Believe me, Dr. Powers, this river valley is the land of tomorrow; with England behind us, we can't fail to prosper here. We'd only wither under the hand of Spain; that's why we've risked everything to take the fort——" The elder doctor had half risen from his chair, only to settle back as he surrendered to a brief but violent spell of coughing. "Once more, you must forgive me for not rising. I've had a rather protracted siege of illness this spring. But I did want to indicate the extent of my landhold. It will help to drive home my point."

"I've already seen much of your estate, sir."

"The view is better from this gallery. Show him, Ned. You know the landmarks."

John moved to the rail with Beasley: Evan Wright continued to speak from the armchair, as though he were consulting a map he knew by heart. "To the north, beyond that clump of cedars, my grant adjoins the Polings'. Now, if you'll count five fire lanes to the south, you'll see where it ends. To the west, it extends to the bluff. Twelve thousand acres in all—the gift of my sovereign. Can I do less than save it for England?"

"Are you the largest landholder in Natchez, Doctor?"

"By no means," said Evan Wright. "At the moment, I'm the largest in residence. Most of our plantations have gone fallow until the political situation resolves itself. Not all of the larger owners have cared to share the burden we assumed when we captured Fort Panmure."

John settled on the veranda rail, and stared down at his brandy. "I gather you felt the burden worth assuming?"

"It was a time for boldness, Dr. Powers—and we were fortunate in our field commander. Colonel Martin assures me that we can hold our position, until General Campbell sends help."

This, John noted, was a somewhat different version of the story Chris had told at the fort. He continued to hold his tongue, unwilling, as yet, to spoil the ambitious picture his host was drawing. "I gather that Colonel Martin has been most resourceful?"

"He has indeed, Dr. Powers. I can't honor him too highly."

"May I ask how this attack was mounted? The militia, I take it, is composed of King's men. Are all of them in your employ?"

"In a sense, I suppose. Look a bit farther—across that gully, between the stand of cypress and the bluff. You'll see another thousand acres of the finest bottom land in North America. That, too, was part of my grant from England. I've parceled it among fifty sharecroppers and their families—on condition they help clear my own land, and assist in my experiments with cotton and other staples. Naturally, they form the nucleus of our militia, and I undertook to supply them with arms."

"Are all these tenant farms the same?"

"Some are larger than others, depending on the family's size. Ned here has already bought back his land, and added more. So has my old friend and pensioner, Colonel Larkin. But even the smallest of my tenants can hope to be a prosperous landlord tomorrow—when Natchez is really England's."

"I can believe that too, sir. Are you sure it isn't too sanguine a dream?"

"So was the conquest of this continent, Dr. Powers. Surely we've the right to keep what we won?"

Moses, thought John, could have spoken no more ardently on his descent from Sinai; in the case of Evan Wright, the promised land was already attained. In every war, it seemed, there were prophets to spell out salvation—and others to lead the faithful to their doom. . . . He felt a premonitory chill as he weighed the possibilities before him. It was now all too evident that Chris Martin had fanned an incipient hostility into flame, for purely selfish reasons. It seemed certain that retribution would strike at almost any hour.

John shook off the mesmerism of Evan Wright's rhetoric and spoke out at last, without measuring the effect of his words. "Colonel Martin advised me not to mention this," he said, "but I feel I must. I bring a warning from Bernardo de Gálvez——" He went on quickly, before the others could speak. "A rather definite warning, I'm afraid. Will you listen with an open mind?"

Evan Wright smiled. "We'll do our best, Doctor."

The gallery was still when John had told his story of the meeting in the Governor's house in New Orleans—so still, that the sudden song of a mockingbird seemed an intrusion far beyond its size. Yet Evan Wright's voice was firm as ever when he spoke again.

"Do I take it I've signed my death warrant, in the Governor's book?"

"Not only you, Doctor—your whole militia company."

"We're over a hundred strong. Would he damn all of us?"

"I'm afraid that's just what he's done."

"The fort was never really attacked. Colonel Martin captured it by a ruse."

"It was still a military action; sentries were killed before the surrender. Did the whole command participate?"

"I'm afraid so, Dr. Powers."

"Are there Whig partisans in the vicinity to supply a list of names?"

"A few—more's the pity."

"Then it's my duty to repeat the warning: you'll be hounded to the last man."

"It's our hope the Spaniards will never return to Natchez."

"What if that hope is mistaken?"

Evan Wright studied the pattern of the blanket across his knees. When he looked up again, his eyes were clear and unafraid. "Wouldn't you say that was the threat of a desperate man, Dr. Powers?"

"I'm sure that Governor de Gálvez meant every word. What's more, he'll be twice as vengeful, now you've tricked him."

"Colonel Martin thinks differently."

"Colonel Martin is acting under orders. He was sent here to create a diversion. Naturally, he's done all he could to make the diversion a success. But it's only a temporary triumph; Natchez will never stand against a Spanish army. When Pensacola falls, its doom is sealed as well."

"You're a gloomy prophet, Doctor." Evan Wright turned to Beasley with the gentlest of smiles. "Do you agree with our visitor, Ned?"

"It could happen, just like he says. Remember Bloody O'Reilly in New Orleans?"

Glancing at Beasley, John saw that his story had struck home. The major was pale under his turkey-red tan; his eyes, rolling uneasily toward the river, seemed to vision a Spanish vanguard, intent on his personal extinction. The farmer turned warrior, it seemed, had a rude grasp of the verities which the doctor-philosopher lacked.

"Perhaps it's unfortunate you didn't arrive earlier, Dr. Powers," said Evan Wright dryly. "Though I'm sure none of us would have listened—including Ned."

"Fair enough, gentlemen," said Beasley. "I'll admit I was hell-bent for a fight, same as the others. I'll also admit I'm scared blue today."

"Suppose I'm right?" asked John. "What are your plans?"

"Most of us crossed over from the Carolinas to get here," said the major. "Reckon we can cross back, if we're warned in time. Nobody's neck is itching for a rope."

"And you, Dr. Wright?"

"As the instigator of this affair, I should take my punishment."

"The people would never stand for that," said Beasley. "If it comes to flight, you'll go along. Even if we have to hog-tie and carry you."

Evan Wright held up a soothing palm. "Aren't we crossing a great many bridges prematurely, gentlemen? We've friends in New Orleans, ready to warn us if Pensacola falls. Until then, I suggest we take what pleasure we can in the conclusion of our little war."

John got to his feet with a sudden resolve filling his brain; while it lasted, the sense of release was like a weight lifted from his soul. "A capital suggestion, sir," he agreed. "I'm sorry if I've spoiled that pleasure."

"You haven't, Doctor, I assure you. I shall continue to hope our good fortune is permanent."

"As you wish. I still felt I should deliver the Governor's warning. If you'll excuse me now, I'll return downriver."

"But you've only just arrived," Evan Wright protested. "Now you're here, we won't surrender you so easily."

"As the bearer of bad tidings, I mustn't wear my welcome out. Will you convey my compliments to your wife?"

"Why not convey them yourself, Doctor?"

John turned in time to see Stella Wright emerge from the rose garden, with a flower basket on one arm. Behind her, a slave trundled a barrow overflowing with azaleas. The smile she offered them began and ended in her wide blue eyes; it made him welcome, before she could speak a word.

There was no hint of coquetry in that smile; the greeting she offered him could not be said to go beyond her gracious role as chatelaine of Trail's End. And yet, John felt a strange surge of emotion as their hands met, a bondage he would never put into words.

"So you've joined us at last, Dr. Powers," she said. "Don't think I'd lost hope—but it's been a long time."

"Too long," he said—and felt the silken net tighten. It was a pleasant bondage, he reflected, part and parcel of this charming scene, of the peace that enveloped this house and garden like an invisible mantle. Try as he might, he could not avoid a sense of home-coming—as though he had been destined to walk into Stella Wright's world on just such a morning.

"You arrived opportunely, my dear," said Evan Wright. "Already, he's talking of returning downriver."

"That I'll not allow," said Stella. "No more will his bride. I've just looked in on her, Doctor—and insisted on an extended visit. May I congratulate you on your good fortune?"

John accepted the compliment with a wordless bow. The urge toward flight had been real enough just now. With one gesture of welcome, Stella Wright had made it seem ridiculous—the impulse of a schoolboy to avoid an authority greater than his own will.

Evan Wright was chuckling in the background. "It seems the

ladies have mapped out your immediate future, Dr. Powers. It's a way ladies have."

"Of course he must stay awhile," said Stella. "In Pensacola, I told him something of what Natchez has to offer a physician. He must see I spoke the truth."

"I can see that now, Mrs. Wright," said John. "As it happens, I'm here for another reason."

"Your wife explained that too," said Stella. "An ultimatum from de Gálvez, full of sound and fury. Now it's been delivered, you can think of other things. For example, the *soirée* I've planned in your honor."

"Hospitality's a sacred word here," said Evan Wright. "The moment we'd heard of your arrival, Stella sent notes to a dozen neighbors. Tonight, they're dining here especially to meet you. Forgive my bluntness, Doctor, but your hands are tied."

"Quite firmly," said Stella. "And I'm in no hurry to loosen the knot. Nor is Mrs. Powers."

"Don't tease him any longer, my dear," said her husband. "You'll find him a willing captive, I'm sure. Especially when he's gone the rounds with me tomorrow, and seen the medical problems I'm facing."

Stella had already moved to her husband's chair; she let an affectionate hand rest on his shoulder. "Evan tries to do too much. He needs help badly. But I explained that in Pensacola, didn't I?"

She was smiling at John over Evan Wright's shoulder, renewing her welcome with no further need of words. He permitted that unspoken bond to tighten still further. Already, he was beginning to understand her a little. The affection she was giving him now (and affection was hardly too strong a term) was part of her love for all the world. Like her husband's acceptance, it offered the home and hearth he had never known, the chance to find himself on his own terms. It was a far cry, he thought, from the dark compulsions that had brought him here: only a boor could fail to meet such warmth halfway.

"I'd be glad to—make the rounds," he said slowly.

"In that case, Evan," said Stella, "I'll rest on my laurels. If you gentlemen will excuse me, I'll arrange the flowers." She bestowed a final smile on John as she beckoned to the waiting slave. "Trail's End is prepared to receive guests at any time—but this is a special occasion."

6

Faith studied her face in the huge oval mirror above the dressing table, and treated her red-brown tresses to a dusting from the atomizer she had bought in New Orleans. The silk print she was wearing (a watermelon green, with an overlay of gold net) had come from a *boutique* in that same town. So had the hoop earrings and the high-heeled silver slippers, already tapping impatiently in response to the harp music that had begun to drift up the stair well. Watching her preen herself, John continued to take his ease on the chaise longue across the room. He could enjoy the luxury of a thoughtful pause before launching into his argument anew.

A measure of calm had descended on his mind after a long siesta. Now, stretching in the comfort of the cushions, he could tell himself that he had been overstrained this morning—that his encounter with the Wrights had never really gone beyond the bounds of hospitality, the genius for welcome for which the South was famous. True, he had consented to remain here tonight and tomorrow—but he could still depart when he chose. . . . Faith's problem, of course, was quite different—and he meant to solve it tonight.

"Even if I should stay awhile to help Dr. Wright," he said, "you'd be safer in New Orleans."

"I feel safe here, John. Safe enough to suit me, at any rate."

"I've said we could divide our cash. Yulee will stay on as your personal servant, after he's sailed you downriver. You can wait out the war in comfort; afterward, you can do as you like."

"But I'm doing what I like right now."

He kept his temper: he had expected her to be stubborn. "I've told you what will happen here, when Pensacola falls."

"You could be wrong."

"It isn't like you, Faith—refusing to face facts."

"Natchez doesn't seem in danger now. Not with Colonel Martin at the fort."

"Damn Chris Martin for a brassbound adventurer!" He found that he had just escaped shouting, and lowered his voice. "And a special damnation for all visionaries who dream of Utopia."

"That's a poor way to speak of Dr. Wright. You just said he's one of the finest men you know."

"He's also an idealist who's been taken in rather badly. And I'll never prove I'm right until it's too late. When that time comes, I want you out of harm's way."

"Stella isn't afraid," said Faith. She opened her jewel case and clamped on a bracelet blazing with paste diamonds. "Why should I turn tail, just because you've moved the Spanish Army into the Wrights' back yard?"

"Believe me, Faith, that's just where they'll be."

"Suppose you're wrong? You'd make me look like a coward. If you're right, our hosts will need all the friends they can find."

Still propped on pillows, John continued to study Faith in the mirror. This was not the first time he had been shocked by her prescience. He was glad now that she had not witnessed his reunion with Stella.

"Very well," he said. "Suppose I do remain here—serve as Dr. Wright's assistant while his illness lasts——"

"You know he's dying of consumption."

"It's all too likely, I'm afraid. Still, he might rally."

"But he won't be active much longer. You can be the first doctor in Natchez. Isn't that what you're really after?"

Faith's voice had been innocent as her manner—but John was

certain that the appraisal in the mirror was a two-way game. He took one of Evan Wright's segars to the tall French window that opened directly to the upstairs gallery. "Naturally it's an attractive prospect," he admitted. "It's also a hopeless dream—if the Spaniards take Natchez."

"Why? As a neutral, your hands will be clean. You can still practice here."

"These people are now open enemies of Spain. The moment de Gálvez moves upriver, they must run for their lives."

"And what if they do, John? *You'll* be in no more danger than the back-country Whigs—or the ones who stood aside."

"You're suggesting I settle here as Dr. Wright's assistant," he said stiffly. "If I decide on that course, I can hardly help taking sides."

"Sympathy for a business partner is one thing," said Faith. "Risking your life for him is quite another."

"Didn't you just say the Wrights would need friends, if trouble comes to Natchez?"

Still at the mirror, Faith lifted nut-brown shoulders in a philosophical shrug, and pinned a brilliant to her décolletage. "I've admitted I make friends easily. Just because I'd like to help the Wrights doesn't mean you must play follow the leader."

He moved to her in a quick, impetuous gesture, letting his fingers caress her shoulders as he met her eyes in the mirror. "I'm afraid that's just what I'd do, Faith," he said. "If I linger beyond tonight, that is. Once I sign on with Evan Wright, I'll probably stay to the end."

"Then we're in this together," she said.

"Were you testing me just now, by any chance?" he asked, with a rueful grin.

"Of course. May I add that you passed my first test with flying colors?"

"Will there be others?"

"Of course there will. Shall we go downstairs before dinner is served?"

"Tell me what you mean."

"I couldn't, so soon. Ask me tonight, when the party's over." She rose from the dressing table on that, and left the room—so quickly that he was forced to lengthen his stride to overtake her at the head of the stairs.

John saw at once that they had lingered too long over their dressing. The hallway below was filled with guests. Some of the visitors had already begun to sample the prodigal buffet over which a half-dozen aproned house slaves presided. Knowing that eyes were upon them, he produced his husbandly smile.

Colonel Larkin, wearing a frogged dress coat of the British Army, strutted forward to escort them to the front parlor, where the Wrights were still receiving latecomers. It was easy enough to drop back a pace, while Faith and that slightly fustian warrior conversed amiably. It was easier still to let his mind slip into a pleasant but dangerous reverie—the Whigs' rebellion ended, Natchez still firmly in Loyalist hands, and Stella Wright's husband already in a hero's grave. . . . The unworthy fancy died when he glimpsed his host, receiving his guests from an armchair, with an urbanity that transcended his illness. Bending above Stella's hand in apology for his tardiness, he could wonder why Faith had planted that image in his mind—and why she spoke of greater tests to come.

Receiving introductions right and left, accepting the welcome of the good Englishmen of Natchez with a heartiness he knew was adequate, John took command of his vagrant fancies. For this evening, at least, he would only observe. Later, he could plot his future course—and Faith's.

To keep his defenses steady, he plunged deliberately into a discussion of the force at Chris Martin's disposal: his informants were Captains Page Hammond and Ralph Otis, a pair of dashing uniformed figures tonight, but Natchez planters in less martial times. As he had surmised, the former sutler had little more than a hundred men under his command. Larkin was rated officially as his adjutant. Ned Beasley (with a foot in both the slave-owning and the tenant-farmer worlds) had been a natural choice as battalion major. So far, the battalion contained but two full companies, under Hammond and Otis.

There were other plantation owners, he learned, eager to command a company (most of them, in fact, were present tonight). The fact remained that many a would-be officer drilled in the ranks, if only to swell the two companies to full strength. There was no doubting the fiery loyalty of each guest at Trail's End. But it was just as true (from what John learned) that the turnout of King's men in the Natchez country had been far below expectation.

Chris Martin himself (and John noted this fact with wry detachment) was conspicuously absent tonight; duties at the fort prohibited his attendance at the gala welcome of a new doctor to Natchez. There was no mistaking the fact that these duties were genuine. Outside, the whole valley was bathed in moonlight. From time to time, the boom of cannon from the bluff was a reminder that the commandant was taking full advantage of good hunting weather.

Faith, laughing on Colonel Larkin's arm, seemed to be enjoying herself thoroughly; when the first cotillion was formed after supper, no lady in that long double parlor was more graceful than she. The cotillion was followed by a reel, in which John was paired with his hostess; after that dance ended, there was a general exodus to the lower gallery, where fruit punch was being poured. Beyond, the moonlight created its own magic above the rose garden and the file of cherry laurels. It seemed oddly natural to be strolling here with Stella Wright.

"Be honest, Doctor. You know you're here to stay."

"You're a persuasive planner, Mrs. Wright," he said. "Do all your plans come true?"

"Call me Stella, now you've gone in with Evan."

"But I haven't, yet."

"You will, John. You can't help yourself. He needs someone like you so badly. And there's no limit to what Natchez can offer you."

For another dangerous moment, he let the reverie that had

claimed his mind in the drawing room return once more. It was much easier to believe with Stella beside him, wide blue eyes pleading, lips soft with concern.

"Faith is willing to settle here. Surely you won't disappoint her —or me?"

"What can I say but yes, Stella?" he asked with a smile.

"You promise readily, John Powers. Do you mean it?"

Was she more than her husband's advocate at this moment? Until today, the revenge he had planned in Pensacola had been his evil star; the thought that it might be effected more easily than he had dared to hope would have brought a surge of satisfaction. Stella Wright was far younger than her husband—and an invalid was no proper mate for a woman in full flower. Yet he could take no joy tonight in the conviction that this flower was his for the taking.

"Please, John—don't disappoint us."

"I trust I'll never disappoint you, Stella."

He looked deep into her eyes, hoping that the words expressed his real meaning. Someone was calling his name from the gallery, and he heard himself answer the hail. Stella laughed gaily, and tucked her hand through his arm.

"Your wife is claiming you for the next reel," she said. "She'll complete my persuasion."

"I'm sure she will," he replied—and led his hostess toward the music with something akin to relief.

7

John remembered little more of the evening—the badinage with other partners, the solemn toasts he drank to the English cause as the uniformed squires called for horses and carriages, and lifted a stirrup cup before riding forth in the moonlight. Evan Wright had retired early, before the slaves began to snuff out the downstairs candles; Stella, after saying good night to the last of her guests, had slipped away to attend her husband, without further teasing.

He smoked another of his host's segars in the gallery after Faith had gone upstairs, to give her time to undress—but she was still in the closet behind the mirrored doors of her armoire when he entered their bedroom.

"I'll be ready in a moment," she called. "Smoke if you like; there's no need to go outside."

Taking out a final segar, he put it down unlighted. When Faith emerged from the dressing room, demure as ever in her quilted peignoir, he was lying on the chaise longue, still fully dressed.

"Well, my dear?" he asked. "Is Natchez all you hoped?"

"Natchez is everything I hoped for," she said quietly. "So was the Wrights' party."

"You acquitted yourself well."

"Perhaps that was because I enjoyed it so thoroughly," she told him, in that same light tone. "I wish I could say as much for you."

The thrust brought him bolt upright on the settee. "What do you mean?"

"You're still troubled by something, John. Whatever it is, I wish I could help."

"You could go downriver, as I suggested."

"It has nothing to do with me. Why pretend it does?"

"Can't I be concerned for your welfare, Faith?"

She had been brushing her hair at the mirror. Now she turned to face him. "Stella told me something I didn't know until tonight. About her brother in Pensacola. The one who prosecuted you at your trial."

"Must we talk of him now?"

"He won the money from the man who was really guilty, didn't he?"

"He did, Faith. But it's something I can't prove—something I've put behind me now."

"Are you so sure of that?"

He stretched full length on the settee again, if only to avoid meeting her eyes: he knew how clearly they could see, when she was in a divining mood. "I'm sure now, Faith," he said.

"In New Orleans, I guessed that something besides the need for work was driving you to Natchez. Wasn't it really a desire for revenge—in some way involving Stella Wright?"

"It's your story," he said, with his eyes still on the ceiling. "Try your hand at finishing it."

"No one can help you, if you won't help yourself," she said.

He risked a glance at her then. All at once, he understood the real reason for his fear. This was no longer the scared girl he had faced in Mobile. Somewhere along the way, she had lost the dewy innocence that is the hallmark of youth. Tonight, a lovely, self-possessed woman had taken the place of the upcountry jenny— a woman who could dance and flirt with Natchez' finest—a woman whose quick, darting mind was far too nimble to suit his self-esteem.

"Be curious if you must," he said. "You've every right."

"Not curious, John—concerned."

"About yourself? Didn't I offer to send you to safety, with half of everything I own?"

"About you, my dear. After that night in New Orleans, you must know why."

"Don't say it, please," he said. "I don't deserve it."

"But you do know I'm in love with you?"

"Not too deeply, I hope."

"Deeply enough to stop you from hurting Stella Wright—if I can."

"Aren't you assuming a great deal?" His voice was harsh, but his anger was more for himself than her. As always, she had put her finger squarely on the cause of his discontent.

"Can't you see that you mustn't, John? That you'd only end by hurting yourself?"

Had she been the voice of his own conscience, she could not have stated his plight more clearly. He could not quite force himself to meet her eyes. He spoke regardless, lest his silence damn him beyond repair.

"Haven't I told you that I'd do my best to help both Dr. Wright and Stella?"

"Is that because you've given up your revenge? Or are you already in love with her?"

"Stella's in love with the whole world," he said. "It isn't hard to love her a little in return."

"Is it possible to love a little, John? You can't move into love by degrees. The water's too deep for that. Deep and cold and frightening—if you must swim there alone."

He saw that she was crying quietly, as she continued to brush her hair with long, rhythmic strokes; no matter what the risk, he felt an irresistible urge to comfort her. Before the urge left him, he yielded to it—moving to stand behind her as she continued to sit before the mirror, and drawing her into a light embrace. Though she neither resisted nor yielded, Faith seemed to melt in his arms. Then, with a sudden, impulsive motion, she freed herself and moved to the open French window, to stare down at the Mississippi—beginning to cloud, now, with the promise of rain.

"Think your future through," she said. "Dr. Wright hasn't long to live. He told me as much tonight at dinner. Already, you've won his confidence, and Stella's. If you take over his practice and care for him in his last years, you'll be his logical heir. Why shouldn't Stella marry you one day?"

"So that's my story," he said. "Complete with happy ending. What's yours?"

"I don't know, John," she said quietly. "Perhaps I was a fool to come this far. And a greater fool to stay a moment more. But I refuse to leave until you've made up your mind, once and for all."

"Don't look too far into the future," he warned her. "It isn't always wise."

"You're right, of course," she said. "Not when the picture's so clear—and so logical."

All of his anger was gone now. He could only feel sorry for her—and admire her for her willingness to sacrifice her own happiness for his. Of course, there was a simple answer to her reproaches, and it was on the tip of his tongue to make it now. He had only to offer to take her before a Natchez magistrate in the morning—to make the fiction of their marriage real. It was no more than such loyalty deserved. At least it would put an end to his own doubting.

He had half turned, with the avowal already on his lips, when Faith spoke again. "Don't say it, John——"

"Can you read my mind tonight?"

"I can read it well enough," she said. "Whatever I may want from you, it isn't pity. And I won't be an escape—for something you don't want to face."

"But, Faith——"

"We've said too much now," she told him. "There's no need to say more. But I think we understand one another—perhaps for the first time."

She left him on that, to go into the dressing closet; though she closed the door firmly behind her, there was no hint of rage in the gesture. For an instant he stood staring at his face in the mirrored surface, while he fought down the urge to continue an argument he had already lost.

Faith, as usual, was right, to the last syllable. Only he could write finis to the dilemma he had so far refused to face. She had every right to be present at that moment of decision.

Ten minutes later, he was still pacing the carpet of the bedroom —and still wondering if Faith was dissolved in tears behind that mirrored panel. He could not deny that the knock on the hall door came as a welcome interruption. Or that he had all but bolted from the room at Major Beasley's news that he was needed at Fort Panmure for an emergency case.

8

In the surgery at the fort, four fish-oil lamps bathed the trestle table in a garish but adequate light. The grizzled boatman who lay there, nursing a jug of whiskey between deep-fetched groans, seemed more bear than human at first view—a somewhat aged bear, John thought, with a fleck of gray about the muzzle, but a world of power in those long, hair-matted arms. Tossing his cloak aside, he approached the table confidently. He had dealt with men like this in more than one language, and understood them well enough.

"Good evening, stranger. Don't you know better than to argue with a British battery?"

"You needn't have hurried, Doc," said the riverman. His voice was thick with alcohol, but cheerful enough. "This ain't the first time I stopped lead."

Once he had stripped aside the rude dressing plastered to the man's left shoulder, John could see the clean puncture of the bullet, the pump of blood in the depths of the wound.

"How did it happen?"

"We come to the bank when they challenged us, meek as lambs. Then they piled aboard, with a red-coated fellow in the lead—Colonel Martin, he calls himself. I said he was no better'n a pirate—and he drills me. Is that a nice way to run a war?"

John frowned as he turned aside to lay out his instruments. He had left Chris Martin a moment ago, too steeped in brandy to give a coherent account of his latest capture. It was not too difficult to imagine his hair-triggered burst of wrath.

"No one else hurt?"

"You bet there wasn't, Doc. Word's already come upriver that they shoot first at Natchez nowadays—and argue later. The dons were more polite, once we'd worked out our bribes."

John selected a porcelain-tipped probe from his case, and called Beasley into the room. "Better take another pull on that jug, my friend. Do they have your name at the adjutant's?"

"Not yet, they haven't: we ain't on speaking terms. Name's Hurt. Obadiah Hurt. I run trap lines in Kaintuck, and deliver cargoes to Orleans."

So far, they had been talking around a problem they shared—the fact that a leaden pellet, embedded somewhere in the muscle of Obadiah Hurt's shoulder, must be probed for and extracted at once, if his arm was to be saved. The Kentuckian's progress toward oblivion was only a means to that end; John's banter, so far, had been just as automatic.

"Next time, you'll know better than to run an English gauntlet," he said. "Stay with that jug. This is going to be painful."

A forcep was ready on the table, in case he found the bullet on the first try; beside it was a curved elevator, honed almost to the sharpness of a knife, in case the lead had found lodgment in a bone. Known as a "spud" in army surgeries, this useful instrument had saved dozens of limbs in John's medical career. He nodded to Beasley, who moved forward to anchor the patient's shoulders. Ready for his first exploration, he laid a soothing hand on the Kentuckian's arm.

"How do you feel now, Obadiah?"

"Drunker'n a owl, Doc."

"Fair enough. Get hold of yourself."

The probe slipped gently into the puckered red mouth of the wound. Working it downward, along the course the bullet had taken, John saw at once that his objective had lodged in bone, or near it, complicating a technique already difficult enough. If only to be sure, he eased the probe even deeper: the porcelain tip grated on lead at last, a solid, jarring sound that made its picture, as accurately as though muscle had been laid bare to the scapula.

"Touched it that time, all right," murmured Obadiah sleepily.

"I'm moving around it now. Steady does it."

The porcelain-tipped steel, defining the lodgment of the bullet with a slow, circular motion, might have been an extension of John's fingertips. On the off-chance that the leaden pellet would yield to the forcep, he inserted this instrument into the wound. The jaws penetrated easily enough, but the bullet refused to budge, since it was impossible to close them firmly.

"We'll have to use the spud, Major. Anchor him as best you can."

The slender arc of metal, entering the wound in its turn, grated upon the bullet—a sound that rasped on John's nerves like the screech of chalk on a blackboard. Sweat beaded his forehead as he strove to dislodge an enemy he could not even see, but he pressed on with all his strength; Obadiah might have stopped lead before, but this particular threat must be dislodged if the riverman intended to keep his arm.

With an abruptness that brought a gasp of relief to the surgeon's lips, the battered leaden pellet popped into view, like a watermelon seed shot from a child's fingers. There was a fresh spurt of bleeding, but no real threat of hemorrhage.

"'Bout finished, Doc?"

He came back to the patient with a start. As always in such moments, his entire being had been concentrated on the wound and the threat lurking in its depths. Smiling down at Obadiah, John felt a sudden rush of friendship for this man from the other side. True, the operation had been only a routine affair—but it had done much to restore his sense of self-respect. Here, at least, he had been master of a situation.

"Stay with that bottle," he advised. "The worst is over. I'm just making sure that ball didn't carry part of your shirt with it." Experience had taught him long ago that leaving a bit of cloth in a bullet's track was sometimes as dangerous as leaving the missile itself. With a clean wound, and Hurt's reservoir of vitality, there would be little chance of pus—or the mysterious, stinking-green suppuration that so often followed in the wake of such injuries.

John needed only a short exploration to be sure no cloth or buckskin had entered the wound. By the time he strapped on a fresh dressing, Obadiah Hurt was snoring loudly enough to shake the table. Standing back to check his handiwork, the surgeon nodded to Beasley, who relaxed his grip at last.

"He'll sleep till morning, Major. Kentucky whiskey's a sovereign specific."

"I'll put the surgery under guard."

John frowned. "Has Colonel Martin made him a prisoner?"

"Those were his orders when we brought him in." Beasley took up his raincape. "The colonel was pretty riled tonight, Doc. Just before he nailed this fellow, a whole flotilla slipped by us, when the moon went under."

"I'll want him moved to a hospital in the morning—if you have one in Natchez."

"We've got one all right. Made-over farmhouse, on the Trace. I'll see he's taken there myself."

Acknowledging the militiaman's salute outside the surgery, they ran together to the major's gig. Rain, still pelting heavily from a leaden sky, showed no sign of lessening in this black hour before dawn. The gig, laboring in the wet sand of the Trace, seemed forever in reaching the gateposts of Trail's End. John was about to step out to the columned portico (where a night light glowed dimly above the doorway) when Beasley leveled his whip into the streaming darkness.

"What d'you know? The Polings are back. Their place is lighted like a Christmas tree."

John's gaze followed the pointing whip. The manor house (withdrawn in its grove of live oaks) had seemed empty as some abandoned mausoleum when they drove to the fort. Now, a dozen windows blazed with candles—a garish glow that seemed all the more bizarre at that hour. Even from the distance, John could make out the silhouettes of the house slaves, as they bustled to make Poling Hall habitable again.

"Is it a good sign, Major—or a bad one?"

"Too soon to guess, Doc. But if you ask me, they figure the war's ended—so far as *we're* concerned."

John paused with one foot already on the driveway. The rain beat its mournful tattoo on his cape, but he was oblivious of that chill discomfort. A deeper cold had invaded his blood stream as he weighed the import of Beasley's words.

"Have they returned to count heads for de Gálvez?"

"Could be. Or they might have had late word from Orleans— and figured it was safe to take down their shutters."

John stared hard at those bright rectangles of light—and the windows glared back at him through the rain. Perhaps it was the lateness of the hour, as much as the tensions of this long day. But he had never felt more deeply alone—or more uncertain of his next move. The lighted casements of Poling Hall were only an added threat—a reminder that forces beyond his control were even now on the move, ready to dictate his future beyond all doubting.

"Good night to you, Major," he said. "Let's hope their return means peace."

"Amen to that," said Beasley, as he drove off into the darkness.

Ascending the stairway of Trail's End, John had expected to drag his feet: he had hardly looked forward to his return to the bedroom he shared with Faith. Strangely enough, he found that he was turning the knob of his door almost willingly. As he had expected, the bed curtains were drawn tightly: Faith's gentle breathing told him that she was deep in slumber.

Tonight, at least, he would have given a great deal for the right to join her there, to lose the worst of his doubts in the haven of her arms. Yet he could still take comfort in her nearness as he lay down on yet another settee to seek what sleep he could. Already, the loneliness that had seemed beyond enduring had vanished, as quietly as a ghost at cockcrow.

Give the devil his due, he thought drowsily. *I may be trapped between two women—and enjoying my captivity. I may find that the trap is too strong to escape when I waken tomorrow. There can be no retreating now. Faith and I are part of Natchez.*

The Trace

*A*s *fortnights went,* the next interval was the lull before the lightning stroke. Recognizing it for what it was, John found that he could move through the days with no real sense of strain.

There was much to occupy him in that time of waiting, once he had taken the load from Evan Wright's shoulders. Like all settlements in these latitudes, Natchez had its share of ague and fever in warm weather. In addition, the fort sent a flow of patients to the hospital on the Trace—aftermaths of Chris Martin's piracies, for the most part, plus a few bitings and gougings from the barracks. Most of these cases were salvaged as readily as John had saved Obadiah Hurt. Others died under his knife, or babbled their way to eternity in a fog of opium. The fortunes of war had their ruthless percentages, even at Fort Panmure.

Because of these heavy duties, John had little time to spend at Trail's End. His glimpses of Stella were brief indeed, his visits with Faith confined to drowsy talks (and an occasional spirited argument) at day's end. In a way, he welcomed this state of limbo, precarious though he knew it to be. Faith had diagnosed his situation accurately enough, but there was no need of definite action now.

Meanwhile, he waited—as did everyone in Natchez—for the next move in the chess game downriver. Whatever gambit de Gálvez might choose, he would play it in his own fashion, at a time and place of his choosing.

John was not sorry when a patient called him to some distant landhold (on occasion, no more than a clearing in the virgin forest that boxed the Natchez bluff). Often he took the excuse to make a shakedown bed beside the hearth. If these absences resulted in another sleepless night, he had only himself to blame. Events beyond his control would shape his destiny. There seemed no point in belaboring the question now.

Obadiah Hurt's shoulder healed rapidly, once the bone had knit; when he was well enough to ride, he insisted on accompanying John to the backwoods. The Kentuckian soon proved himself a friend, as well as a philosopher of sorts. He had followed most of the trails around Natchez; between trips to New Orleans, he had kept himself informed on the fast-changing politics of the frontier. After a talk with Obadiah, John could not help feeling that Evan Wright, for all his burnished mind, was a spokesman for yesterday. Obadiah was surely the voice of the future.

"It's our time, Doc, not theirs," said the Kentuckian. "General Clark holds the west for the Whigs, give or take a few corners. Clinton's whipped in the East. Lord Cornwallis is sweating every day of the week, and twice as hard on Sundays——"

"Surely England can hold the Floridas."

"East Florida, maybe—just to keep a pawn for the peace table. West Florida will belong to Spain when de Gálvez puts the plug on Pensacola Bay. If you ask me, the dons will get the whole thing when the smoke has settled—*and* this river valley, clear to the spot we're tramping now."

"Don't say that out loud in Natchez."

"Never you fear. But hasn't de Gálvez earned as much, after his job of back-stabbing?"

"And what becomes of the Wrights?"

"I couldn't say. Would the old doc settle for a nice, dry cell in the Cabildo?"

"De Gálvez promised to hang him—in my hearing."

"Then he'll hang—if he doesn't head for the canebrakes."

"Must you put it so bluntly?"

"A Spaniard's a Spaniard, Doc. And a King's man's, a Tory. How else can I put it?"

John shrugged off the query; in this time of waiting, he could hardly question such earthy wisdom. English pride would never strike its flag to Spain—nor would English caution trust Spanish clemency. Once the Loyalist position here was untenable, there was no choice but retreat or death. Augusta (far upriver on the Savannah) was the nearest sanctuary—and at least five hundred wilderness miles separated that haven from Natchez.

Evan Wright grew weaker as the days went by; John found that he was handling most of the calls that came to Trail's End. These included appeals for medical aid from Poling Hall—or from Rodell's Bluff, the handsome river plantation that was the Wrights' southern neighbor. Both houses blazed with light each evening— though the owners themselves held aloof. John was positive now that many eyes were fastened on Trail's End, while Natchez awaited word from New Orleans.

He had no doubt whatever that the news would be bad. Why else would these cautious straddlers open their blinds? More than once (when he was lancing a boil in the quarters, or setting an arm in the overseer's house at Poling Hall), he all but yielded to the impulse to storm into the mansion itself, and demand an accounting. On each occasion, common sense had intervened. These prudent landowners were as ignorant of events as he— though they were convinced the insurgents had lost their gamble. Until that conviction was verified, he would hold aloof—serving both camps with what skill he had, and giving homage to neither.

2

When the news came at last, it was no less unsettling, for all the portents that had preceded it.

John had been upriver for three days, in Yulee's sloop, to perform a difficult amputation; until the worst of the aftermath was over, he had not dared to leave the patient. Warping into the pier at Rodell's Bluff (which served as a landing for Trail's End), he had sensed the change of air before the dock boy could catch his painter. Avoiding the manor house itself, he could feel the stir of defiance within, though the windows were eyeless as ever in the declining day.

Obadiah, riding in from the fort when John and Yulee reached the crossroads, brought the latest bulletin. Pensacola had fallen long ago; the news relayed from New Orleans via the river trail had reached Evan Wright only a few hours after John's departure. Already, every Loyalist home on the bluff was astir with preparations for departure as fearful portents wafted upriver.

De Gálvez, it was said, had assembled a punitive force three thousand strong, using an armada of keelboats and sloops as his transport. Only yesterday, he had been reported at Baton Rouge. A second report (an hour old) announced that he was camped a mile downstream, ready to pounce on Fort Panmure. Regardless of his exact whereabouts, there was no doubt that Loyalist heads would soon be falling. A manifesto had announced as much, in blood-chilling terms. (No one could produce this broadsheet—but there were dozens who could quote it verbatim.)

"The old doc is waiting for you now," said the Kentuckian. "Been asking for you, ever since this song-and-dance began."

"It's true, then?"

"Pensacola's gone," said Obadiah. "The English have stacked their arms. I couldn't rightly say if the dons have moved their army, so far. But it's only a question of days before they send calling cards. The Wrights won't be here to receive 'em—you can lay to that."

So Evan Wright was resigned to the inevitable. John felt a strange pang at his heart. In the old doctor's book, England had planted her standard on the Mississippi for all time—with Natchez as the inevitable nerve center. It had been a stubborn dream, and he had clung to it beyond the bounds of reason.

"Take my horse," said Obadiah. "You'll find him in his office."

John remembered little of that headlong gallop to Trail's End.

He needed only a glance at the faces of the house slaves to catch the note of disaster. Bales and trunks were stacked in the corridors, as though the owners, no longer in residence, had abandoned their possessions wholesale. Stripped of their carpets, the long parlors had a shrouded air. Invisible cobwebs had already meshed above the tall window frames—and ghostly mice dared to squeak behind the baseboards. . . . Though he had spent but little time in the house, John had loved its dignified repose. Today's desolation was ominous proof that an era had ended here.

He found Evan Wright in his study, at a desk piled high with ledgers, in the act of signing a sheet of foolscap. London stood by to receive this document; he left on the run, the moment the ink was sanded. The elder doctor offered John no formal greeting; his voice was as composed as his manner.

"Another bill of sale," he said. "This time, I'm disposing of the slaves—and such gear as Sam Poling will find useful."

John fumbled for words of sympathy that did not come. He had not expected the Wrights to dispose of their Negroes; the casual announcement had shocked him deeply.

"Don't think I'm unfeeling," said the elder doctor. "My slaves are men and women to me; I'm putting their welfare above my own sentiments. Sam will make an excellent master. In my place, would you expose them to the hardships I'll be facing?"

"You're selling *all* of them?"

"All but London. He's spent his lifetime in my service, and refuses to leave my side." The master of Trail's End smiled wanly as he made an entry in the debit column of a ledger. "In the circumstances, I think Sam gave me a fair recompense. Naturally, he wanted the bill of sale in hand at once."

"If Poling is taking your Negroes, why couldn't he close the deal himself?"

Evan Wright put down his pen. Though his eyes were kind enough, his voice was wintry. For no valid reason, John felt he was back in Pensacola again, facing a court-martial—and a sentence couched in a tongue he would never really comprehend.

"Englishmen perform most transactions in the open," said Dr. Wright. "Others are handled through factors. The transfer of my slaves is one of them."

"I'm afraid I'm still confused, sir——"

"It's simple enough, John. I am now *persona non grata* in Natchez—a fugitive, in fact, who must leave the bluff before his neck is stretched. In such circumstances, one doesn't meet his neighbors directly. It's just possible they'd absorb the taint."

"There must be some way to come to terms with de Gálvez. What if you struck your colors? Or asked for a truce?"

"It's a bit late for that, I'm afraid. I'm cutting my losses, and leaving Trail's End." Evan Wright could not have spoken more casually had he been discussing current prices on the New Orleans levee.

"Do I gather you can absorb the blow, sir?"

"I'll tell you a secret, John. Ever since you brought me the Governor's ultimatum, I've prepared for the worst. If need be, I could quit this house at an hour's notice."

"What of the others?"

"Most members of our faction have managed to sell out too. We're marching at dawn tomorrow—with Colonel Martin to guide us."

"May I ask your plan?"

"I've stated it. We must run for our lives."

"Without a formal threat from New Orleans?"

"You've delivered that threat, John. It isn't your fault that I wouldn't listen."

"You won't consider a white flag? Or a plea for mercy?"

Evan Wright got to his feet. John was vastly heartened by the spring in the old doctor's step. Here, surmounting its fragile outer shell, was the spirit that had planted Britain's banner in every corner of the globe.

"I've found that there are Englishmen willing to live under a different king," he said. "Whigs are English too, I'm afraid—and I won't dignify their government with a name. I'm an Englishman with just one sovereign. I'd die rather than take orders from another."

"That's still your privilege, sir."

"I hope you're right, John. I must move fast, if I mean to exercise it."

"You've arranged for an adequate guard, I trust?"

"A hundred and fifty of us will move out together. It will be a long journey. At least we'll protect one another."

The simplicity of the declaration gave it added impact. Though he had realized the extent of the revolt, John had not visioned so large a migration. It was an impressive tribute to the Wrights.

"You've chosen your route?"

"Indeed yes. We've done some rapid planning since you went upriver. Our first thought was to cut across country and take the Creeks' Lower Path——"

"The Lower Path *would* be the shortest march," John agreed warily. Eager to know if Chris Martin had endorsed the route, he was careful to say no more. Familiar as he was with the maps that linked these backlands with the Mississippi, he knew the dangers of this particular trail.

"Even the Lower Path seemed long enough," said Evan Wright. "At the best, we're facing a hard test. Most of us will be traveling by families—groups that came here at my urging. I tell myself I'm thinking of them—not of my own fate."

John nodded soberly. Like a patriarch of old, Dr. Wright had led his people into the wilderness; he had seen it blossom under their hands. It was a cruel stroke of fate that he must now lead them out again, before the first real fruits could be harvested.

"I gather you hope to survive this journey, sir?"

"I think it's reasonable to expect as much. There are few ventures I wouldn't face with Stella beside me. Of course I'd never last without her."

"Where do you plan to settle?"

"I'll answer that when I reach Augusta. Eventually, I suppose, we'll go on to East Florida. I've extensive holdings there, in Stella's name." The elder doctor closed the last of his ledgers. "Waste no tears upon us, John. We plan to reach our goal."

"By the Lower Path?"

"That was my original plan—but Colonel Martin vetoed it. The route strikes east and south, across the headwaters of the Pearl River. The land is swampy, and apt to be treacherous in this season."

For once, thought John, Chris Martin had been honest. As chief architect of the Natchez war, it was imperative that he make good his escape. Evidently he had decided that his salvation lay with the migrants. If this assumption was correct, Chris could be invaluable to the Wright party, since he knew the country thoroughly, and had a large acquaintance among the Creeks and the lower Choctaw tribes.

"Did Chris suggest another route?"

"He felt we should move along the Trace, until we reach higher ground—then take the Middle Path. It's farther, of course. But we'd end among what the Creeks call their Upper Towns. And the going will be easier."

It was an excellent suggestion. So excellent, in fact, that John found himself examining it warily. "Yulee will be a great help in the back country," he said. "So will Obadiah Hurt. They've both volunteered as outriders."

"Why should they concern themselves with our problems, John?"

"Call us a team, if you like. Where one goes, the others follow."

"Does that mean you're joining us?"

"*We're* a team, Doctor," said John steadily. "Unless you feel you won't need me."

"Your presence would be invaluable, of course; but I've no right to ask such a sacrifice. You came here to establish a practice—and you've a wife to support." The old doctor put a paternal arm about John's shoulder. "Surely *you've* nothing to fear from de Gálvez?"

"In New Orleans, he offered me Spanish citizenship and a land grant—if I persuaded you to spare the fort." John found he could smile, not too ruefully, at this glittering might-have-been. "Probably I can still count on his patronage. I'm afraid I would never accept it on his terms."

"Stay on—make sure."

"I'm sure of that much now."

"Don't pretend you're ready to call yourself a Tory."

"Perhaps I can't go that far. I'm still an ally of the Wrights."

The old doctor stacked his ledgers precisely, and began to stow them in a pair of saddlebags. He seemed hard put to control himself when he spoke again.

"I must admit this makes me easier in my mind," he said. "Both for myself and for Stella. Naturally, I hoped you'd cast your lot with us—even in exile, as it were. So, I might add, did Faith."

"Would you repeat that, sir?"

This time, Evan Wright's smile had all its old warmth. "She's upstairs now, fitting Stella to a suit of buckskins—and designing one of her own."

"Perhaps I should thank her—for knowing me so well."

Clambering over the boxes that encumbered the stair well, John was glad of this excuse to cut short the old doctor's thanks. In the upper hall, he paused for breath before the door of his bedroom and listened to Stella and Faith chattering inside. Try as he might, he could catch no note of false courage in the women's laughter. Lifting his hand to knock, he let it drop to his side: this was no time for a formal expression of gratitude. He had always realized that Faith would stand by the Wrights. His own decision to join them had been just as inevitable.

We'll each have our task on this migration, he thought. Stella Wright's was simple—to preserve her husband's life during the rigors of the journey. As for Faith, she would remain at his side, whatever the perils, until he made his final choice. . . . *Your own task,* he added grimly, *is the simplest of all—to watch Chris Martin like a patient hawk, until Chris has proved himself by deed as well as word.*

3

Later, when he looked back on the beginning of that exodus, it was the silence he remembered most vividly. He had scarcely expected Godspeed from those who remained; he had realized that the fugitives themselves would be muted to the point of tears. But he had been unprepared for the stony emptiness of Natchez itself, when the straggling cavalcade wound down from the bluff in the dawn, on its way to the Trace.

That morning, the settlement might have been a deserted village. No children played under the fresh-leaved umbrella trees in the yards. There was no bustle of slaves in the breezeways, no chatter at the kitchen doors. Brooding on that silence, he understood it well enough. Though it clung stubbornly to its rejection of these infidels, Natchez was ashamed to show its face today; it would wait for the dust of their passing to settle before it came alive.

"The way of the exile is hard," said Evan Wright. "Perhaps this is the proper time to remind ourselves that trouble brings wisdom. It's a poor consolation now. It may be worth remembering later."

He drew off beside the trail, where John and Chris Martin had reined in, while the latter re-formed the long line of travelers. Watching him narrowly, John saw that no cavalryman could have sat more firmly in his saddle; even in the full light of morning, the old doctor seemed sturdy as the horse he rode. He guessed that Evan Wright had drawn unexpected strength from the challenge confronting him—to say nothing of the loyalty he read in the honest English faces that streamed past this vantage point, like a homespun army in review.

It had been decided that Chris, Dr. Wright, and John should lead the cavalcade this first day. Next came Colonel Kirby, also on horseback—the leader of the first group of migrants. Major

Beasley led the second group, at the same brisk pace. Page Hammond and Ralph Otis rode as rear guard, to cover a string of pack horses. Yulee and Obadiah Hurt covered the expedition as outriders—exploring the flanks of the Trace for possible enemies, or cantering ahead to report on the state of a road that was, in places, no more than a game trail.

Stella and Faith, in new buckskin kirtles, marched with the family groups that made up the bulk of the procession. As John had noted instantly, most of the company were sturdy, back-country folk, long since inured to the hardships of the wilderness. From the oldest paterfamilias to the smallest toddler, Evan Wright's cavalcade was seasoned for the task ahead. All in all, the old doctor had reason for his quiet pride, as the last marcher filed past the clearing.

Chris Martin had planned his expedition well; on the basis of his first inspection, John was willing to give the ex-sutler his due. Marching in two compact groups, with outriders on each flank and a musket on each man's shoulder, the migrants were well protected from assault, immune to the marauding bands that had always roved the Trace. Thanks to that long string of horses, the women and children could ride in turn; the youngest could be nested among the packs, or ride pickaback among the small groups of slaves who had joined in the exodus.

Most of the travelers were leaving Natchez richer than they had entered it, thanks to the largess of the Wrights. Shrewd bargains had been driven by those who remained: slaves had gone for but a fraction of their value, and those who had disposed of homes and land had been forced to accept the buyer's price. But the brief period of English triumph at Fort Panmure had paid handsomely: a fortune in pelts rode among the packs that followed the marchers. A second fortune jingled in Evan Wright's saddlebags—the product of his own prosperous years on the bluff. This he proposed to divide among each family to reach Augusta, share and share alike.

John had expected Chris Martin to cry out against this arrangement. To his surprise, the sutler had applauded Dr. Wright's decision to share both the booty and the cash. A common misfortune, said Chris glibly, had drawn this group together: there was nothing like a common reward to insure its success. For his part, Chris wanted no more than the others. He had gambled and lost at Fort Panmure: he was eager to use his woodsman's skill to lead them all to Augusta. . . .

Today, riding side by side with John, easing his mount a little to give Dr. Wright the honor of setting the pace, Chris offered his familiar, crooked smile. They had crossed swords more than once while final plans were settled. John had probed their self-elected leader as skillfully as he could—if only to assure himself that the real Chris Martin, and the wilderness guide who jogged beside him, were one and the same. Even now, he could not resist a final prod.

"We'll have few chances to be alone," he said. "Isn't it time you explained why you're here?"

"Misery makes strange trail mates, Doc."

"Do you expect me to believe you're guiding us to Augusta for unselfish motives?"

" 'Course I don't. I'll take my share when this picnic's over. Right now, I'm in good company, and safe from de Gálvez."

"This isn't going to be exactly a picnic, you know."

The sutler's grin broadened. "Now you mention it, we may run into a mite of trouble. But we're long on grub and gumption. Most of us are trail-wise. Just you believe in me, Doc, and follow my blaze marks. You may sweat blood before you're through. You may be hungry enough to eat your moccasins. But I'll take you to the Savannah River."

John could only mutter a grudging assent to the other's good humor. A shadow continued to hang over his mind, deepening with each word Chris uttered. "Why did you let me come along?" he asked dourly. "Aren't you afraid I'll spoil your game?"

"For the last time, there's no game to spoil. Now you've raised the subject though—just why *did* you join us?"

"Maybe to keep an eye on you."

For an instant a flash of anger wiped the grin from the sutler's lips. "Seems like you and I'll never cotton to each other—don't it, now? We can at least pretend to, so long as we're on trail together."

What Chris had just said was reasonable enough: there was no room for personal dislike at a campfire. And yet, as he admitted this obvious fact, John's doubting persisted. "Frankly, I'd have been happier if you'd just cut and run," he admitted. "If I've misjudged you, I'll be the first to apologize. I may even shake hands with you, if we reach Augusta. But don't expect it now."

He rode back down the Trace, telling himself that his words had been both churlish and unfair. It was a relief to put the sutler from his mind as Stella Wright came into view in the line of march.

No man, unless made of stone, could have failed to enjoy the sight of her. With her head thrown back proudly and the green, filtered sunlight gleaming on her blond hair, she might have been a Viking from a simpler age, marching toward a battle still unjoined. Knowing she was aware of his eyes, John did not prolong his staring. Instead, he dropped to the ground just before she could draw abreast—and, seizing her elbows, lifted her to the saddle in his stead.

"Your husband insists you join him for a while," he said.

"I've *never* ridden astride, John."

"That's your lesson for today, then. Don't mind the scandal."

Stella looked down at him from her unaccustomed elevation. For that instant, at least, they were cut off from the dusty world about them—a dangerous isolation which John broke promptly by handing her the reins.

"Anchor yourself to those stirrups, and guide him with your knees," he advised. "You'll find it's far easier than sidesaddle."

"I can see that now. But I don't deserve to ride so soon."

"Others will take their turn later. The Wrights should lead us to our first camp."

Stella did not look back: he guessed that perhaps she, too, had felt the danger when their hands had touched. Now that her back was turned, he dared to admire her without fear of detection— noting the patrician way she handled the ancient plow horse, her serene unawareness of the glances she drew from other women in the cavalcade.

"Walk with us awhile, John?"

He turned to find himself eye to eye with Faith, who was following the trail with long-legged grace, and matching the two lanky Hammond girls stride for stride.

"Tess asked if we'd stop for a nooning," she told him. "I said we can't lose a moment of daylight. Not while we're on the Trace."

He fell into step beside them, and smiled at Tess Hammond —wishing that he could enjoy this adventure with her lighthearted acceptance. "Anyone who gets hungry can ask for molasses and corn pone," he said. "But you must walk while you eat. Colonel Martin won't have stragglers."

"I can wait until camp, Dr. Powers," said the girl. "That's my sister's stomach you hear growling, not mine."

Sarah Hammond replied with an insult that was just as spirited. Hearing his own laughter mingle with Faith's, John could not help wondering if jokes would come as easily after a month on trail. He put the worry aside instantly: Tess and Sarah Hammond were the daughters of pioneers. Like their elders, they could be trusted to keep their nerve.

He was glad when the girls scampered on to join a game of touch-tag. There were questions to put to Faith: it hardly mattered if they were the same queries that had plagued him since that strange, almost clairvoyant midnight at Trail's End. Somehow, Faith seemed far closer, now that they were really marching out the first lap of this grueling journey.

He made a cautious start, if only to test the depth of that new understanding.

"Have we been walking together three minutes or forever?"

She flashed him a loyal smile. "You were giving Stella her lesson just now. Shall I give you one in turn?"

"You'll find me a willing pupil," he told her.

"Forget about time, John: time is a dream on the Trace. Today is all that matters. Tomorrow, you'll think you've been born here."

"Now that we've settled with the calendar," he said, "can you explain why I'm here at all?"

"You answered that in Natchez."

"Speak for yourself, then. At least you're a free agent."

"These people call me Mrs. John Powers," she said proudly. "You may not realize it, but that's a rather important title. Would they trust you, if I'd turned coward and stayed behind?"

"Is that your only reason?"

"Of course it isn't. I'd have joined this march without you—and you know it. The Wrights can use all sorts of help."

"Let's forget the Wrights a moment—and talk about us."

"We can't, John. *Us* means *everyone* now, not you and I." She was still smiling, but he saw that her eyes were grave enough. "Of course that's lesson number two. You'll find it a bit harder."

"Aren't you putting things rather bleakly?"

"Perhaps it's the very lesson you've needed," she said quickly. "Living from day to day, with no John Powers to trouble you. Settling each crisis as it comes—and never mind tomorrow."

He glanced down the long, dust-caked column, and began to see her meaning dimly. Would it really be possible to draw this wilderness about him like a cloak, shutting out a future that seemed insoluble? When the one real problem was survival, would those other dilemmas drop into perspective at last?

"Thanks for the lesson," he said. "I'll begin studying it at once."

"See that you do," she said, with those same grave eyes. "There'll be others as we go along."

"May I say I'm fortunate in my teacher?"

"I'll accept the compliment," said Faith Gordon. "After all, you've just walked into my world. I know the landmarks."

Her hand closed on his, as a song moved down the marching column. With no sense of transition, he found that his voice had mingled with the others.

One morning, one morning
The weather being fair
A mother and a daughter
Went out to take the air
And as they went a-walking
I heard the daughter vow
I must and will get married
I'm in the notion now.

It was a melody from English hedgerows, rich with Anglo-Saxon melancholy. But these migrants did not sing it sadly as they swung along the Trace. Feeling his own heart lift, John saw that shared courage could be a real and vital thing—that these sturdy marchers, who had already tamed the Mississippi wilderness, could face a second wilderness unafraid.

Swinging into the next chorus, he knew that he had begun to learn Faith's second lesson.

Suppose you were to try it
And could not find a man?
Oh, never mind, dear mother,
For there is miller Sam
And there is Jack the farmer
A-whistling at his plow
I must and will get married
I'm in the notion now.

4

They camped that first night in a pine grove, a spot of dry ground blessedly free from insect pests, where a floor of aromatic needles made a natural mattress for weary bodies. They had come less than twenty miles from Natchez, but it seemed well to test their muscle by degrees, until they grew hardened to the march.

The outriders had each brought in a deer, which they had butchered before the arrival of the main party. A feast of venison, augmented with stores from the packs, gave those first campfires a gala air—as though this were a bizarre outing, with home and hearth over the next bend in the trail.

Listening to the twang of a guitar on the grassy plot before the cook fires, and the shouts of laughter and song that passed from tent to tent, John told himself that the migration was off to a good start. True, they had done no more than break into the routine of the trail, but the cavalcade was now fairly launched. Chris had announced a thirty-mile goal for tomorrow, and these hardy folk had taken the order without a murmur of protest. All of them recognized the importance of speed on this first long leg of their march.

As the crow flew, Augusta was perhaps five hundred miles distant from tonight's encampment. But these trampers knew (almost to the last child) that the actual journey would be far longer. Worn down by generations of boatmen, this portion of the Trace was simple enough to follow. Once they struck east, into the virgin forest of the Middle Path (which was no path at all, but a dimly blazed Indian trail), they would often count themselves lucky if they averaged ten miles each day.

As the camp settled slowly for the night, John moved from fire to fire, spreading what cheer he could while he checked on the health of his charges. Save for a case of ague in the Otis brood, a sprain or two among overeager young marchers, and a few blisters, there was no work for a doctor tonight. Yet he could feel that his presence spread assurance among the tents that had mushroomed here beneath the pines.

For all the surface bravado, there were gaunt faces beneath those canvas flaps; minds had begun to turn back to a past forsaken forever, or fumbled, just as vainly, at a future shrouded by doubt. It was good to have a man of medicine here tonight. Though John realized that his potions would never be as popular as those of Chris Martin (circulating with a jug in each fist and a laughing word for everyone), he was sure they were valued none the less.

There was time for a visit with Evan Wright, though he was careful not to prolong it. So far as he could judge, the old doctor had come through the day in excellent spirits. Preparing to sample the comfort of a folding camp cot, he protested but mildly when Stella insisted on making her own bed in a nest of blankets at his feet.

"When I brought my wife to Natchez," he told John, "Trail's End was ready to receive her, down to the last teacup. Tonight, she chooses a couch of pine needles. How can she be so cheerful?"

"Evan simply won't believe I'm just as contented," said Stella. She was spreading a quilt across her husband's cot: as always, she managed to efface herself deftly while he was speaking.

"She even has a reason for her contentment," said the elder doctor. "The fact that *I'm* doing what I think is right——"

"Perhaps you've a wife in a million," said John. "It's a fact that few husbands recognize."

"This husband is keenly aware of his blessings," said Evan Wright. "I hope you will say as much for your own campfire, John. While you were playing the healing shepherd among my flock, your wife was pitching your tent without help."

"We offered to send London," said Stella. "But Faith wanted to prove she could do everything herself."

Understanding that impulse perfectly, John moved across the camp to find that Faith had raised their canvas abode beneath a cedar tree, at a little distance from the others. She had made an ideal bivouac—with a double shelter from the drenching dews that would fall before morning, a fire banked expertly to burn through the hours of darkness. The canvas overhead was familiar: he recognized the extra sail from Yulee's sloop, which had served Faith as a tent on their voyage upriver.

Tonight, the bivouac was constructed for two. Faith herself, bundled to the eyes in a Spanish serape, was already asleep; a similar bedroll at her side awaited his occupancy. With eyes still upon him, he had no choice but to roll into his own poncho. Faith, it seemed, had taken her declaration of the afternoon quite literally. Already, she was an integral part of the camp, submerging her own problems in the greater needs of the many; secure in her knowledge that she had proved herself as adept as any woodsman, she could sleep the sleep of the just. Reminding himself to compliment her in the morning, he found he could drop into a repose as dreamless as her own.

It was not quite dawn when he wakened. The gentle tug at his ankle was repeated: he recognized the silhouette of Yulee, crouched between the shelter and the glow of the fire. Moving cautiously so as not to waken Faith, he joined the half-breed in the outer circle of tents. With Yulee's hand at his elbow, he moved beyond the camp, still deep in sleep, and wrapped in a silence broken only by the pawing of the tethered pack horses, an occasional basso-profundo snore.

"Señor Hurt is on sentry duty," said the half-breed. "He felt I should waken you."

"Is something wrong?"

"We are not quite sure, *jefe*." Yulee was speaking a quick, pidgin Spanish now. "Colonel Martin has been gone since midnight. He slipped past his own pickets like a snake."

"You followed him?"

"*Naturalmente, Señor Médico*—as you ordered." Yulee's voice dropped to a whisper. "He has only now returned to his shelter. No one marked his absence."

"Say what you mean, Yulee."

"Colonel Martin was searching for something he did not find. Mostly, he moved up the Trace itself. Twice, he scouted the brush to the east. He discovered nothing."

"You're sure of that?"

Yulee's teeth flashed in a smile. "Colonel Martin can see in the dark, *jefe:* but I have trailed his kind before. I think he searched for Indian sign."

John nodded soberly as he led the way toward the central campfire: the sentries that Chris Martin had posted so importantly last night had begun to return to the camp, shaking the dew from their ponchos. Already, figures were moving quietly among the tents, to begin preparation for the communal breakfast: the snore that issued from the ex-sutler's shelter was most convincing—and John avoided it by instinct to seek out Obadiah.

He found the Kentuckian seated on a pile of saddlecloths beside his own fire, gnawing a cold venison steak. His calm reception of the half-breed's report was sobering enough: John had long since realized that Obadiah could face most brands of skulduggery with detachment.

"Answer me this, Doc. Did you ever meet a sutler you could trust?"

"What's he after?"

"We'll know soon enough, I reckon. If I was you, I'd try to find out even sooner."

"Chris plans to meet Red Shoes later, to arrange for guides across the Middle Path: he announced that much in open meeting."

"So he did, now you mention it. They don't come slicker than Chris Martin."

"Do you think it was a blind?"

"Call it dust in our eyes," said Obadiah. "*He* knows that Yulee and I will pick up Indian sign any day now; if we do, he wants us to think it's *honest* Indian."

"The Choctaws helped capture Fort Panmure; they're supposed to be allies of England."

"Not Red Shoes, Doc. I've brushed with that stinkard before; it's true he's hand in glove with the traders, but he's more wildcat than sachem. I doubt if he's sat at a council fire for years."

"Surely he won't risk attacking us."

"I wouldn't put it past him—if Chris don't give him his reward for that hoax at the fort." Obadiah considered his next words carefully. "'Course, I could be dead wrong; it takes all kinds of Indians to make a wilderness. But if I was you, I'd keep Yulee on that sutler's tail."

"Perhaps we should consult Dr. Wright on this. He's the leader of this group."

"The old doc's a fine man," said the Kentuckian. "But it happens he lives inside his head. Turn *him* loose in these woods—he'd walk in circles till he died."

"I'd call him a fair judge of men."

"And so he is—to a point. He let you and me and Yulee join up, didn't he? He's a just man, too. That's why he paid Yulee full value for his sloop, and gave us a bonus for working as his outriders. Trouble is, he's apt to fall over backward being fair to everyone. Chris Martin plain don't rate the job of captain. By rights, you should be giving the orders."

"He's still a hero to these people."

"So he is—for now. Ain't that why we're here? To prove he's a stinkard too?"

There was no time for more, since the camp was now astir: Chris Martin himself had come yawning from his tent to give his first commands of the day. Despite his conviction that the man was a potential traitor in their midst, John could not help admiring his assurance as he whipped the cavalcade through breakfast. The pines of their campsite were still misted with dawn when they entered the Trace again, determined to break their first day's record.

All that hot, clear morning, the travelers plodded northeast along a deep-notched trail, with no pause for the traditional nooning. Old and young alike were given rides on a turnabout basis; Hammond and Otis, riding a patient rear guard, had no need to report stragglers today. When the sun had moved to the west, the road turned sharply at last, carrying the cavalcade into a region of dense canebrakes, broken by rust-colored sloughs and alive with the mournful arguments of bird life. More than once, it was necessary to drive snakes from the path—cottonmouths for the most part, with an occasional diamondback that continued to rattle defiance from the shrub.

Just before the trail lifted to high ground again, Obadiah planted a musket ball between the eyes of a young alligator, as the saurian rose from its nap on a mudflat. The creature's powerful tail, cut from a still-twitching carcass, was added to the larder as a *pièce de résistance* for tonight's menu. 'Gator tail (as Obadiah explained to the skeptical John) was a rare delicacy, once it was properly broiled over a bed of lightwood coals.

Shortly after midday, Chris had ridden ahead quite openly. On the surface, there had been nothing unusual about that departure. Obadiah, who knew the Trace blindfolded, had been assigned to lead the marchers in the other's absence; Evan Wright, still riding proudly at the head of his band of pilgrims, continued to set the pace.

"Chris is getting bolder," said the Kentuckian, in an aside to John, after Yulee had quietly picked up the ex-sutler's trail. "Mind you, I'm not ready to accuse him of planning an ambush. But it does hurt my feelings a mite that he should think we're so blind."

John glanced down the trail. Faith, taking her turn on horseback today, was carrying the Beasley baby in her arms. Far back in the steadily moving file, Stella was leading the others in a revival hymn, a sovereign spirit-lifter in the hot, midafternoon drowse. Viewed from this angle, the emigrés still seemed on a kind of extended outing, an adventure far removed from the evil designs of man. It was hard to believe that death might be lurking behind a crossbow in the next thicket, or waiting to pounce from those mossed limbs that hung above the trail.

"Should I speak to Dr. Wright now?"

"Leave Chris to Yulee, Doc, just like I said. If he's that careless, it means he'll trip himself in time."

5

In the midmorning of the third day, the wisdom of Oba-diah's advice was brought home to John with stunning force—and, like so many crises, almost without warning.

Chris Martin had gone cantering ahead once again, with the excuse that he must test the trail—and Yulee had ghosted into the brush, at a nod from Obadiah, to keep him in view. John himself had served as outrider that day, in the hope of flushing another deer for the larder—and had just reined in his horse at the top of a long, steep rise. It was the first break in the flatlands of the Mississippi Valley, a warning that they must soon leave the comparative ease of the Trace for the rigors of the Middle Path.

Drowsing a little in his saddle, aware of no real sensation beyond the beat of sunlight on his bared head, John was only mildly surprised to mark a spurt of dust ahead. Even before the rider himself came into view, he guessed that it was Yulee, returning with another report. Steeped as he was in the gentle melancholy of solitude, he merely raised one hand in greeting as the half-breed pulled his mount into an awkward, four-footed stop. His mind reacted but tardily to his scout's first breathless words—that Chris had found Red Shoes at last.

"Didn't Colonel Martin *say* they'd meet?"

"You must come quickly—and see for yourself. Dr. Wright might not believe, if I am the only witness."

John was alert now. Yulee would know at once the difference between a casual contact with the Choctaw leader—and something far more sinister. He spurred his own horse into a gallop, as Yulee wheeled back into the Trace.

"You saw the meeting yourself?"

"It is a powwow, Doctor—with a war party."

So their long-nagging suspicions had borne fruit at last. "Shouldn't we warn the others?"

"There is no time. You must see and decide."

Yulee did not speak again: there was no further need for words as they drove down the trail. Riding Indian-fashion, with both fists in his horse's mane, the half-breed continued to outdistance John, who was forced to dodge more than one branch in his effort to keep his companion in view.

When they had covered some four miles, Yulee swung to the right, and vaulted to the ground, in the shelter of a palmetto thicket. Beyond, in a clearing, a tethered horse cropped at the sun-bitten grass. The musket thrust muzzle down in the saddle boot was evidence enough that Chris considered himself secure while he made rendezvous with the Choctaws.

"Where's the powwow?"

"In the next ravine, *jefe*." In his excitement, Yulee had slipped back to Spanish. "*Hace prisa*, I beg of you. Already, we may be too late."

"Is it safe to come this close?"

"Follow me, *Señor Médico*. I will show you how."

John turned sharply, to find that Yulee had vanished. The half-breed's voice, ghosting from a dense mass of dog fennel, pulled him into the green ambush beside him.

Dodging from tree to tree, nursing every scrap of cover, Yulee led the way to a steep downslope, masked in a tangle of palmetto scrub. When they had covered some two hundred yards of this difficult approach, the half-breed pulled back abruptly, on the lip of the ravine itself. Here, he parted the screen of leaves, with the gesture of a mathematician completing a demonstration in geometry.

"See for yourself, Doctor," he whispered. "There is no danger— these dogs feel they are safe."

The ravine, John saw, was roughly circular in shape. Perhaps a half-hundred braves were gathered here, in the ritualistic pattern of the war camp. In the precise center of the grassy plot, a fire burned. The warriors sat in two tight circles, feet pointed toward the flames, their guns and powder gourds suspended on forked sticks behind them.

Each man was naked save for an apron of otter skin, decorated profusely with bird feathers. There were crane feathers in their scalp locks, and their glistening, copper-red bodies were daubed with white hieroglyphs. Around each mouth was the characteristic blue tattoo of the Choctaw—or, rather, that part of the nation whose hunting ground embraced the delta formed by the Yazoo and the Mississippi. The fact that this party had strayed from its traditional preserve told its own story instantly. Red Shoes and his braves, having played their part as English allies at Fort Panmure, had returned as simple marauders.

The chief himself sat before the fire, his shaven skull decorated with a barbaric headdress of egret feathers. There were silver plugs in his ear lobes, and moon-shaped amulets of silver on his chest. John would have recognized him even without the bright vermilion moccasins. Red Shoes was a head taller than his tallest warrior. The deference of his four captains (whose ornaments were only a shade less magnificent than their leader's) set him apart instantly.

At the moment, he was in the act of passing a calabash pipe to Chris Martin. The sutler, who sat cross-legged before the fire, seemed entirely at home: his arrogance was a match for Red Shoes' cold-lidded stare. Only the quick dart of his eyes betrayed an inner agitation. John could understand that fear when Red Shoes took up a tomahawk and whirled it about Chris Martin's head. The circle burst into a roar of primitive laughter.

"What are they saying, Yulee?" John asked in a whisper.

"Red Shoes is telling Colonel Martin how they treat enemies."

"Can you hear more?"

"Not at this distance. I will go closer. You must return to the horses, and wait."

"I can't let you take that risk."

"There will be little risk. Colonel Martin brought two jugs to the council. Most of them are drunk as goats."

Once again, only the whisper marked the spot where the half-breed had rested; the faintest of ripples in the dog fennel told John that Yulee had begun to move toward the outer circumference of the powwow. Since he had no other choice, he dropped to hands and knees, and began to retrace his own route to the clearing where Chris Martin's horse was tethered.

His mind still whirling, he could welcome the absolute concentration needed to cover his progress. Though he could never equal Yulee, his return journey was a respectable achievement. Moving in a wide circle to take full advantage of the patches of dog fennel, he needed a good twenty minutes to reach the clearing. When he tumbled into it at last, he was still breathless, and his mind continued to recoil from conscious planning.

Yulee had not yet returned. If only to lighten the ordeal of waiting, John led both their horses deeper into the scrub and tethered them on short ropes, where the sounds of their grazing would not betray their presence. Back at the clearing, he checked the sutler's saddlebags for possible clues to his intentions. The search uncovered nothing but a pint of whiskey, and a few rounds of ammunition for the musket, still upended insolently in the saddle boot. John's hand had just closed on the stock when a familiar voice addressed him from the palmettos.

"That gun's hair-triggered, Doc. Wouldn't play with it, if I were you."

Chris Martin lurched rather than walked into the clearing. Preoccupied as he was, John had not heard his approach through the yielding curtain of dog fennel. He stared at him now, across the horse's flank, and cursed himself for his neglect.

As a cadet of the Pennsylvania Rangers, he had learned long since that a man's life could hang on small things—the snap of a twig, the sixth sense that anticipates destruction before it can take tangible form. Thanks to his carelessness, he had tossed his own life away in a matter of seconds, as casually as though the knife (now balanced on the sutler's palm) was already quivering in his throat.

"Lift up your hands, Doc," said Chris. "And keep facing me. Won't help to back up, 'cause you're in my sights right now."

The boast, John saw, was justified. Drunk though he was, Chris was quite steady. The hand that held the dagger seemed carved in stone as it half lifted above his head, then hung there motionless. All too vividly, John remembered how the sutler had split playing cards at ten paces in the taproom of the Royal George, after hours of wassail.

"Why should you want to kill me?" he asked—and knew, even before the words were out, how grotesque the question was. Chris Martin had meant to destroy him for a long time. He had only awaited the proper moment.

"Put it this way," said the sutler. "You know all about me now, and why I came this far. That's more'n I could allow even my best friend."

"Aren't you going to ask how I got here?"

"Doesn't matter now," said Chris. "You came to spy, and I've caught you. *That's* what counts——"

So Yulee had been trapped on the lip of the ravine—and Chris had come here for his revenge. Perhaps his red allies were closing in now. The threat of the knife might be only a blind—an anticipation of more ingenious torture. John heard his voice force the issue. The hoarse croaking seemed to come from a great distance.

"Can't you get it over with?"

"Sure, Doc. Whenever I like." The sutler's feet were uncertain in the sandy clearing, but his knife hand was still motionless overhead. "Just thought you'd like the whole story first—so you'd have something to take with you——"

Torture, John perceived, could take many forms. Listening to the sutler's plans, as Chris outlined them step by step, he could grasp the man's almost fiendish thoroughness. Save for Yulee's skill as a trailer, the trap might well have been sprung on the Natchez migrants without a hitch. . . . Then he remembered that Yulee's discovery (like his own intervention) had come too late. It would be easy for Chris to return to camp that evening and put his ruse in motion. Easier still to shrug off the disappearance of a pair of scouts who had ridden too far, too fast.

"Never mind the rest, Chris!" he half shouted. "You knew I'd expose you, if I could. Why let me live this long?"

"Maybe I *did* miss a trick there. But I figured you were too lovesick to pay me much mind."

Even with the shadow of eternity upon him, John felt his throat swell with rage. "You don't overlook much, it seems——"

"Maybe that's why I'm still alive. Tell me this, Doc. Which one of the girls will miss you more?"

John flung himself at his tormentor—though a good three yards of sand still parted them. Strangely enough, Chris Martin made no move to hurl the knife. The smile on those full lips seemed frozen; the hand bent backward above his head (with death's messenger balanced on the palm) remained as strangely immobile. It was only when he heard the bowstring's twang (a split-second after the thudding impact of the arrow) that John saw why.

For that small segment of time, Chris himself seemed frozen in mid-air. The snout of the arrow, winking blood-red in the sun, had smashed through his chest wall from behind, driven at point-blank range from the dog fennel. Then the knife hand crumpled; the blade slid smoothly from the inert palm, to sink haft-deep in the sandy loam. Chris coughed just once as he pitched face forward. Save for the deep, soft-plucked note of the bowstring, it was the only sound in the clearing.

Yulee emerged from the thicket on silent feet, unlimbering the six-foot longbow as he advanced to gentle the sutler's mount, which showed unmistakable signs of bolting from the presence of death. He knelt briefly to snap the feathered shaft of the arrow before he tossed the body over one shoulder, carried it to the horse, and tumbled it across the saddle.

"They were really drunk as goats," he said. "It was an easy matter to steal a bow."

"Did you—follow him here?" Too amazed, for the time being, at finding himself alive, John could hardly stammer out the question. He was still on hands and knees, where he had flung himself by instinct to avoid Chris Martin's knife.

"Of course, Doctor. What else? It was time for this man to die. A time when an arrow was better than lead." The half-breed's voice was dead calm, but his eyes were bitter with controlled rage. "I knew he would taunt you before he struck. It seemed best to let him speak—to reveal his own plan."

John laughed softly, but his laughter still held a note of hysteria. "You mean you—stalked him? As you'd—stalk a deer?" The words came in short, breathless bursts. The voice was not yet his own.

"When a man digs his own grave, it is best that he dig deep." Yulee glanced contemptuously at the body that lay across the saddle. "Not that this carrion is worth burial. We can dispose of it along the Trace."

John staggered to his feet at last. It was good to be alive—and he would savor his reprieve in a moment. For the present, it was simpler to stumble in Yulee's tracks—and to accept the half-breed's hand at his elbow, while he lifted himself to the saddle of his own mount.

"Did I—remember to thank you, Yulee?"

"There is no need for thanks, Doctor. Follow me, please. There is much to do."

Neither of them spoke again as they cantered into the Trace, with Yulee in the lead. Little by little, John could feel his mind edge back toward reality. He had joined the cavalcade with just one purpose—to challenge the sutler's shoddy claim to leadership. Today (to put things bluntly) he had come forward to prove himself the better man. . . . True, he had just escaped a fatal blunder—but the chance to prove himself was still there.

His vision had cleared completely now: he could ride as bravely as Yulee in their headlong dash to rejoin the marching column. It was only when they had driven a good two miles down the Trace that the memory of Chris Martin's last taunt exploded like a delayed rocket in his brain.

Somehow, the sutler had plumbed his deepest secret—the desires John had not admitted fully, even to himself. It was the crowning irony that Chris, of all people, should force him to face his problem squarely, at the very moment when he was dashing hell-for-leather to save the lives of the Natchez migrants.

Just in time, he remembered Faith and her hard-won wisdom. In the wilderness, he reflected, a man solved each problem as it arose. At the moment, simple survival was all that mattered. Tomorrow, or the day after, he would attack this other problem and surmount it. He was not the first male in history who had been tempted by two women, and could settle on neither.

6

Evan Wright heard them out in silence. Obadiah Hurt, holding his mount on a tight rein, emitted a few back-country oaths as John and Yulee finished their macabre recital. The empty saddle on Chris Martin's horse was a potent reminder of the tragedy that had just missed striking a death blow at the cavalcade. It might still strike, if the leaders of today's march could not devise a plan to meet it.

The Kentuckian spat a final curse. "Where's the carcass?"

"In a slough, a mile down the trail," said John.

"Won't the Indians spook, when they find he's gone?"

"The powwow was over when Colonel Martin left," said Yulee. "Red Shoes did not expect him to return."

"How do we account for his absence here?"

"Chris spent most of his time scouting," said John. "No one will be troubled, if he doesn't appear tonight."

"You intend to march straight on?"

"It's a chance we'll have to take."

"I still think it's suicide to pass the war camp," said Obadiah. "How can we be sure they haven't set an ambush?"

"It's high noon," said John, glancing up at the sun. "Every man in our column is armed. Not that we'll be trading shots on the Trace. Yulee says that Red Shoes and his braves are too drunk to leave camp before dark. Besides, it's part of the plan for us to pass by."

Evan Wright spoke in a voice that seemed oddly remote from the business at hand. "I still can't believe it——"

"Yulee heard the whole plan, sir."

"Tell it to me again, John. Not that I care for details—but I must get it in my mind."

John glanced at Obadiah, who gave a wordless shrug. Both of them understood the older doctor's hesitation. To the idealists of this world, it is a bitter shock to discover that some men are purely evil. So far, Evan Wright's mind refused to grasp the fact that Chris Martin had plotted the death of one hundred and fifty persons, solely for his personal gain.

"Chris was to direct us to a campsite where the Trace joins the Middle Path," John said. "At dawn, he would have called in the pickets: that was to be Red Shoes' signal to attack. Naturally, they'd have to butcher the lot of us: Chris could hardly afford witnesses. When it was over, the Choctaws would claim the pelts, and such gear as they fancied. Chris would have taken the cash in your saddlebags—and a free path to the Savannah."

Obadiah cut in, with just a hint of impatience, "Then so far as Red Shoes knows, Chris is still alive? And the trap's to be sprung on schedule?"

"That's our trump card," said John. "I'm afraid we must play it."

"Why not take fifty men, and bottle 'em in that ravine? If they're as drunk as Yulee says, we could bag the lot."

"Not in cold blood," said Evan Wright quickly. "I could never sanction that."

"They'd do it to us soon enough."

"I agree with Dr. Wright," said John. "We must let Red Shoes make the first hostile move."

"Have it your way, gentlemen," said the Kentuckian. "But when we do meet, let's meet head on—just like Chris planned. We'll never get the chance again."

"Obadiah's right, sir," said John, as Dr. Wright covered his eyes with his hand. "You know what chance we'd have in a running battle with fifty Indians."

"Very well, John. Let's say we make camp—and lie in wait. How can you be sure we'd survive?"

"We outgun 'em, almost two to one," said Obadiah. "Give us a few hours to dig in, and place our rifles. They'll never know what slapped 'em down."

"What of the women and children?"

"Sorry to put it that rough, but they're part of the bait. Right again, Doc?"

"That's only the beginning," said John. "We must keep this to ourselves until the last moment. At the very least, until we're in camp tonight."

Evan Wright's voice was still a gray whisper. "I'm afraid I'm not that finished a performer."

"Then you must stay at the head of the column and speak to no one." John's voice was intentionally blunt; he could see that the older man's eyes were still clouded with doubt.

"It's easy for you to be a realist, John. You almost lost your life. But I can't assent to wholesale killing so readily—even if it's a mortal enemy."

Again, Obadiah and John exchanged glances. "Don't make us put it to the vote, sir," said the Kentuckian. "You know what the result would be."

"There's no need for a vote," said Dr. Wright. "You and John are the natural leaders now. The most I can call myself is a spiritual mainspring. If we're alive tomorrow, I'd suggest that one of you be named our captain."

"Doc Powers is my boy," said Obadiah. "I know he's Yulee's. And I'll lay odds the camp picks him too."

Evan Wright smiled wanly—for the first time since his shoulders had sagged under the weight of John's report. "May I make the vote unanimous?"

John spoke with his eyes on the trail ahead. "It's a post I won't take willingly," he said.

"Consider yourself elected as of now. What's your first order?"

"To keep marching as before," John told him. "With a song or two, if possible. I'll see to that now."

A dozen times in the long, hot day, he rode down the column to make sure that there was no slackening of the pace. The spot Chris had chosen for a camp was far along the Trace, and it was essential they arrive there in good time. It was quite as essential that the faces of the marchers reflect no change from their prevailing mood. Yulee had assured him that the war party would snore away the daylight hours; but it was possible that Red Shoes had posted spies along the route—so they must act as if they suspected nothing.

John needed all his discipline to play the part of a happy outrider, with time for a laugh and joke for everyone. He had no doubt that his performance was convincing—indeed, there was too much at stake for it to be otherwise. Stella and Faith, with whom he paused for extended chats, seemed taken in by his chaffing, and responded in kind. Without seeming obvious, he took care to ride close to both of them while the cavalcade wound past the little clearing where Yulee's arrow had found its target. Already, it seemed incredible that he had escaped death there; it was hard to picture a half-hundred Choctaws, bedded in a ravine a scant half mile to the south and dreaming of scalps and glory.

"You *are* in good spirits, John," said Stella, when Faith had dropped back to help amuse the children. "Why did you laugh just now, for no reason at all?"

"Must we always have a reason for happiness?"

"No, my friend," she said, with lowered eyes. "But it helps—doesn't it?"

"I'll tell you mine, since you insist," he said. "I'm learning to live on trail. Or should I say, to live in the present—and to rejoice in it? Right now, I've just one responsibility—to make camp safely tonight. Beyond that, I refuse to look; only this afternoon is real."

"Would you object if I let my imagination stray a bit farther?"

"Don't, Stella, I beg of you. Think only of the corn pone and venison awaiting you at sundown. We'll be in Augusta soon enough."

"Aren't you looking forward to Augusta, John?"

"No. Are you?"

"Why not, if we can take up our lives there?"

"Right now, I'm in no hurry to take up any life but this. Don't forget we'll be saying our goodbyes in Augusta."

"Must it be goodbye, John?"

"You and your husband will be going on to St. Augustine——"

"So will you—I hope."

"I'm told that East Florida is full of fundless Tories. There will hardly be room for me."

"Evan will need a long rest to regain his health——"

If he ever regains it, thought John. Their eyes had dueled briefly on that; he knew that she had shared the unspoken thought.

"He'll rest easier if he knew you were helping me."

"And how could I help in Augustine?"

"We've estates to stake out—a whole new life to build. Eventually, you could both go into practice again."

"I'm not sure Faith would care to live there."

Stella offered him a slow, revealing smile: once more, her eyes said more than her lips. "Faith told me your whole story, John— that last time you were upriver. You've been more than chivalrous, caring for her as you have. Surely it needn't go on forever."

So the offer is definite, he thought—and she's making it from the kindness of her heart. A new life in British Florida, now that Natchez was behind them. A chance to prove himself, as her counselor and friend—and, eventually, the chance to take Evan Wright's place entirely, when the disease that wracked his body had claimed him. No one, he felt sure, would be happier at such a consummation than the old doctor himself. Stella was beautiful, she was gracious, and she was rich. And, as Faith had said, he was at least half in love with her.

"Let's not confuse tomorrow with today, Stella," he said quietly. "We've enough dangers to face now."

He left her on that, with a quick, laughing salute, though there was no laughter within him. The evasion, he knew, was worse than no answer at all—but he had none.

Thanks to the driving pace he set, the long line of fugitives reached Chris Martin's chosen campsite a good hour before sunset. There was no mistaking that depression on the hillside where the two trails met. It was only when the night had settled in the forest behind them that John cupped his hands to call for general attention. Obadiah and a picked squad of helpers had worked busily to raise a low breastworks at the circumference of the hollow, and to level the palmetto scrub that lay, like a dusty green wall, between the campfires and the Trace. Using the palmetto fronds to mask their rude defenses, the Kentuckian had further strengthened his position by sinking rifle pits on the flanks of the western redoubt, which would surely absorb the first shock of the Choctaw onslaught.

It was not the first time the camp had dug in for the night—and John knew it would not be the last. Still, it seemed wiser to explain their situation fully.

He would never forget that moment of revelation—the tight-packed circle of faces, the gleam of firelight on a hundred staring eyes, the soft-voiced wailing that broke out among the women when the news sank home. For that instant, he feared that panic would sweep the camp. Then, as the low murmur died, he was shamed by his own doubting. There was no real fear in those staring eyes—only a stubborn will to live.

Faith summed up for the others, when her voice rose in the

hush. "Most of us have fought Indians," she said. "We'll handle them tomorrow."

"*We'll* handle them, my dear," said John. "You'll be where you belong—with the other ladies, in the precise center of camp."

"I can load a rifle as well as any man. So can other women among us."

And fire one too, if need be, thought John. "If you really want to be useful," he said, "you can serve as Dr. Wright's nurse. He'll be setting up his surgery between those two cabbage palms, in case one is needed. If we can believe Obadiah Hurt, no enemy will cross his breastworks—but there's no stopping their bullets. They're armed with muskets."

"English muskets, at that," said Colonel Larkin. "The Choctaws are supposed to side with us, same as the Creeks."

"These stinkards are more renegade than Choctaw," put in Obadiah. Framed in firelight as he leaned on his long-barreled fowling piece, he seemed a tower of strength in that muted babble. "I'm mighty proud to see that no one's afraid. There's no reason to be. Not if we keep our heads, and hug the ground."

"Obadiah is in command," said John. "Beginning now, no one stirs without his orders. Is that clear?"

Dr. Wright spoke for the first time. "How can we be sure the attack won't come before dawn?"

"That's one good thing about an Indian," said Beasley. "He'll trail and steal by night—but he won't kill or be killed before sunrise, if he can help it. Seems he's afraid of losing his way to the Happy Hunting Grounds, if he takes off in the dark."

"Then I'd suggest a good night's rest, if such a thing is possible," said the elder doctor. "Naturally, we'll keep our sentries at full strength until morning. Red Shoes will be expecting that."

John was glad to observe that his colleague's tone was now quite composed. "For all we know, he may be listening out there now," he said. "A few songs might not be amiss—if someone will lead us."

Stella rose from her place at her husband's side, and took the guitar that Page Hammond offered. Watching her narrowly, John was sure that she was facing the coming crisis as resolutely as Faith. If Stella's self-possession had a dramatic overtone, he could understand that too. Like the new soldier about to smell powder for the first time, she was determined to appear more casual than the most grizzled Indian fighter.

As though by common consent, she was allowed to sing the first verse of her song alone. Her clear soprano, floating into the void of the wilderness, should have seemed lost and alone. Instead her voice laughed back at the night—mocking its terrors, until they dissolved clean away, and only the warm, vibrating melody had meaning.

> *O fare you well, my own true love*
> *O fare you well awhile*
> *I'm going away, but I'm coming back*
> *If I go ten thousand mile.*

Faith's contralto came in on the second verse. One by one, the women at the campfires joined in—hesitant, at first, to pour out unspoken fears in song, yet oddly cheerful, once they had found the pitch.

> *O don't you see yon pretty girl*
> *A-spinning at her wheel?*
> *Ten thousand guineas would I give*
> *To feel just like she feels.*

The men were singing now, a deep, crashing chorus that built its own barrier against loneliness and despair. On the third verse, one hundred and fifty English voices cast their defiance against the treacheries of the night—with a childish treble tossed in here and there, as the children of the Natchez cavalcade rocked into slumber in their mothers' arms.

John, singing as lustily as the rest, could only pray that the song had reached the Choctaw camp.

7

That night, the women and children slept in the first circle of tents—deep in the hollow that Chris Martin had chosen as their final resting place. In the outer circle of canvas and tarpaulin, seventy-odd riflemen composed themselves to uneasy rest, while they awaited the spring dawn. Beyond the camp, the sentries made their rounds, eyes glued on the dark forest mass that hemmed them, ears tuned to catch the first bird song—or the first hoot of an all too human owl.

Despite Obadiah's protest, John had insisted on taking a turn at sentry duty.

"Sleep while you can, Doc. You'll soon be busy enough."

"Could you sleep, if someone else was doing your job?"

"'Tain't the same. I can smell a Choctaw before I hear him. So can Yulee. Don't you fret—we'll wake you in time for the show."

"I'll still feel happier on my feet."

Occupied as he was, Obadiah had offered no further protest. All through the night (as he paced his rounds on the edge of that grassy hollow) John knew that the Kentuckian was in ceaseless motion about the camp, counting noses by touch rather than sight. At three o'clock, when the forest was still cloaked in black, he began to place his riflemen, using infinite care to move each unit of his command in utter silence. John, returning from his tour of duty, stumbled on a palmetto root and found himself gripped instantly in Obadiah's arms. The knife at his throat was uncomfortably accurate, pressing hard over the carotid artery in the second before he was recognized.

"See what I mean?" the Kentuckian whispered. "You'd be safer behind a log."

"Did you think I was Red Shoes?"

"Why not? They're thick as lice in August, and they're closing in."

"How can you be sure?"

"Ask any trapper, and he'll admit he doesn't rightly know. But I can *feel* 'em, inside my nose. They're holding back, so far. Nary a man amongst 'em will raise a war whoop, until he can see the next one's topknot. When they come, they'll come fast as thunder."

"Did you warn the women?"

"Just passed the word. They're to lie flat and bite grass."

Obadiah met John's eyes as they crouched in the graying light. The dimensions of the camp were small; it was easy to imagine the destruction a few tomahawks could wreak, if the enemy drove past the breastworks.

"I'd be happier, if you'd order Faith and Mrs. Wright to join the others."

"So would I, Doc. But *there's* a pair of ladies who won't take orders. They aim to be useful in this hoe-down, or die trying."

John glanced toward the far side of the camp. The light was changing from gray to pearl. He could make out the contours of two stumpy palms, midway of the northern and eastern breastworks. It had seemed the best spot for a field surgery; he hoped it would not be caught in a cross fire. He considered checking on that fear; instead he took up a short-barreled shotgun, and found his place in a rifle pit. Stella and Faith would insist on taking their risks with the others.

The other sentries had begun to return to camp, as the silhouettes of the lightwoods took shape against the dawn. John was glad to note that they moved casually, without so much as a final glance at the forest wall. No observer in that ready-made ambush would have guessed that this huddled group of tents was staring wide awake.

Obadiah moved down the breastworks on hands and knees to whisper final instructions. "You may be Tories," he said, "but this time I want you to fight like Whigs on Bunker Hill. Don't shoot until you see the white of a Choctaw eyeball—and I'd squeeze my trigger even then. If you hold your fire, we'll drop half of 'em on the first volley. The fellows with shotguns can take the rest."

There were a few murmurs of assent. Hefting his own shotgun, careful to keep his head below the shelter of the palmetto fans, John drew a bead on an imaginary enemy. The tops of the pines had caught the sunrise now—but the underbrush at their base still held the night in a firm embrace, and the mist that had begun to spiral up from the bottom lands obscured the vision still more. The open space between the camp and the nearest thicket seemed pitifully narrow. How could Obadiah stop the attack before it overflowed the last tent?

"They are moving, Doctor."

It was Yulee, speaking at his side: John had noticed long ago that the half-breed's vision was far keener than his own. Obadiah had just whispered the same comment. Try as he might, John could discern no movement in the underbrush beyond camp.

"Sure there weren't more'n fifty, Doc?"

"Yulee's count tallied with mine."

"They're fixing to jump us from the west, like we hoped. Check your priming, boys—and stop breathing, if you can."

John took a second sight along the barrel of his shotgun. Loaded with a double charge of powder, it would be a deadly weapon at this range. His finger had crept under the trigger guard before he remembered that he must hold his fire until the second volley.

The ragged curtain of mist had lifted a little—light had begun to invade the forest floor. Now, for the first time, he saw what Yulee and Obadiah had already noted—patches of darker shadow, hunching into human form, to scuttle from bush to bush, to vanish and reappear again in the shelter of tree trunks. A muted bird call, picked up instantly from a thicket a scant hundred yards from camp, seemed the signal for a general advance, though John had yet to glimpse the face of the enemy.

Save for those matched bird notes, the woods were silent. Even the forest denizens seemed to feel a battle in the making—and waited breathless for the outcome.

For all his choked-down fear, John could admire the precision of Red Shoes' maneuver. Though the advance was concerted, it was impossible to pick out individuals in that dark, slow-moving mass. It was as though the night itself had risen on two legs, to ghost from ambush for a life-and-death struggle with day.

Would the Choctaws move into the open at last and overwhelm the camp? Red Shoes could still scent the trap, and recoil—though there was no visible evidence that his supposed quarry awaited him en masse, with a battery of rifles primed and ready. It was almost a relief to see the first paint-smeared face lift above the grass. A dozen others burst into view at once—until the whole space before the camp swarmed with copper-red bodies, inching forward at an unhurried pace and flairing the morning breeze like so many hounds.

John saw at once that the Indians were totally unaware of the reception that awaited them. If they still moved warily, it was only the caution of the hunter, approaching his kill on silent feet. They were near enough to count now, as the last of the war party wriggled into view from the farthest thicket. John felt the pressure inside his skull relax a trifle when he saw that the renegades had committed their entire force to a single assault. Believing that Chris Martin was within the camp, that the migrants were sleeping save for a few drowsy sentries, Red Shoes had counted on surprise to sweep the field.

For the last time, John glanced down the row of silent marksmen in the rifle pits. Cheek to stock, eyes riveted on their sights, each man in that company had picked his target. Immobile as wooden carvings, they awaited the crack of Obadiah's rifle, which would signal their first volley.

He saw Red Shoes at last, at one wing of his force, his shoulders humped as he waddled toward his objective. Ungainly though he seemed on hands and knees, the Choctaw's threat was real enough. John found himself fingering his musket a second time: the command to fire seemed forever in coming. True, the enemy were still elusive targets, while they crept from hummock to hummock. Yet he could pin Red Shoes cleanly in his sights: the savage seemed near enough to touch.

A bird call sounded from the far wing of the Indian advance— so naturally that John would have sworn a lark had just risen to try its wings in the sunrise. He saw the chief's lips shape an answer to the call, watched his arch enemy rise to his full height, a scant fifteen feet from the outer limits of the camp. All down the line, the Choctaws popped into view. Red Shoes lifted his rifle high. The bird call changed to a war whoop, a high-pitched scream that poured like ice water down John's spine. Moving in a tight arc, their feathers brave against the sunlight, the Indians charged the camp, hatchets and rifles at the ready.

Obadiah held his fire even now. When the tension seemed beyond enduring, his rifle barked its signal—a short, decisive bark, followed by the thud of lead against flesh. John saw a brave tumble headfirst with the bullet in his heart, as the slamming volley and the great whorl of smoke from seventy gun barrels blotted the enemy from his musket.

The second volley, fired from another rifle pit the instant the smoke had cleared, seemed to blunt the echo of the first and choked the last war whoop into silence. Staring up at the faltering red tide, feeling a strange detachment from the others, John saw that fully two-thirds of their attackers had already gone down: every Choctaw had been a standing target, and virtually every bullet had scored. Pinned to the lip of the hollow where they had expected to reap scalps and plunder, the survivors paused just long enough to collect their wits. Then, as rapidly as it had advanced, the attack broke and fled. Of the original advance, only Red Shoes and a subchief still hung above the breastworks—and, even as he watched, John saw the second warrior go down like a squirrel before another rifle crack.

The crash of twenty shotguns, fired point-blank at the retreat, blazed a finale to the Choctaw debacle. In all, less than a dozen

Indians escaped the field; several of these were dragging wounded limbs as they scrambled for the thickets. Bemused as he was by the smashing triumph of the defense, John had made no attempt to join that final volley. He could hardly believe his eyes when he saw Red Shoes come raging through the smoke to leap the breastworks. Driven by a force that transcended reason, it was clear that the leader of the attack preferred death to dishonor.

The tomahawk flashed in the sunlight, with John's head as the target. His vital forces rose to the emergency, shifting the musket to his shoulder. There was no sound beyond a faint click when the hammer fell. Rolling desperately with the threat of death upon him, he knew that the flint had missed fire.

A great roaring filled his ears. Choked by the blast of gunpowder, he watched the tomahawk falter in its descent, caught the look of stunned surprise in the Choctaw's face as his knees buckled. Spread-eagled in the palmettos, with a full charge of buckshot in his chest, Red Shoes made a last, angry effort to rise. With the death rattle in his throat, he was still the epitome of his race, still eager for a white victim.

John's heel ground the tomahawk into the earth as his enemy gave a last, convulsive shudder. Faith, kneeling on the edge of the rifle pit, the shotgun still at her shoulder, gave him a cheerful smile, though her cheeks were pale enough.

"I told you I could load as well as any man," she said.

Still on one knee, with the wood-smoke stench of the dead Indian in his nostrils, John continued to stare open-mouthed.

"How did you get here?"

"I can crawl like an Indian too," she said. "Aren't you glad I joined you?"

"You might have been killed, Faith——"

"So might you. In fact, that hatchet missed your head by inches."

He got to his feet to stare wildly at the battlefield. Smoke still hung above the breastworks, but the riflemen had moved into the open. John had a glimpse of Obadiah, in the act of lifting enemy hair; he saw Colonel Larkin, a clubbed rifle in his fists, go charging into a thicket to smash the skull of another would-be murderer. Turning aside with no desire to complete the ghastly inventory, he put out a hesitant hand to touch Faith's arm. Even now, he could not quite believe she was real. Or that she had knelt there, just behind him, at the moment he needed her most.

"First Yulee, now you," he said. "It's more than I deserve."

"Why shouldn't I save your life, John?" she asked. "Isn't that what wives are for?"

Perhaps she hadn't lifted her lips for that reason, but it seemed perfectly natural to kiss her. The moment cried out for jubilation.

Faith rested but an instant in his arms before she moved toward the inner circle of tents—alive with children's wailings, now that the threat of doom had receded. Falling into step beside her, John gave her hand a final, grateful pressure. Someday, he would thank her as she deserved—he had no words this morning. Certainly this was not the time or place to confess that she might have saved him for another woman.

The Tombigbee

*A*x *and machete* had carved their path through the Mississippi canebrakes; in the last weeks, they had used those same trail breakers in the densely forested lowlands that spread, like an endless apron, from the flanks of the mountain wall to the north. It had been a hardslogging, backbreaking month—an interval when the mind was too numbed by distance to think beyond the next bend in the trail, the next brambled hillside.

They had crossed gullies and ravines where the brush was thick enough to shut out the sky, and the markings of the Middle Path were almost too faint to follow; they had wallowed through bogs where only the compass enabled them to tell north from south, where quicksands bubbled beside the trail and leeches by the dozens fastened to their flesh. For three blessed days they had marched through a great, park-like glade that, Obadiah insisted, marked the dividing line between Choctaw and Creek, a neutral ground untouched by Indian moccasin. Here, they had dared to steal a short rest while the stock was watered and children romped.

Finally, as the second month of their pilgrimage began, they had breasted the last of many rises, to find themselves looking down on a brown prairie, already sere in the June sunlight. Behind them, to the northeast, the outposts of the great Appalachian chain were only blue mirages. Ahead, the pine barrens seemed to stretch into a dusty infinity, until they merged with the heat haze on the eastern horizon.

Riding a bit ahead of the cavalcade, with Yulee and Obadiah

on either side, John eased his mount to a stop and opened the map case on his pommel. He had reined in by design, for there was no real need to halt. The Path was in plain view on the flank of the hillside. Still, it had seemed a natural spot to pause, now that another phase of their journey lay before them. Without glancing back, he knew that the marchers had settled to the earth, glad of this short respite.

The Romans map on his knee was a memory book of sorts— as accurate as the log Evan Wright had kept so meticulously in his leather-bound diary. For no good reason, John found himself checking the trail they had already covered, rather than the unknown hazards ahead. Here (for a starter) was the neat red cross that marked their short and bloody meeting with the Choctaw marauders. He needed only to close his eyes to see that field again, strewn with windrows of Indian dead, and the breastworks where Red Shoes lay tumbled, as grotesquely as a broken toy.

In a very real sense that would-be massacre had marked the start of their journey. It had been followed by his election as leader; the load that had settled on his shoulders that day had been a tangible thing. . . . It had also marked the division of the company, since nearly fifty members of their group (shaken to their souls by the Indian attack and visioning worse dangers ahead) had chosen to turn back to Natchez and throw themselves on the mercy of the Spaniards.

As Obadiah had said, it was a crisis that occurred in every wilderness camp, a time when the men are separated from the boys. No one could deny that the stalwarts who had marched behind their chosen captain these thirty days were the stuff of which empire-builders are made.

It was strange that this flight from Natchez was retracing its footsteps, as it were, to wind back through the wilderness to an older, safer world. Now that they had been tested by the trail, John felt that his companions could have marched to the Pacific, had they so willed. It was doubly strange that he (of all possible leaders) should head this column today. Or that he should have found his dedication there, his reason for being.

2

He glanced back just once before he returned to the map, and his usual conference with Obadiah.

There was Faith (in the vanguard, as always) chatting with the Beasleys—Faith, who had saved his life in the Choctaw attack and had preserved his sanity no less surely in the days that followed. Though she did not look up, he could tell that she felt his eyes; he looked away with a feeling akin to guilt. With a trail mate like Faith Gordon, it had been simple enough to face each problem as it arose on this endless journey; he had learned that most problems could be solved, once they were tackled squarely. The problem of Faith herself, when they found that all journeys had an ending, was another matter.

Stella, he saw, was marching with the Hammonds today; at the moment, she was charming the two Hammond girls with some fanciful tale that had already sent them into gales of laughter. Now that the migrants had turned southward, both Stella and Faith had discarded their buckskin kirtles in favor of cooler homespuns; thanks to the merciless sun, Stella had long since tanned as darkly as Faith. Still, there was no mistaking that patrician figure in the cluster of sunbonnets beside the Middle Path. A stranger blundering into their midst would have guessed instantly that this was a queen in transit, for all her dust-caked garb—a queen who gave few commands, yet expected them to be obeyed.

John began to check distances on the map, if only to put thoughts of Stella from his mind. So far as he could judge, they had covered more than half the distance to their first objective, the Creek town of Talassee, where he hoped to find an ally in the person of the nation's king, Alexander McGillivray. Once at Talassee, he told himself solemnly, his obligation to these migrants would end. If McGillivray's people proved friendly (as they must), there would be guides and horses to take them on the last lap of their journey to Augusta or East Florida.

What came after, when he had resigned his post as trail captain, was something he would face when the time arrived. Today, he could only be thankful for the responsibilities of leadership, for the endless details of the march that combined to shut out all thoughts of the future. While they were still deep in the barrens of the Middle Path, with survival itself in doubt, he could refuse to concern himself with tomorrow, or any reality more distant than their next bivouac.

True, the perils they had imagined after the Choctaw attack had failed to appear. Indians had skulked on their flanks, while they worked out of Red Shoes' country; but these had been mere shadowy pilferers, not daring to show their faces by daylight. When they reached the glade that divided the two nations, even this petty marauding had ceased. Now, more than ever, John was convinced that Red Shoes had been no more than a maverick, disowned by the responsible chieftains of his tribe. Like Chris Martin, there had been no one who cared to avenge his demise.

The expected threat of sickness had also failed to materialize, beyond the inevitable aches and pains of a long journey. Ralph Otis had suffered a broken arm after the Indian attack, but the bone had knit snugly. Old Amos Dexter (who had been the Wrights' overseer at Trail's End) had pulled a tendon on their last climb down from the mountain country; he rode on horseback today, beside Hal Duffy and the younger Borland boy, whose teeth still chattered from the aftermath of summer ague. So far, these had been the only casualties.

The most trying problem in the past few days had been a persistent shortage of water—and, as an inevitable corollary, a scarcity of game. The easy days of the Trace, when the outriders had never failed to bring in deer or partridge at day's end, seemed remote as Eden now. Thanks to this early-summer drought, most of the game had retreated to the coolness of the mountains; the water holes Obadiah remembered from former trips through this region had been bone-dry. Even the upper branches of the Tombigbee (which he recalled as roaring freshets) had been reduced to mere muddy trickles.

Thirst was never far from them, the need to find water a sharper goad than any fear of a second Indian attack. They had marched on short rations all of yesterday—and the vista ahead was hardly encouraging, though the sight of open country was a welcome change after their weeks in the piedmont.

John looked up from his musings as he heard Obadiah stir in his saddle. To the best of his knowledge, they had covered close to three hundred miles in that long (and sometimes heartbreaking) month, perhaps half their total journey. Yet other tests awaited them before they could set foot on the track to Talassee. He could understand why the Kentuckian was anxious to put that sun-bitten plain behind them.

"How far to the Tombigbee?"

"Three days, at the outside," said Obadiah. "That is, if the fine weather holds—and our tongues ain't dragging in the dust. I wouldn't have prayed for rain in the hills, but I'll put in a request right now for an old-fashioned cloudburst. This neck of the woods could do with a soaking, same as us."

John nodded sober agreement. The fine summer weather had been a blessing in the hills, so long as springs were abundant; even on the hottest days, it had been possible to water the stock adequately at each campsite. Now, with a three days' drive in prospect before they could reach the Tombigbee (the first full-sized stream they had encountered since the Mississippi), the threat of drought was ominously real.

"Any chance of finding a spring before sunset?"

"You won't believe it, Doc, but we'll turn up water by nightfall. See that line of trees—yonder to the right? I've camped there more'n once, when I was hunting in these foothills. It's a prime spot for game, when the fens still hold the rain."

"They'll be powder-dry now."

"An all-weather spring feeds down to that hammock from higher ground. You'll see it plain enough, once the trail has crossed the next hump. What say we head out and prove I'm right?"

John lifted his hand to signal the resumption of the march before he followed the Kentuckian over the last ridge of the foothills. Yulee wheeled in at the head of the column, which heaved up from the grass with a precision that was almost military. These weeks on trail had done more than harden the marchers into a close-knit unit. Long practice in surmounting the perils of the Middle Path had given each member the precision of a puppet. Faces were haggard with fatigue today, and dust lay thick on every shoulder when the column snaked out into the plain. But there was no word of complaint to cloud the purpose of that final, driving pace. The migrants had long since learned to conserve their breath for the last, bone-shaking hour before making camp.

Obadiah and John reached their selected bivouac just before sunset. As the Kentuckian had promised, there was abundant grass in this cleft; thanks to the all-weather spring which bubbled in a rocky cup, the vale had been spared from the parching heat of the barrens that surrounded it. It was a blessed relief to unsaddle both mounts, and watch them roll beside the spring—to stretch one's own limbs before preparing cook fires, and staking out tent sites against the arrival of the main column.

There was time to splash naked in a pool below the spring, while the dust cloud on the prairie translated into the weary bodies of their companions. Lolling in the delicious coolness of the water, John felt his mind drift back to quieter times . . . The back garden of his home in Germantown, filled with the murmur of bees and the whisper of the brook that ran through his father's apple orchard. The Schuylkill in the rain, after a day's fishing in his brothers' skiff: he could still remember their boyish shouts of glee, as they had lifted their faces to that refreshment, after hours of parching heat. . . . Were those brothers still alive today—and had the war they had fought so valiantly ended at last? It seemed unlikely that their paths would cross again. But he no longer felt an uneasy stir of shame when he thought back to the adventures they had shared. He, too, had earned his victories; they would have no right to reproach him now.

"I'll give odds it rains by morning," said Obadiah, as they sunned themselves dry on the grassy bank. "Leastways, that's what my private barometer says. Did you know I carry one in my carcass?"

"Don't tell me I overlooked a bit of lead at Fort Panmure."

"This is a bullet in my right shin—a present from a Shawnee. Never know it's there, until the weather changes. Then it starts teasing the bone a mite. Right now, it's talking of thunderstorms."

John smiled drowsily at the news. Evan Wright's glass had fallen several points since morning; it was good to find that a human barometer had registered the same change. Stretching mightily before he donned his clothes, he offered the Kentuckian the last of his Havana segars; they had been husbanded rigorously for this moment of repose at the end of a long day's drive. Obadiah had already poured two pannikins of his favorite potion from a jug in his saddlebags.

"Here's to the Tombigbee—and a safe crossing."

"Can't ask for everything, Doc. If it rains here tonight, it'll probably pour in the mountains. We'll be lucky if that river's inside its banks when we fetch it." The Kentuckian continued to grin, despite the gloom of his prediction. "Reckon we can swim as good as we can walk?"

"Right now, I'd call it a welcome change. Still, I wouldn't frighten the others until we're sure."

"Believe me, it'd take a lot to spook these folks now. They've turned into first-rate trail beaters. They'll more'n likely be good mud turtles too."

Obadiah's rain had not come when the camp settled for the night, a scant half-hour after sundown. At each bivouac, it seemed, the tents were up faster than before, the last fire lighted in record time. But the near-picnic mood of the Trace had long since been replaced by a harsher reality. There was no singing tonight, and even the pre-supper games of the children were muted by weariness.

In a matter of minutes, it seemed, the tents were wrapped in silence. Sleep claimed their inmates in its blanket of oblivion; the footfalls of the pickets (pacing the higher ground to the north, the lip of green earth where dale and prairie met) were the only sound to break the repose of the summer night.

3

John had long since trained himself to plummet into sleep the moment he had murmured a good night to Faith. Tonight, he was more angered than startled to find himself wide awake, a few hours after he had slipped under his poncho. He knew instantly that a far-off crash of thunder had roused him, though the distant booming had not intruded on Faith's repose.

The thunder repeated as he raised on one elbow. Apparently the storm was building in the mountains, for the thrust of the hillock above the camp had blacked out the glimmer of the lightning. Only a spatter of rain had touched them so far, stirring an acrid odor of dust in the bone-dry ground outside the camp. It was quite possible that the rain would skirt this area entirely, to follow one of the wide northern valleys in the Appalachians, the foothills of whose southern terminus lay a little to the north.

Cursing the vagaries of weather, John prepared to compose himself for sleep again, when he saw that Obadiah had just come into camp. There was no mistaking his tall, stooped figure as he paused before the central fire, then moved toward John's own tent.

"Hoped that thunder had wakened you, Doc. Better come to the hilltop; there's something I'd like you to see."

Knuckling the sleep from his eyes, John stumbled along in the Kentuckian's wake. When they stood together on the spine of the ridge that fenced their camp to the north and west, he rubbed his eyes a second time to wipe out the unwanted vision. The solid wall of flame was still there when he looked again—a towering red wall that seemed to rumble closer with each breath, to lift and rear until the sky itself was part of its almost incandescent glow.

He had seen other forest fires blaze into being and run their maniac course—but he had watched from a place of safety, where he could savor the infernal drama. Tonight, with the breeze from the north and the fire raging on the last slopes of the foothills, he saw that the slash pines on the prairie itself would soon ignite. Standing here on the ridge, with the bushy green sea of the barrens before him, he could feel the breath of that distant blaze—as though some demon from the underworld was pumping a monster bellows, and chuckling darkly at his work.

"Any idea how it started?"

"Must have been the storm. Wasn't enough rain to taste down here, but there were lightning bolts to spare. One bolt in a dead tree would spark that sort of tinder."

"Any chance it may pass us by?"

"Not if that breeze holds. Once the pine woods catch, they'll burn like torches."

"No use to break camp and try outrunning it?"

Obadiah shook his head. "Better to stay here—and thank God there's a little green wood around us. Not that it'll stay green for long, if there ain't some rain mixed with that wind."

John's mind, shocked wide awake by this not unexpected threat, had already jumped ahead of the Kentuckian's whispered estimate. The cordon of live oaks surrounding their camp was still green enough to resist that fearful heat, if the fire itself could somehow be deflected from the ravine. But if it rolled unimpeded to the edge of camp, it would devour them as casually as so many spitted birds before an open furnace.

"There's one chance left," John said. "We'll have to backfire."

"Wind's right powerful, Doc. What if the main blaze catches up?"

"We'll burn the underbrush in strips. The first fire can start at the top of the ravine. Are you afraid to try it?"

"Not me," said the Kentuckian. "Just wanted to make sure you saw the risk."

"How else can we keep from roasting?"

"Go rouse the camp," said Obadiah promptly.

He was already kneeling beside a clump of dry grass, to pour out a pinch of powder from his horn. Shielding the area with his body, he struck the barrel of his rifle a quick, glancing blow with his hunting knife. Sparks leaped into the windy air; on the second try, the powder flared, igniting a ready-made torch, which the Kentuckian plucked from the earth.

"Bring out your firemen, Doc. We'll need 'em in the next hour."

John did not pause to watch Obadiah range down the curve of the ravine, setting a man-made conflagration as he ran. There was no time to break the news gently to the camp below. Indeed, more than one tent was now astir, as sleeping migrants began to flair the smoke. A dozen men were running to help the Kentuckian before John could bark his first orders. The spout of flames, as the fat lightwoods just outside the ravine began to ignite from the burning underbrush, had already rivaled the howling menace to the north.

It was John's plan to set his first fires not more than fifteen feet apart. Thanks to the organization of the camp (which had lived and worked by groups since the first day), it was easy to assign men to these separate tasks. The older boys were sent to gentle the pack horses. It was too much to hope that they could avoid a stampede if the fire really entered the camp—but John meant to salvage what he could of the string.

Racing to the top of the ravine again, he had a glimpse of Faith, already wide awake and calling orders of her own to the boys. He had assumed that she would take over the leadership of that area. The children of the camp were used to following her, however much they might wish to join the men on the fire lanes.

A band of flame several yards wide was already crackling at the top of the ridge. Beyond, where the second fire lane had been staked out, the underbrush was sizzling into combustion. John had forgotten how solidly a pine tree could burn, once it was fairly ignited. It was as though the core of fire, blooming like a blood-red rose in the tree's heart, had waited until the last possible instant before exploding into a geyser of sparks and hissing coals.

Not all the trees had caught: here and there, a gaunt sentinel remained. But their margin of safety was widening fast, as new backfires were laid down in ever-widening half-circles. At the same time, another group of torchbearers, working in a broad V-pattern on both sides of the ravine, were establishing a second barrier.

In the next half-hour, the entire company was soot-blackened to the eyes. Women and children, working within the camp itself, dampened the grass along the ravine and stood ready to snuff out wind-blown sparks. The wide, free-burning V's, arrowing away to the south, were laying down their own paths of destruction in the piney woods below the camp, but they had wiped out all danger of invasion on the flanks. The critical point was still the head of the ravine, which would receive the full onslaught of the flames.

John and his cohorts had now established a backfire perhaps two hundreds yards in depth—a roaring threat of its own that all but invaded the camp at times. A few clumps of bushes, ignited by spontaneous combustion within the ravine, were allowed to burn themselves out, thus increasing the area of scorched earth. Once the main blaze was upon them, everything burnable within that green hollow would be a deadly threat.

The men on the outer circles worked for the most part in sweating silence. The only sound to lift above the roar of that holocaust to the north was the scream of a horse, signaling that yet another animal had broken the cordon and charged into the night. Now and again, John had a glimpse of Faith—a soot-blackened Amazon, her voice raised in a warning to her youthful charges. Oddly enough, he had no thought that she might be in danger. Faith, who understood horses in all their moods, would know when an animal could be roped into submission—and when it was impossible to stop another charge into the red-rimmed dark.

Stella had joined the fire fighters at the northern end of camp —where it was difficult, at times, to distinguish the backfires from the bubbling hell-broth beyond. If Faith seemed a bit larger than life tonight, Evan Wright's wife was insubstantial as a wraith as she hurried to do her part. But there was no mistaking Stella's dogged courage—or the fury with which she charged upon each fresh tongue of flame. More than once, in that panting half-hour, John found an excuse to cross her path, while he hurried to fulfill his own tasks. There was no time to speak, or even to advertise his presence; but he knew she had been lifted up with the others, in that communal drive toward survival.

The main blaze was marching upon them with terrible speed— exploding the piney woods tree by tree, raging across the swampland, where the crackle of burning reeds resembled the roar of small-arms fire in a war beyond mortal ken. The backfire still seemed a pitiful obstacle in the face of that red juggernaut. Working in the last of the burned-over bands, with Ned Beasley at his side, Obadiah ranging to the other flank, and Yulee behind him, John saw that they had accomplished what they could. He cupped his hands in an order to retire; it was time to gain their defenses (such as they were) or risk blundering into a trap without an exit.

Obadiah echoed the order from his own singed whiskers. The air was full of shouted curses, all but drowned by the detonations of the blaze, as the men yielded their posts one by one in the general retreat to the ravine. Calling for Beasley to follow, John turned back with the others. He had run perhaps fifty yards with the pressure of the holocaust like an incubus on his shoulders, before he realized that he was alone.

"Where are you, Ned?"

There was no answer when he repeated the call, though he was sure he had heard a groan, somewhere in the sooty darkness behind him. Despite the glare, it was hard to see clearly, because of the billows of greasy smoke that had begun to roll before the blast. There was no mistaking the groan when it came again, though he could not locate it precisely. From that distance, it resembled the cry of a wounded animal. All kinds of game had coursed through their backfire in the past hour—deer, rabbits, woodchucks, a pugnacious hog or two.

"Are you there, Ned?" John called again.

This time, the groan seemed to rise from the ground at his feet. He stumbled into the path of the fire, and all but tripped on Beasley's body.

The man was sprawled beside a stumphole—one of those treacherous, rotted-out pits impossible to avoid in the dark. Stunned by the violence of his fall, the major did no more than moan faintly as John knelt to examine him. Ned's foot had evidently crashed through the shell of rotten wood, snapping the bone at the ankle.

"Up you come. We'll have to move fast."

Despite his thin frame, Beasley was a dead weight in his arms as John struggled to lift him on one shoulder. He forced himself to kneel there in the soot, while Ned's mind groped back to consciousness: without an effort on his part as well, they would both perish.

"Leave me lay, Doc. You'll never make it."

"We're making it together, Ned."

Beasley struggled feebly, and managed to raise himself on his good leg, until his body was draped over John's shoulder, and one fist had anchored in John's belt. It took a bone-cracking effort, but John managed to stagger to his feet. Already the smoke was so thick it was impossible to pick out landmarks: he could only guess at the location of the camp. But there was no time to seek out directions now: the roaring wall of destruction behind them took care of that.

The going proved hard in the backfire. More than once (as he stumbled there, ankle-deep in soot and glowing cinders) John found himself teetering on the brink of other stumpholes, or recoiling from thickets that still made minor holocausts of their own.

The hell-mouth of the major conflagration sucked at his heels with a thousand tongues. He felt his shirt catch fire, and knew that Ned was doing his poor best to beat out the blaze.

For one dreadful moment, John was sure he had circled the ravine, only to blunder into the flaming cul-de-sac to the south. Then he stumbled in earnest, and knew he had reached the grassy margin of the camp. Willing hands relieved him of his burden, and with no sense of transition he somehow managed to limp across the rim of the ravine, where he pitched into Faith Gordon's arms.

The roaring of the fire was still in his ears as he slipped gently into limbo. He was aware of voices and bustle all around him and knew he had not quite fainted, after all. Then a dipper of water touched his lips: he drank gratefully and looked up into Faith's begrimed face. Her eyes, he saw, were red from smoke, her hair wild as that of some Valkyrie fresh from combat.

"They reached you just in time," she said. "Ned Beasley's clothes were already burning."

"He beat out mine when they caught. Is he——?"

"They carried him to the spring. Obadiah said he'd be all right." Faith looked up when a figure John dimly recognized as Colonel Larkin loomed above them. "What about Dr. Wright?" she asked, in a quick whisper.

"We got him back," Larkin said hoarsely. "A little singed, that's all."

John attempted to sit up, but his head began to swim, so violently he was grateful for the cradle of Faith's arms. "What happened to Dr. Wright?"

"He heard that you and the major were still out there—and tried to find you. The others stopped him before he got too far."

The conflagration seemed nearer than ever now. John could feel its deep, panting breath in the air above him, and understood the stormy heaving of the bosom where his head was pillowed. Like himself, Faith was finding it hard to breathe in the partial vacuum created by the back draft of the blaze. He tried to sit upright again, but the wave of dizziness returned. He was glad to let her restrain him with arms that seemed, for the moment, far stronger than his will.

"I must see about Dr. Wright and Ned."

"You've been hero enough for one night," said Faith brusquely. "If you'd swallowed a bit more smoke, they'd never have found you."

"What about the fire?"

"It's passing around the ravine now."

He found that he could lift his head enough to observe the solid ring of men along the sides of the ravine, with pails and dampened blankets poised, ready to beat down the showers of sparks that erupted from the wall of fire still raging just beyond. Even from where he lay, it was apparent that the blaze had exhausted itself, on the threshold of the backfire they had carved out with such backbreaking toil. Already, the core of the holocaust had moved down the long arrows of the Vs they had burned on the ravine's flanks.

"Yulee was on his way to rescue Ned," said Faith, still with more than a hint of anger in her voice. "Why did you have to outrun him?"

Before he could frame an answer, Stella Wright came into his fast-clearing vision. She knelt on the bank beside him, her face white and her eyes bright with concern. "Evan sent me, Faith," she said. "To see how he was."

John stirred in Faith's tight embrace and felt her arms relax at last. This time, he found he could sit up after a fashion.

"There's nothing wrong with him that a good dose of fresh air won't cure," Faith said. "Plus another dose of common sense."

He saw the two women's glances meet. Had his thoughts been clearer, he might have understood the smile that passed between them for what it really was.

"Now we're on the subject," he said, as he got to his feet, "I'll have a look at Dr. Wright myself."

With Faith steadying his arm and Stella close on the other side, he circled the spring to where Ned Beasley and the old doctor lay. Ned's ankle was a clean break, as he had hoped—the kind of fracture that could be held easily with splints to insure a good union of the bone. Evan Wright lay propped up against a saddle, with a pad of blankets under his shoulders. His lips were bloodless and his face devoid of color, but his eyes were brightly alert.

John grinned as he knelt to examine his colleague. "They tell me you made a hero of yourself, sir," he said.

Dr. Wright returned the smile wanly. "When I heard you were out there with the major, I seem to have lost my head. Still, my impulse was sound. These people could hardly go on without their leader."

Faces were thick about them now, as the fire fighters drew back from their work: John spoke for their benefit as well as Evan Wright's. "In this smoke, anyone could get things turned around. Don't forget they'll always need you far more than me."

"It's good of you to say that, John, but——"

"No buts, sir. People need strong hearts as well as bodies on a march like this. I'll do my best to guide their feet, but you must give them heart. That's why you've got to take a little better care of yourself."

A rumble of thunder, followed by a quick spurt of rain, wrote its own signature to the moment. Stella bent quickly to help her husband to their tent. As John called for men to move Ned Beasley, he saw Faith stoop forward to assist the old doctor too. Both of them were thoroughly soaked when they ran hand in hand to their own shelter, but they could still join in the cheers that rose on all sides at this timely intervention of the elements.

4

Once it was under way, Obadiah's downpour proved worthy of the name. Rain was still pelting from a darkened sky when the migrants took to the trail in the dawn. Ned Beasley, with his splinted ankle in a sling hooked to his saddle horn, rode in the vanguard today, between the Kentuckian and Yulee; Evan Wright came next, his white warlock lifted to the deluge, his voice raised bravely in a hymn of thanksgiving the whole cavalcade was singing from overflowing hearts. With each step the marchers took, the miracle of their survival was more apparent.

The wide swathe of the fire, reduced long since to sodden ashes, had spent its force in the hammocks to the south. As far as the eye could reach, the rain-wearied landscape resembled nothing so much as a colossal frying pan, neglected too long by some drunken cook. The cavalcade, wading knee-deep in soot in its slogging effort to stay on trail, resembled a file of gnomes before the first hour's march was behind them. Like underground demons, they seemed to walk in a gray-green gloom that was neither earth nor water, though it partook of the worst features of both.

It was only with afternoon that the humid half-light dissolved a bit along the horizon's rim, and Obadiah was able to take his bearings. So far as they could judge, they had waded a bare dozen miles from their campsite. The compass told them that they were still working their way south by east, in the general direction of the Tombigbee. In the aftermath of last night's disaster, one mile was much like another. Even when they paused at last to gnaw on a makeshift meal of corn pone and jerked venison, it was impossible to believe that they would outmarch the fire's fury on the morrow.

More than half of their pack horses had been lost at the ravine —and they had been forced to abandon much of their gear when they broke camp. There were still enough mounts for the sick and wounded. Essential articles, such as sacks of flour and the powder and shot that would be invaluable when they had outmarched the region of drought and found game again, were carried by human pack horses now.

The hard cash they had brought from the Mississippi still jingled in Evan Wright's saddlebags; the men of the party shouldered their share of pelts, grievous though the burden was. Once they had crossed the Tombigbee, it was John's plan to head straight for the next river on the map, the Tascaloosa. Here, it might be possible to raft their burdens downstream to the junction with the Koosah, near whose bank Talassee stood. Long before they gained this objective, he hoped to replenish their stores, and to buy fresh pack animals in one of the Indian towns of that region.

Rain had been still pelting down when they took to the trail, after their dreary encampment. It was falling when they climbed to higher ground, and left the ravages of the fire behind them at last. The Middle Path (though it had long since ceased to deserve the name) was now a mere muddy trough in the forest bed. At times, it threatened to dissolve entirely, and change into another of those deep-walled creeks that flowed to join the Tombigbee.

At least they were making progress of a sort—or so John reasoned, as he rode back from scouting the country ahead, and surrendered his horse to a foot-weary marcher. Chins were still held high, and there was no audible murmur of complaint, beyond the wailing of tired children, or the sigh of exhaustion that escaped some ancient for whom no horse was now available. It was good to hear the shout of joy that ran down the cavalcade when the sun broke through at day's end, revealing another stretch of open country at the top of the long rise.

Next morning the trail was well marked again, the march easy— but it was four days, not three, before they began their actual approach to the river. The Tombigbee's current had been swollen by rains in the mountains, to say nothing of the downpour that had deluged its own valley. Thanks to the bluffs that confined it at this point, it had yet to overflow its bed, but the ford marked on the map had long since been covered. John needed but a glance at the heavily forested banks to realize that it would be necessary to spend a day in camp, while the party was rafted through that turbulent current, and the horses swum across.

With woodsmen by the dozens in their ranks, it was no problem to construct a floating platform large enough to accommodate twenty-odd passengers. Built of halved timbers, with a lashing of dry logs beneath, their raft was hardly a thing of beauty—and, despite the number of willing hands, it had taken a long, sun-burned day to convince Yulee and Obadiah that it would prove seaworthy. Both of these rivermen agreed that the actual cross-ing should wait until the clear light of morning. Since several trips would be required to transport the party and its gear, it was also decided to make a second camp on the eastern bank, where the cavalcade could enjoy a well-earned rest.

"Let's hope this is the last big leapfrog," said the Kentuckian. "Country's easy enough beyond, until we hit the Tascaloosa. In-dians should be friendly, too, once they've found this is an English party on its way to the Savannah."

"Friendly enough to sell us horses and provisions?"

"Why not, when you were asked by McGillivray to be head doc-tor to the nation?"

John sighed wearily, as he stepped aboard the raft to test its balance, there in the heavy current. "I hope you're right, Obadiah," he said. "Now that I look back, my talk with McGillivray seems to belong in another world. Right now, I can't push my mind be-yond tomorrow's crossing."

"A good leader wins his battles one at a time," said the Ken-tuckian. "The one we'll fight tomorrow may be worse than it looks from here. If you like, Yulee and I can make a trial crossing now."

With a cheering audience to mark their progress, Obadiah and the half-breed stripped to the waist and spurred two pack horses down the steep descent to the raft. Forcing their mounts to wal-low into deep water, they kicked free of their saddles and swam side by side with the animals, guiding them as best they could to the far bank. Viewed from this angle, the crossing seemed easy enough, if one discounted a moment in midstream, where the horses seemed all but helpless in the spin of the current. John could well understand the excitement among the younger mem-bers of the cavalcade, to whom a tussle with the Tombigbee seemed a welcome change from the dust of the trail. For his part, he slept uneasily that night, wishing that the ordeal of the raft was behind them.

Men and gear made the first crossing on the raft next morning, with Yulee leaning on one of the guide poles and John himself snubbing hard with another. By giving their vessel its head in midstream, it was fairly simple to quarter into the current as it slackened, then spin the rocking platform into quiet water along the eastern shore. Here, by leaning on the poles, a landing was managed, on a gently shelving beach that gave, in turn, to a meadow deep in summer grass.

John breathed a sigh of profound relief, now that his own trial run was behind him. The scene ahead was a peaceful one. Several of their pack animals (swum across by Yulee and his wranglers just after dawn) were grazing in the fetlock-deep grass, and axes rang cheerfully in a bower of live oaks. Walking into cool shade after the unloading, John saw that the early arrivals had staked out a perfect campsite—an amphitheater perhaps two hundred yards in diameter, framed in mossy greenery and cheerful with the bubbling of a spring. It seemed a good augury for the days ahead that they should have blundered into this pleasant glade.

Perhaps it was the refreshment of that glimpse, joined to the intense activity of the next two hours—but John could feel his foreboding diminish with each crossing. Four trips were needed to transport the men of the party. Though the children begged to come aboard each time, John forced himself to refuse their pleas, until he felt more adept at this cumbersome ferry service.

All but two of the horses were swum across in the raft's wake. Before noon, their new camp was a solid reality. Only the women of the party and a dozen young ones now remained on the western side of the river. The fifth and sixth ferry ride brought the mothers safely across, leaving Stella and Faith with the restless children, and a rider for each of the two horses.

John gave Evan Wright a reassuring salute as he stood knee-deep in the shallows, to help ease the raft into the Tombigbee for its final crossing. A towpath of sorts had long since been hacked out along the bank, permitting the two boatmen to jockey the ferry upstream for its return. Here, the old doctor paused briefly, with one hand lifted to shield his eyes from the sun motes that danced on the current.

"You could have brought Stella and Faith on that last trip, John."

"They refused to leave the nursery. The children will be quieter if they're aboard."

"You take account of everything, my boy."

"Not quite everything, sir. It was Faith's idea to wait for the final crossing, not mine."

On the east bank, a dozen small fry swarmed aboard with eager shouts, almost before Yulee could step ashore to help. After he had given a hand to Faith and Stella, John placed his passengers with care. Compared with their earlier trips, the raft seemed underladen for this final duel with the Tombigbee: it was necessary to place stones on the platform to trim ship, and the children were ordered to remain in the center, with folded arms. Easing into the current one more time, with the two horses blowing noisily in their wake, John felt the pole in his fists lose contact with the bottom, and set himself for the moment in midstream, when they were virtually at the mercy of the river.

What happened next came too fast for conscious thought. He had not realized that one of the horses had lost its head in that plunge for deep water, or that it had shaken free of its rider. Before either he or Yulee could brace themselves, the fear-crazed animal had come abreast of the raft with forefeet raised. With a high, banshee whinny, its hoofs crashed down upon the platform, missing the half-breed by inches, and sending their ballast to the bottom.

The sudden pressure, combined with the loss of their ballast, had thrown the raft into a near-fatal yaw. Yulee, dropping his pole, spread arms and legs in time to save the children from pitching into the river. John, by leaning hard on the far side, managed to right the platform after a fashion, until they were drifting toward shore again. He saw that the discarded rider, swimming far astern, could never come to their assistance. The second horseman had dropped even farther behind, in a hard-fought effort to keep his own mount from bolting. Watching the maddened horse prepare to charge again, John knew there would be no way to keep the raft from capsizing.

A shout rose from the bank; he felt the raft bound beneath him and realized Faith had plunged overside, that she was swimming in the path of those lethal hoofs. He saw the russet head submerge in time to dodge the expected blow, watched it pop into view again, on the animal's flank. With that maneuver, Faith had somehow knotted the reins in one fist. The first toss of the horse's head almost lifted her clear of the river; on the second toss, both animal and girl vanished briefly in a welter of foam—but the strip of water between raft and animal was steadily widened.

On the third try, Faith jerked the horse's head below surface and forced him to change course. One foot was in a stirrup now, a free fist knotted in the mane. With an incredulous gasp, John saw that she had lifted a leg across the saddle, then sprung lightly to the animal's back. For an instant more she clung to her dangerous perch, whispering into the cocked-back ears, controlling the horse's efforts to buck free with the knees of the born rider. Then, per-mitting the head to lift again, she drifted into slack water, where mount and rider swam calmly to the bank.

Half waiting for the expected cheer from shore, John was startled to hear a babble of advice instead. He understood when he heard a faint cry from midstream and saw that Stella had some-how been pitched into the Tombigbee at the same moment that Faith had made her dive. Now, clinging to a bit of driftwood that had spun within her reach, she seemed unable to quarter into the current, or even to lift above the swirling surface.

"Steady the raft, Yulee! I'm going after her."

John plunged as he spoke, a long, raking dive that carried him free of the raft—just before that clumsy vessel, turning in a last, crazy spin, slipped into the water along the bank. He looked back as he swam downstream and saw that Faith had already dismounted and was wading hip-deep in the eddies to help with the landing: a dozen others had followed promptly to lift the children ashore. Then he kicked off his boots and began swimming after Stella, with all his remaining strength.

Afterward, he would remember that he had gone overside with only a passing thought for the safety of his remaining passengers. He would reproach himself bitterly for clinging to the raft when Faith had plunged to save them all—only to leave it, like a copybook lifeguard, to help Stella Wright ashore. And only a deeper probe of his emotions would reveal his assurance, even then, that Faith was fitted instinctively (by both inheritance and training) to rise to such an emergency, while Stella was not.

At the moment, it mattered little to him by what means tragedy had been turned aside; there was even a comic element in his haste to reach Stella, to steer her impromptu buoy ashore. *Hero and Leander,* he thought, as a bubble of laughter began to expand in his brain. *Only this is the Tombigbee, not the Hellespont—and neither of us is likely to drown today.*

5

He swam to the downstream end of the sandbar where the log had stranded at last, careful to stay clear lest it contain quicksand. At first glance, he was sure that Stella had fainted, though she still clung to the driftwood: thanks to that boisterous current, it had been a long and arduous pursuit. Then, as he was about to call her name, she lifted her head and gave him a smile that was half ashamed—and totally unafraid.

"Just hold on as you're doing," he told her. "I'll work the log ashore."

Making sure that she was still tightly anchored, he freed the driftwood from its lodgment, and eased it into the current again. At this point, the eastern bank was too high to make a landing feasible; he quartered gently toward shore, until he could round the next bend, where he discovered a stubby, cedar-crowned point and a crescent of sandy beach. Once he had rounded this promontory, it was a simple matter to trap the log in the backwater at its foot. The log was now far easier to manage; after a few thrashing kicks, he felt solid bottom under his toes.

Stella had continued to cling to the log without attempting to speak while they worked inshore. Now, she lifted her face in another tremulous smile—and swooned dead away, as he rose in waist-deep water and lifted her clear of the river.

Her faint, after all, was but a natural reaction to her ordeal; he knew that she would soon emerge from it. It was only a short walk to dry land, and the sun-warmed beach was clear of debris. A small watercourse, tumbling down a gully to join the Tombigbee, made a cheerful murmur in the background. He placed his burden on the sand, and went to fetch water in a twist of wild grape leaf. Stella opened her eyes before he could press this cup to her lips.

"I must look a fright," she said drowsily.

"You never looked lovelier."

It was a compliment from the heart. Disheveled though she was, with daubs of river mud on cheeks and hair, Stella Wright was simply a woman today, a beautiful and desirable woman who bore only a faint resemblance to the mistress of Trail's End. The eyes that looked up to him now were warm with gratitude— and the laughter they were already sharing.

"Do you mean that, John?"

"Of course I mean it."

"Then why must I nearly drown myself to be alone with you?"

He knew that much of this was the product of near-hysteria, yet he could not keep down his own response. "For the time being," he said, "we've this part of the world to ourselves. Do you mind?"

"Not if we can stay awhile."

"I'm afraid we can't linger long. They're sure to worry."

"They must have seen me catch that log," she said—just a bit too quickly. "Everyone saw you swim after me."

"So they did," he said, in the same tone of forced lightness. "Shouldn't we prove their confidence is deserved?"

"How far did we drift?"

"Two miles, at least."

His arm was still beneath her head as he held the water to her lips; now she put the leafy cup aside to look at him directly. Her eyes were warm, but with an emotion that went far beyond gratitude. "I almost wish it could have been farther, John. What if they never found us?"

He made no attempt to answer her with words. Being no more than human, he could not help being stirred by the eagerness in her eyes, the softness of her half-parted lips—and the promise of surrender they offered. And yet, he somehow managed to hold his desire in check—for the moment.

"That wasn't a fair question, I suppose," she said. "No one can drift forever. We must go back."

"Back to camp and the Middle Path, Stella. On to the Koosah and Talassee—and what comes after."

"What *will* come after, John?"

"I don't know."

"Can't I help you to decide?"

She had pulled his head down to hers before he quite realized what the words implied. This time, he could not have resisted her had he tried. The mouth that met his own was warmly demanding —and as sweetly eager as he had pictured it.

For a moment he returned Stella's kiss—and the steel of his resolve floated away like chaff in the wind. The harsh, laughing cry of a blue jay broke the spell in time. He stared up resentfully at the bird on a tree branch overhead. The beady, cynical eyes were fixed upon him, for all the world like a sardonic incarnation of conscience.

Stella's glance had followed his—and he knew that she understood the meaning of that interruption well enough. It was not integrity that had come between them—or the thought of the frail, half-dying husband who awaited her so anxiously upstream. Happenstance alone had kept him from possessing her completely, there on the bank of the Tombigbee.

"I suppose we should be starting back to camp," she said—and her tone could not have been more composed, had the whole wide river flowed between them. And yet, for all her apparent poise, she made no move to leave his arms.

The blue jay had taken flight long since, but not his conscience. Even now she was daring him to finish what she had begun so recklessly—though she knew, in her heart, that their moment of abandon had somehow escaped them.

"I suppose we should," he said. "After all, we'll both be needed there."

He lifted her in his arms before she could speak again, and carried her along the slope of the gully where the small stream joined the river. No matter how he prolonged them, he knew that each step he took forward was a stride away from temptation.

"It's good to be needed, John," she said at last. "At times, it can be a burden too."

He set her on her feet at the forest's edge, where the tangle of water oaks opened to a wide vista of grasslands. "Can you walk, Stella?"

She swayed against him, and he saw the sparkle of tears in her eyes. "Yes, John," she said. "Too well, perhaps."

He put down his desire, though it took his last shred of will. "Integrity can be a burden too," he told her. "It's one you can't surrender. I know you too well for that."

"You're right, of course," she said. "We must both bear it—for a time."

So her offer was in the open at last. He faced the fact gravely as her arms stole about his neck again. The kiss she had given him beside the river had been born of passion. This time, her lips were more a pledge to the future than an invitation to surrender.

They were still locked there in each other's arms when the drum of horses' hoofs brought them back to the present. At first, it seemed no more than a distant echo from another world. Then, as John stepped from their leafy bower, he saw Faith, riding at a hard gallop across a stretch of grassy prairie to the south. A short distance behind her, Obadiah Hurt was thundering down the edge of the bluff at the same gait.

6

"So they found you at last. I knew they would."

Evan Wright smiled up at them from his vigil at the edge of the camp. Behind him, the migrants stood on the slope of the natural amphitheater, like a group of pilgrims fresh from prayer. The Bible in the old doctor's hands completed the picture; so did the shout of welcome that went up as John dismounted and lifted Stella down to her husband's arms.

"Faith swore she'd bring you both back. But we passed an anxious hour, just the same."

Withdrawing a little from the general rejoicing, John could only marvel at his own glib response. "We stranded some two miles downstream, sir. It took them awhile to find us."

Faith had tossed her own bridle to Yulee; she moved now to join the group. "Usually I'm a better beagle," she said. "So, for that matter, is Obadiah. But we knew they were safe; we saw John steer the log ashore."

John would recall that casual attitude later, along with the look Faith turned in his direction as she settled on a stump and started fanning her brow with the slouch hat she had worn to their rescue. The look spoke a language of its own, had he known it—an assurance that she was prepared to accept today's events at their face value.

"It's quite all right, my dear," said Evan Wright. "You did bring them safely here again. At least John's score is perfect now."

"My score, sir?" John heard his voice enter the discussion. He had meant to hold aloof, as befitted a hero in the making. A hero in name only, he added silently—wondering what Evan Wright's reaction would be, if he knew the facts of that hour downstream.

"Don't you realize you've brought us through flood and fire and Indian attack without a single casualty—if you'll overlook a broken bone or two, and a few cases of ague?"

John moved to the stump where Faith sat, and grinned solemnly as he knocked wood. "Our journey isn't ended," he said. "I'll save my rejoicing for later." He raised his voice for the benefit of the others, still grouped on the slope above the half-made camp. "In fact, I'd suggest we raise our tents and put out sentries, while daylight's on our side."

"There's time to spare for that," said the old doctor mildly. "We were awaiting your return to hold a service of thanksgiving to God for bringing us safely across the river. Now we have added reason to be thankful."

It was John's turn to yield, as it were, to an authority higher than his own. He remembered agreeing to Dr. Wright's suggestion that they open this camp with a prayer. The wish seemed all the more fitting now. Eminently fitting, he thought (as he knelt with the others), in view of the temptation he had just resisted beside the Tombigbee.

"With the company's indulgence," said Evan Wright, "I will read the Twenty-third Psalm."

John took a quick glance around the circle before he bowed his head. Faith knelt at his side; Stella knelt just beyond, as submissively as he. There was no trace of guilt about her, no hint of secrets she could not share. He counted other companions of the trail beneath half-lowered eyelids. Larkin and Hammond and Otis with their sunbonneted wives and their young; the Borland boys and Hal Duffy; Beasley and his overflowing brood; the turtle-like solemnity of Amos Dexter; Yulee's proud and impassive profile; the solidity of Obadiah Hurt, who clung to his long-barreled flintlock, even in prayer. . . . These are your people, John told himself; this is the flock you must guard with life itself. Until you've led them into Talassee, you can't forget them for a moment.

> *The Lord is my shepherd, I shall not want.*
> *He maketh me to lie down in green pastures.*
> *He leadeth me beside the still waters!*

The well-remembered thanksgiving flowed through his mind like a litany, as his lips repeated it, along with a hundred others. Thanks to the alembic of prayer, he could feel himself lifted above the tyranny of self; for this moment, at least, he could believe that the miracle of their survival would continue to the end. Evan Wright had never spoken a truer word—a miracle was the only way to explain their presence here, without a single death to mark the long flight from Natchez.

How else could one justify their escape from the Choctaw tomahawks, their survival in a ring of fire, the rescue of the raft? How else could he account for the sudden, unreasoning impulse that had made him refuse Stella's offer of surrender? How, above all, could he dare to ask for absolution now—unless he knelt with the others and knew he came with clean hands?

Surely goodness and mercy shall follow me all the days of my life
And I shall dwell in the house of the Lord forever.

Faith's eyes, he saw, were closed tightly; she was drinking in each word the old doctor was speaking, as he told of the perils they had faced on the trail—and gave thanks to an all-wise Power that had granted them safe-conduct. His glance moved on to Stella, in time to see a tear slide down one cheek. He knew the genesis of that tear, as well as he understood Faith's quiet strength and trust.

It was Faith, far more than he, who had helped to bring this cavalcade to safety, he admitted now. From the start, she had put the welfare of the group above her own. If she had twice saved his life between Natchez and the Tombigbee, it was to preserve the symbol of the leader, the rallying point.

Somehow, he must learn to be worthy of that title—though a demon in his soul still reproached him for the opportunity he had lost beside the river.

The Deserted Village

Seven days later, traveling by forced marches that began at dawn, they reached the west bank of the Tascaloosa, not too far above the falls. They camped here beside a ford, within sound of the cascade; the Middle Path was now a well-marked trail, and both Obadiah and Yulee were confident that the Upper Towns of the Creek nation must lie on both banks of the river. It was agreed that John and the Kentuckian would scout ahead until they made contact with the Indians. In the meantime, hunters could bring in game to replenish a larder long since reduced to the danger point.

The two scouts had departed from camp while the migrants were still plunged in the deep repose that exhaustion brings. It had been an effort for John to wrench himself from his blankets when a sentry called him a half-hour before sunrise; it had taken courage to wade into a waist-deep stream in the dark, with the thunder of a waterfall not too far below. But he knew that it was necessary to strike out boldly at this point; both supplies and transport were essential, before the cavalcade ventured farther.

As Obadiah had expected, they came upon a Creek village below the falls, a silent circle of huts with fish weirs in the pool below the cascade, and acres of cultivated land along the riverbank. The settlement appeared empty, though it was hard to be sure in the darkness. It was often the custom for a village to move en masse, for no reason visible to white men's eyes. But it seemed odd that this particular village should be deserted with corn tall in the furrows, and several canoes at the landing.

Neither John nor Obadiah were in the mood to complain at this last bit of good fortune as they selected the lightest of the craft for their trip downstream. They could pay for its use later, if the Indians returned. Meanwhile, skimming southward with a breakfast of corn pone and venison under their belts, it had seemed easier to move with the current, and hope that the Creeks would show their faces later.

Yawning prodigiously as he studied the riverbank in the sunrise, the Kentuckian had voiced only a mild concern. "'Course we're only borrowing this dugout. If the varmints come back unexpected, they might call that a fancy name for stealing."

"Yulee knows the Creek tongue. He'll explain why we're camped at the ford."

"Maybe we should have waited for sunup and explored a little. But I reckon you're still itching to reach the Koosah."

"I can't rest until I've found McGillivray—and made sure he'll help us. Our luck won't last forever, Obadiah."

"Have it your way, Doc. I'm not arguing. But there were still fish in those weirs—and their corn was waist-high. Why did them Indians move out so fast, along with their dogs?"

2

The mystery was still unsolved in the later afternoon, when the lodge poles of another village showed above the brush. Viewed in broad daylight, the lodges themselves were typically Creek—square or rectangular in shape, and constructed of willow withes plastered with the red clay of the region, which had long since dried to the hardness of brick. The roofs were thatched with sun-faded grass, giving the lodges an odd resemblance to crofters' cottages in Britain. Only the painted birchbark scrolls that framed the doorway of the chief's hut, and the talking gourds that made their own mournful music on the lodge poles, reminded John that this was the dwelling place of a savage people.

This time, it was impossible to doubt that the Creeks had left in haste. The keel marks of many canoes were visible along the bank, and the lodges had been stripped of their last sleeping mat. John turned to Obadiah for enlightenment, but his companion merely snorted and moved on to explore the perimeter of the town.

While he waited for the Kentuckian's return John continued to circle the hard-packed earth and peered into the empty huts again while he fought down a rising sense of dread. His memories of the Creeks were still fresh; he had expected a far different reception in this neatly built village—which must have resounded only yesterday to the shouts of naked children sporting at the river's edge and the slow, even throb of the council drum. Here was the platform where headmen had deliberated from dawn to dark—slow-voiced arguments that grew more animated as gourds of the "black drink" circulated, a frothy, aromatic mixture brewed from the cassina shrub, which a visitor sampled at his peril. Here, before a dozen cook fires, squaws had pounded corn into meal, and laughed at their work. . . .

Did he hear an echo of that laughter from the gourds overhead, or was it only the cry of a nesting heron? In the past, it had been good to discover that the Indians were a gay and forthright people, when left to their own devices; he had been proud to share in the Creeks' games and laughter, since it proved that they had accepted him as a brother. He had hoped for such an acceptance today—or at least something besides this oppressive silence.

Obadiah stalked back to the council ground. "They sure left for keeps, Doc. Any guesses why?"

"Perhaps there's a powwow at the Hickory Ground. That's their meeting place on the Koosah. These are summer towns, you know; the nation generally moves south ahead of bad weather. They could have moved early this year."

"You mean—because something besides weather ran 'em out?

Cherokees, maybe? Or Whigs from Georgia? But there ain't a sign of fighting. Besides, if it had been Cherokees, they'd have burned the town."

"What's the answer, then?"

"Doc, there's just one thing that'll make a whole village hit the trail and leave good food behind. That's disease."

"You mean, an epidemic?"

"White man's disease, they call it. Indians think it floats in like fog, and puts a spell on every lodge. I've seen 'em move out from under that fog overnight. Fact is, they usually go in the dark, so it can't follow."

"Have you any evidence to prove that theory?"

"Plenty. And you better hold your nose."

Half guessing what Obadiah had found, John followed him to a path that led upward from the village. His companion set a brisk pace until they reached the summit of a low ridge. Here, in a clearing open to the four winds, stood a high, stoutly built trestle. John recognized it immediately as an open burial ground, even before the river breeze had brought to him the sick-sweet odor of death. He needed only a glance at the dozen bodies, tumbled grotesquely on that platform, to see that Obadiah's proof was definite indeed.

"The ones that lived skedaddled fast," said his companion. "No wampum or food for the Hunting Grounds; not even a blanket for the long sleep. Shall I say what killed 'em?"

John shook his head. Only smallpox could strike with such fearful aftermath. No other disease left those white crusted elevations as its hallmark.

"I've seen it take whole towns on the Ohio," said the Kentuckian.

"How could it come this far?"

"Traders, maybe. Plenty of 'em work these valleys in summer. Don't need but one spark to start that kind of fire."

They had already quitted the place of the dead; by common consent, they circled the village until they reached their canoe.

John permitted himself a real breath only when they were paddling briskly upstream. It was an absurd precaution, since he had been inoculated against this menace while still a student in Edinburgh.

"Did you ever take the disease, Obadiah?"

"Had it when I was still a boy. You'd see the marks, if 'twasn't for these whiskers. That puts me on the safe list, don't it?"

"By all the rules we know."

"What about yourself?"

"I'm safe too. I had a mild case in Scotland years ago." John was still rejoicing at the disastrous threat the migrants had avoided —including his choice of Obadiah as a companion on this scout, rather than a possible victim. He could hardly pause to explain the mysteries of inoculation now.

The Kentuckian chuckled as he lifted his paddle. He had not quite risked a backward glance at the village; but he seemed his old self again, now they were in midstream.

"Guess the folks in camp are luckier than they know. Leastways, *we* won't be bringing 'em a case of pox."

"We won't bring guides or canoes either."

"Look at it this way, Doc. Wherever the disease hit first, it's moved downriver. Why don't we march upstream instead of down? Trail's broken both ways; we can dicker for horses instead of boats, and go overland to Talassee—or straight for the Savannah. Might be an easier trip at that. It stands to reason it'd be shorter."

John found that he, too, was more cheerful now. He had looked death in the face, and knew it had many forms; smallpox, after all, was a more fearful end than most only because the scourge had the power to strike so mysteriously. As Obadiah had said, they had uncovered the threat in time, at no personal risk; from the migrants' viewpoint, the epidemic downriver could be a blessing in disguise, if it shortened their journey. Now, more than ever, John would not draw a really tranquil breath again until they had reached Talassee.

3

They made camp that night on an islet in midstream; all the next day, they drove hard for the falls, hoping to reach the camp while daylight lasted. Dusk was falling on the misty pool below the cataract when they sighted the lodge poles of the first deserted village. On this stretch of the Tascaloosa, it was possible to skirt a long stretch of swampland on the eastern bank and avoid the channel entirely. John had just taken his turn at the bow paddle when he heard a shout from his right. To his astonishment, he saw Yulee, waist-deep in the darkening water, in the act of impaling a frog on a homemade spear. On his left shoulder, the half-breed carried a sack heavy with similar prizes; he deposited his last catch of the day as he waded toward the canoe.

"I've been gigging all afternoon," he explained. "Dr. Wright is fond of frogs' legs."

John lifted his paddle, to permit Obadiah to snub the dugout against the swampy bank. "Aren't you a long ways from camp, with the sun almost down?"

"By no means, *jefe*. The camp has moved below the falls."

"What are you saying, man?" John managed to keep his voice calm, though the stab of panic at his vitals was real enough.

"Dr. Wright had a slight setback. The hunters had already found a village. It seemed best to Mrs. Wright to put a roof over his head, and post a lookout for your return."

"Get in the canoe, Yulee. We'll go to him at once."

"He is much better now, Doctor—after a day's rest in bed." The half-breed tossed his sack over the gunwale, and took the bow paddle from John's willing hands. "Mrs. Wright hoped to surprise him with a dish of frogs' legs tonight. She is a fine nurse."

"Did you say *bed rest?*"

"We carried him across the ford at noon yesterday, and took

him to the chief's house. Mrs. Powers had me put your gear in the next lodge."

So the migrants had taken over the deserted village to the last hut. No impulse could have been more natural; even without Evan Wright's illness, John could understand the urge that had led them down the path below the falls. After weeks in the wilderness, a Creek lodge would resemble a palace to their tired eyes. The fresh vegetables from those garden patches, the corn in the fields, and the fish weirs below the cascade must have been welcome supplements to the dry rations of the trail.

"No sign of the Creeks so far?"

"We found their trail above the falls, sir. It seems they marched overland toward the Hickory Ground. Colonel Larkin is sure they've gone to a summer powwow."

Clearly, he could not pause to curse the colonel's error—or give way to the tide of panic that had chilled him to the finger ends. Instead, John kept his voice level—and looked ahead for his first real glimpse of the village below the falls.

"I hope you've put out pickets?"

"Of course, *Señor Médico*." Yulee sounded faintly hurt. "We were aware that the Creeks might return at any time. Dr. Wright feels that they will be friendly, when they find we can pay well for food and shelter."

The village was in clear view now, its circle of lodges lighted by the flames of cook fires. Despite the fast-fading light, children were swimming in the warm, bubbling pool below the falls— whooping with laughter when the thrust of the current sent them tumbling, ignoring calls to supper until the last possible moment. The cavalcade could hardly have looked more settled had it built this village from the first twist of willow withes.

Leaping from the canoe before it could ground in the shallows, John felt a deep surge of pity for them all: there was something infinitely touching about that fumble toward hearth and rooftree, after their weeks of sun-bitten marching. He picked out the chief's house at the top of the council ground and hurried toward it with long strides. Greetings were shouted from all sides, but he contented himself with a quick wave of the hand—hoping that his face was an adequate mask for his gnawing fear.

Stella was seated on the platform before her lodge. A glance across her shoulder told him that Evan Wright was dozing on a pallet of blankets just inside the door. The scene had a domestic note that was oddly restful; no matter how rude her bivouac on the trail, Stella had always managed somehow to give it the color of home.

Mounting the ladder that led to her door, offering a formal salute with the eyes of the camp upon him, John managed a smile, despite his sense of apprehension.

"I hear our patient's better."

"Much, John. Did you have a good trip downriver?"

"That can wait," he said quietly. "I'm camp doctor first—and then explorer."

Evan Wright came out of his drowse as John knelt beside him to feel his pulse. The beat was fast but weak, and the older doctor's skin seemed more transparent than before. But John could see that the setback was not serious. With extended rest, and a nurse like Stella, his colleague was in no real danger at the moment. Whether he would escape the scourge that threatened the whole camp (if John's fears were justified) was a question he could not face as yet.

"Is anything wrong, John?"

"Not with *you*, Doctor. You're doing famously."

"I feel guilty for making this move without consulting you. Still, it's done us all a world of good to sleep under a roof again."

"We won't argue that," said John. "Do you mind if I check tonight's pickets before we talk about our scout downriver?"

"There's something on your mind," said Stella quickly. "Can't you tell us now?"

"Just give me time to make my rounds. I'll be back later." He turned in the door, while he fumbled for a more reassuring exit.

"It's—a danger I can't explain adequately now. Bear with me—
I don't mean to be cryptic."

A little pale afterglow lingered among the pines that bordered
the village. John needed only a cursory inspection to make sure
that his sentries were well posted; from the corner of his eye, he
saw that Obadiah was conducting a similar check at the far side
of camp. At least there was no smell of death about this village;
when he skirted the burial ground (on a bit of high ground to
the north) he found that the platform was empty of bodies. He
could even allow hope to rise that his fears were groundless. It
would take no more than a rumor of smallpox downstream to send
this village to the bush.

"Anything amiss, Obadiah?" he asked, when the two met in the
thickening dusk, just beyond that tenantless place of the dead.

"Not so far, Doc. I've left the sick-house for last."

John nodded, even as he suppressed a groan; he had forgotten
the single hut that was an integral part of these Indian towns, the
place of banishment for those beyond help. Obadiah had already
taken a path that led into the dense scrub to the north.

"Pray God it's empty."

The lazarette stood in a wide clearing; even here, it was necessary to give the spirits of the dying room to escape. Above the low-
eaved doorway, a torch smoldered in the dusk. The sight of that
winking flame (like a demon's eye framed in beetling brows)
was enough to confirm his worst doubts.

"Don't tell me they left a medicine man?"

"Yulee said the village was empty," growled the Kentuckian.
"Reckon he didn't scout this far."

John moved forward, snapping a dry branch to make a second
torch. Both men recoiled a little when they found themselves facing Faith Gordon—a pale, disheveled Faith, whose eyes answered
their question before she could utter a word.

"Yulee and I found them yesterday," she said. "I made him promise not to tell."

"*Stand back, Faith!*"

"It's a bit late for that order, John. I had already done what I could to help before I found what was wrong." She did not add what he knew was true—that she would not have run away, even then.

John lifted his improvised torch, and stepped under the low roof of the lazarette. Prepared though he was for the sight that met his eyes, he could hardly keep from retching a little—though the horror that twisted his heart was for Faith's sake, not his own.

Two Indians (both so ancient it was hard to tell their sex at first glance) lay side by side on a pine trestle. Both were skeleton thin; their eyes were muddy with fever, their skin parchment-yellow rather than red. From forehead to toe, their bodies were almost solidly stippled with the kind of festering sores that had but one meaning to a doctor's eyes. Evidently they were in the final stages of the disease—too weak, in fact, to utter anything beyond the feeblest of moans when the torch struck their faces.

"You know what this is, of course?"

"I've seen smallpox on the Perdido, John."

"And yet you nursed them?"

"They'd been left here to die."

"It's the Indian custom, Faith."

"I—didn't touch them, or stay inside the hut. All I did was bring them food and water."

"No one knows of this but Yulee?"

"He's been in charge of the sentries: they were posted outside that thicket. The others were too busy settling in the lodges to explore this far."

From the darkness outside, John heard Obadiah fetch a deep groan. Both of them had noted how thoroughly the migrants had taken over the village. Some had brought food from the storage houses beside the river; others had already used the pots they had found on the hearths, and the bed skins the Indians had discarded in their headlong departure. All of them had bathed in the pool before the village, and drunk from the spring that gushed from a rocky outcrop near the falls. Whether the pox came from an invisible miasma or bodily contact, they had blundered into a death trap with no visible exit.

"What will we do now, John?"

It was Faith's voice, raised in a cry of despair. He stepped quickly from the hut and put his arm about her; it gave him a strange thrill of pride to realize that she had called on him for help at last.

"First we must talk with Dr. Wright and Stella. Then we'll call a council."

"Do you have a plan?"

"A definite plan. If it succeeds, I've you to thank."

"I don't understand, John."

He kissed her gently. "If it weren't for you, those two Creeks would no longer be alive. This is one time when a live Indian's worth more than a dead one."

"Do you mean *they're* part of your plan?"

"A definite part. But I'll do my explaining to Dr. Wright, if you don't mind."

He had made his tone light to reassure her, but he knew that no danger they had faced so far could approach this hideous threat. This was an enemy that could not be conquered with guns; the weapon he must use was more bizarre than the most ancient amulet in the witch doctor's bag. Yet nothing else could save them now.

4

Evan Wright and his wife heard John out with only a few whispered interruptions. It was clear that the older doctor had grasped the terrible problem that faced them all. As for Stella, she continued to sit unstirring at her husband's side. John had no way of translating the meaning of her withdrawal—but he suspected that it went far deeper than personal fear.

"It's my fault, of course," she said, when he had finished his grisly story. "I insisted that Evan be brought to the village."

"Don't reproach yourself," said her husband. "I was as eager to settle here as anyone."

"You were too feverish to think clearly," said Stella. "The fault was mine. We should have followed John's orders, and stayed above the falls."

"Does that matter now? The important thing is to hear his plan —if he has one."

"John always has a plan," said Faith. Like Stella, she had sat quietly—in the doorframe of the lodge, with her hands folded on one knee. Somehow, that air of confidence had heartened John for the difficult task he faced.

"Let me say this, first of all," he told them quietly. "If Faith hadn't saved those Creeks from starvation, we'd be really helpless."

"Few of us would have had her courage," said Evan Wright. "As for the Indians—I almost hope I've misunderstood your meaning."

"You haven't, sir. What I propose is wholesale inoculation of our whole group—using the two Creeks as a source for the material."

"Is such a procedure feasible?"

"When I was a medical student in Edinburgh, it was already widely used in Scotland. I've a scar on my arm to prove it can succeed."

"Surely it's too late to be effective here."

"I think not. Smallpox rarely develops less than ten days after exposure. The inoculation practiced by Dr. Dimsdale runs its course in seven days—sometimes less."

"Can Dimsdale account for the difference in time?"

"Not precisely. But it seems evident that the introduction of matter from a smallpox pustule directly into the patient's skin hastens the development of resistance to the disease itself."

John paused as he saw Stella Wright shiver. He had not meant to draw so graphic a picture. "Believe me, it isn't so fearful as it sounds," he added quickly. "There's usually only local inflammation over that seven-day interval. Sometimes there's fever—but it breaks in a day or so. And when the fever has run its course the patient is well again—and immune to the disease thereafter."

"You make it sound simple enough, John," said Evan Wright. "But there's tremendous opposition to the Dimsdale method in America."

"Perhaps the doctors here feel it's still too experimental," said John. "Or should I say too risky?"

"Does real smallpox ever develop from this inoculation?" Stella asked.

"Cases have been reported," John admitted. "I've never witnessed one."

Stella shuddered again, but her chin lifted. "And you feel it's our only chance, John?"

"Without it, our whole party could be wiped out, save for the few of us who are immune. Those it spared might be too weak to reach civilization." He offered the black threat deliberately, as his eyes moved from face to face in the lodge. "As I said, it's sheer good fortune that we've the means at hand, and time on our side. I think we should take the risk." John's glance returned anxiously to Evan Wright, who was still lost in thought on his camp bed. "What's your opinion, sir?"

"I'm no longer the leader of this party, John. It must be your decision."

"I'd like your opinion, Doctor."

"It's a difficult thing to decide. I had a mild case of smallpox as a boy—so I won't be in personal danger. But I'd do a great deal to spare Stella."

"I'll take my chance, if it's what John wants," said Stella. "Make up your mind to that, Evan."

"I was sure you would, my dear. Give us your orders, John— we'll follow them."

"Why not put this to a vote?" said Faith suddenly. "We should all have a voice in something so important."

"An excellent idea," said Evan Wright. "With John's permission."

John nodded a grateful assent; the suggestion had lifted a heavy weight from his mind. "Will you call a meeting, sir?"

"Now, or tomorrow?"

"At once. If we decide to carry out inoculation, I propose to complete it tonight. Every hour that we delay is dangerous."

"As you wish, John." The old doctor raised himself on one elbow to survey the scene before him. "It seems we've a ready-made council ground—and a platform for your speech."

"The people should hear from their real leader, sir," John said simply. "If you're well enough to speak, of course."

Evan Wright smiled wanly. "I can always talk, John. Especially if I'm speaking in your behalf. When it comes to deeds, I'm afraid you must take charge."

5

Supper was over now, and most of the migrants were gossiping about their new-won firesides. It took no more than a double blast on an empty powder horn to bring them clustering around the chief's lodge. John put down a deep sense of foreboding as he heard their carefree bursts of laughter, and the easy hum of talk that spelled contentment. Clearly, the camp expected an encouraging report on his scout downstream—perhaps even the news that a flotilla of canoes was on its way to transport them to the sanctuary of Talassee. The cheer that went up when he stepped to the platform (with Evan Wright leaning on his arm) did little to raise his spirits.

Falling back a pace to permit the older doctor to open the meeting, John fumbled over the words he must force himself to speak. These were frontier folk: all of them had seen the ravages of smallpox in some form. He would need no special eloquence to convince them of their peril. Would it be as easy to persuade them to submit to a therapy they might not even understand—and would surely suspect?

Clearly, this was the acid test of his leadership. He bowed his head as Evan Wright (with one hand anchored to the lodge pole) began to speak in a clear, firm tone.

"My friends and neighbors," said the old doctor, "we have called you together tonight to discuss a grave threat that confronts us all——"

The cough that shook Evan Wright's slender frame was in no sense a rhetorical pause, though it served the same purpose. The blank silence that clamped down on the council ground was followed by a rising murmur; Dr. Wright stilled it with a peremptory spread of his hands, as he seemed to lift himself from that spasm of pain by will power alone.

"Dr. Powers is ready to describe that threat—and the means we have chosen to combat it. It rests with you to endorse or reject that choice. I will say that I accept his proposal wholeheartedly. We've no other means of—saving ourselves."

Dr. Wright settled in the camp chair that Stella had brought from the house. John found himself meeting familiar eyes as he moved to the front of the platform. But they were happy no longer: the faces lifted to catch his first words were blank with dread. Yet he could sense that the crowd was on his side; thanks to past performance, it might well continue to follow his lead. But if he dared presume on that blind urge to obedience, he must be sure of the rightness of what he proposed.

"I've no speech to make tonight," he said—and dropped to one knee, that he might be nearer that intent circle. "With your permission, I'll speak to you as a doctor."

No one stirred while he described his discoveries downriver. When he had told of the ghastly presences in the sick-house, a woman's voice lifted from the silence in a thin and piercing wail.

"My father died of the pox—and my two brothers. It'll kill us all if we stay here."

"It will kill just as fast on the trail," said John, in a shout that topped hysteria in the making. "I tell you there's a chance, if we keep our heads. Will you trust me to do what I can to stop an epidemic?"

The offer quieted the wailing for a moment. Ned Beasley (his broken ankle propped on a crutch) hobbled forward to lift his voice. "Give us Beasleys our orders, Doc. You saved my life once; I reckon you'll save it again. My family will do what you say."

"And mine," shouted Colonel Larkin.

A dozen others took up the chant, until John was forced to shout for quiet. Warming though the response had been, he realized that he must spell out the peril.

"This is a drastic remedy for a drastic situation. How many of you have had smallpox?"

Seven hands in all went up around the circle.

"We will take your names later," he said, "and assume you're protected. The disease rarely strikes twice. Has anyone here been inoculated?"

No one spoke for an instant: John could see that the word itself was strange to his listeners. Then, to his relief, a small, broad-shouldered Scot came forward, fingers hooked in belt, to stare up at the platform with a certain defiance.

"Is that where they make a little slit in your hide and rub in pus?"

"That's the treatment. Have you taken it?"

"Ten years ago, Doc, in Glasgow."

"Can you remember what happened?"

"Felt a mite anguished for a few days. My arm was sore where they cut me, but that was all. And I never took the pox."

"You've heard what Will Cronin said." Again, John raised his voice to still a rising babble. "Inoculation caused him no harm—and he's been immune ever since. It's my plan to do as much for all of you."

This time, the war of tongues seemed to cut in many directions. It was Beasley's turn to still the murmur as he hobbled up to stand below the platform.

"Don't want to sound gloomy, Doc. But you said this business was drastic. Can you tell us more about it?"

"I didn't mean it's painful or dangerous. Sometimes, I'll grant you, the treatment brings on real smallpox. But such cases are rare."

He was glad he had put the threat into words before it occurred to someone in the crowd to raise the query. Now that he held their attention, he felt he should complete the pattern quickly. "Will Cronin has already described the inoculation," he said. "If you're still willing, I intend to scratch every arm in this camp, and rub the matter from an active smallpox sore into the cut——"

"From the Indians in the sick-house?" It was Colonel Larkin who bayed out the question.

"Precisely, Colonel. To be effective, exudate from a living victim must be used."

"Will that make me part Creek?"

The whoop of laughter that rose from the council ground told John the worst of his trial was over. "Many of us are already blood brother with some friendly Indian," he said. "Why shouldn't they help us tonight?"

"D'you guarantee this cure, Doc?" asked Beasley.

"That's something no doctor can do as yet," John admitted. "You see, Ned, it's more protection than cure. I won't deny that there are risks involved, but it's our only way out tonight." He had already shucked his jacket, making it a simple matter to bare his left arm to the shoulder. "As you can see, I took the inoculation myself, years ago. Here's the scar. I was none the worse for it— and I'm safe from smallpox now."

The sharp intake of breath in the space below was proof enough that this display had brought his point home: if the medicine had saved the physician, how could it fail the patient?

John pressed his advantage swiftly. "I can begin these treatments in a few minutes," he said. "I won't stress the importance of time. Nor will I remind you that we must rest here until we're sure our remedy is successful. Once you've submitted to inoculation, this village becomes a hospital. Obadiah and I will help nurse if we're needed; Dr. Wright will assist us later. Others who are immune will serve as hunters and cooks. Is that agreeable?"

"You're still the doctor," said a voice, far back in the crowd. This time, the cheer that followed was convincing enough. John lifted his voice above it.

"We've not put this to a vote—but we will, if anyone wishes." When no such proposal was made, he looked out across the wide circle of faces, letting his words sink into the silence. "We'll proceed at once, then. Yulee will bring torches to this platform, and a worktable. You can form in line, and file past me, one by one. I'll go now and prepare."

He jumped down from the platform, sensing the hesitation even before his feet touched the ground. It had been easy enough for the crowd to endorse his medical opinion. It was another matter to form in single file, for a treatment that might endanger all their lives. He started to speak again, but realized that no words from him could break this natural inertia, now that he stood eye to eye with his patients. Then, as he hesitated in turn, a voice rose out of the silence to wipe the last doubt away.

"I'll be the first, John."

Without turning to look, he knew that Faith had spoken.

6

He stood aside to let Faith take her place beside the ladder, and watched her bare her left arm to the shoulder. Nervous laughter rose in the darkness as both men and women moved forward to line up behind her, or turned to the lodges to rout out their offspring. John made no attempt to thank Faith as he moved on, though his eyes spoke his gratitude feelingly enough. Somehow it was fitting that she should have been the first to step forward; he had expected it from the start.

At the lazarette, he found Obadiah (a vinegar-soaked rag pressed to his nostrils) fanning the two sweating patients on the trestle bed. With the aid of the torches, John allowed himself time for a thorough examination, which convinced him that both Indians, despite their advanced years, had broken through the crisis of the illness. Though their bodies would be pitted with a thousand crater scars to remind them of their ordeal, there was a better than even chance that they would rise from this bed again. This, too, seemed a fitting aftermath, in view of the help he would ask from them now.

"It's in the declining phase, I'm sure," he said. "Will you spell me here awhile longer?"

"I'll be honest, Doc," said the Kentuckian. "Squaws have nursed me through breakbone fever on the Ohio: I reckon this is only turnabout."

Obadiah listened with sagging jaw, as John outlined the procedure he intended to follow. He was still staring when John bent above the shoulder of a comatose ancient, lifted the depressed crust from the largest crater he could find, and scooped out the whitish material beneath. A half-teaspoon of this noxious exudate, collected in a pannikin, was more than sufficient; he took a trifle more, if only to dumbfound the Kentuckian further.

"Speaking of medicine gourds and shamans, Doc——"

"The first rule of nursing," said John, "is to hold one's tongue while the doctor's working. Call me at once if they look worse. I've a busy night ahead."

Returning to the council ground with his precious toxin, John rehearsed his textbook memory of the Dimsdale method. It was the custom of the famous English physician to prepare his patients carefully. Nine days of fasting usually preceded inoculations; the formidable medicines administered during this time included a concoction of calomel, tartar emetic, and ground crabs' claws, which was followed by a titanic dosage of Glauber's salt. John had often wondered if such progressive weakening of the system was advisable. As a military surgeon, he had observed that such standard remedies as bloodletting and massive purgation could both kill and cure. Obviously, no such regimen could be followed here.

Returning to the chief's hut, he observed that Yulee had already set up a table on the platform and opened his medical bag. He selected two scalpels and brought forth a bottle of brandy as well, in case of fainting fits. Massed torches in the wall brackets behind him threw the scene into strong relief. He was aware of Evan Wright, sitting bolt upright on his pallet, of Stella's anxious eyes as she hovered at her husband's side—but there was no time for further reassurance. Striving hard to make his signal casual, he summoned Faith to the platform.

She joined him without a word, and laid her bare arm across the table. With a knife balanced in his palm, he stared down at her warm brown skin, and felt a great reluctance to mar it, however slightly.

"Don't be afraid, John," she whispered. "I'm not."

It was all he needed to break the inertia.

The scalpel moved as fluently as though the steel were controlled by a force outside himself. He watched the point prick Faith's skin, so delicately that it showed only a thread of blood at the depths of the tiny wound. A second cut was repeated, a few inches above the first: the fingers of his left hand tensed the skin between, so the two small incisions opened wide.

Using the second scalpel, he lifted a droplet of the whitish exudate and touched it to each wound, turning the blade slightly to press the toxic liquid into the tissue. Thanks to the skill in his hands, the whole process was over in a few seconds.

Faith, smiling down at the waiting line below, announced that it had been quite painless.

"Does it need a dressing?" she asked.

"The incisions can remain exposed. Just be careful not to rub or wash them right away."

He let Faith step back, now that their instant of personal contact had passed. For the next two hours, he was far too busy to ponder on risks. Now that she had helped him over that first flash of indecision, he was only a hard-working doctor, absorbed in the task at hand.

The migrants shuffled past his table in seemingly endless line. Though he read terror in many eyes, there was no real hesitation— save when the inevitable fainting occurred at the sight of blood. As always (John noted, with a certain grim humor), it was the most stalwart males among his patients who collapsed under the flick of the knife. The women in the cavalcade accepted their inoculations with an almost stoical calm. Even the children, after a few preliminary whimpers, turned out to be good soldiers.

Stella was the last to bare her arm for the knife.

He looked at her out of weary eyes as he rubbed the whitish exudate into her skin. She had winced under the scalpel. Now her lips drew down in another grimace that had no relation to that all but imaginary stab of pain.

"At least I'm glad you and Evan will be spared," she whispered.

"What are you saying?"

"I feel this was my fault, John. You might call it a judgment of God."

He put away his scalpels, conscious of the fact that they stood alone on the platform. He had known that his patients would hasten to their lodges, where they would lie in the dark through a sleepless night, waiting for symptoms that could never develop in so short a time span. On his couch behind the open doorway of the hut, Dr. Wright had dropped into slumber, wearied by the tensions of the past two hours.

Struggling to emerge from the well of his own concentration, John studied Stella with real concern.

"Call it a mistake, if you insist," he said. "You mustn't blame yourself."

"Walk with me to the falls," she whispered. "Tell me I don't deserve to die."

The council ground was deserted when they stepped down from the platform; the lodges that ringed it seemed empty as the day he had gone downriver with Obadiah. Save for the sleepy cry of a child, and the glowing embers of a few cook fires, there was no hint of human tenancy. Death might have put his seal on each doorsill, before moving on to other matters.

At the river's edge, they paused with fingers laced and stared upstream at the misting of the falls. The mutter of the cascade seemed an ideal obbligato for the moment.

"I need your help tonight, John," she said. "For a week now, I've been struggling with my conscience—like Jacob with the angel."

"Since the Tombigbee?"

"Since the Tombigbee."

"We couldn't help wanting each other that afternoon."

"It was more than wanting, John. So much more. That afternoon in your arms—I was completely happy, for the first time."

"So was I, Stella."

"Perhaps it's wrong, to steal that kind of happiness," she said. "This may be God's way of reminding me."

"Not even an Old Testament Jehovah would take a hundred lives for what we've done," he told her quietly.

When she spoke again, her voice was so low he could barely hear it above the pulsing beat of the waterfall. "Don't you see, John? *I'm* the only one who should die. It would be my atonement."

"Atonement? For a sin you didn't commit?"

"I tried to give myself to you," she whispered. "Can you deny it?"

"The fact remains you didn't."

She was weeping quietly now, but her voice had steadied a little. "We can't go on this way, John—half in love, not daring to be alone together for a moment. And yet I know I wouldn't send you away at Talassee; I couldn't face the thought of losing you entirely. Wouldn't it be simpler if I was the one to go? To leave both you and Evan——?"

He could tell that she was near hysteria; the pressure of desire, joined to the long anxieties of the trail, had simply burst all bonds. It was quite like Stella Wright to insist that she, and she alone, must shoulder a burden of guilt too great for one mortal to bear. It was even more in character that she should face this emotional impasse clearly. Hypocrisy was not among this warmhearted woman's vices. Here in the wilderness, at long last, she too had matured—enough to give her passion its right name.

"Don't speak of death again, Stella. I won't have it——"

"Tell me what to do, John," she said. "I'll try to follow orders."

"You must live for his sake—as well as mine."

"That's how I'd planned it. I meant to bring Evan safely to East Florida. I hoped you'd wait there for me—until he died. After what happened on the Tombigbee, I'm afraid we couldn't wait at all——" Her voice was trailing into hysteria again, but she controlled it with an effort. "Unless you could be strong for us both—as you were that afternoon——"

"I can try, Stella."

"Suppose you're right—about this inoculation? Suppose we're all spared, and reach Talassee. Will you promise to be wise? Enough to save all of us—from too much unhappiness?"

"I'll do my best, Stella."

"That's enough for now," she said. "You keep your promises."

"I haven't always."

"You'll keep this one," she said. "I'll go back to Evan now. You needn't be afraid, John. I won't behave badly again."

7

If Stella had placed her future in his care that night beside the falls, he soon realized that the whole cavalcade had done likewise. The fact that they had accepted his judgment in the matter of the inoculation was a measure of their trust. In the two weeks that followed, their eagerness to believe in his therapy was, at times, a little frightening.

At the end of that first week (or, at the outside, ten days) he had hoped for the classic aftermath—in effect, a mild case of the disease, with fever and a rash, but few if any pustules or scars. This was the usual sequence, when inoculation was a complete success. Almost invariably, the patient recovered quickly, with none of the severe symptoms that would occur with smallpox itself. It was here that the value of the procedure lay—for that mild attack seemed to confer upon the sufferer a degree of resistance to the disease itself sufficient to offer permanent protection.

To John's surprise and dismay, however, his cases did not follow this pattern. By the third day, he could see that nearly all of them were developing a definite pustule at one or both of the spots where he had scratched their arms. Each day thereafter, these spots grew larger and more virulent—though there was, as yet, no sign of rash elsewhere, and little if any fever.

As for the two Indians in the lazarette, their recovery was little short of amazing. Faith had insisted on doing her share of nursing, and John had yielded to her pleas after a prolonged argument: he was sure that her care, and the nourishing broths she provided, speeded their convalescence. At the week's end, both ancients were as good as well, though their bodies were hideously pitted. It hardly surprised him when they slipped into the forest—taking with them a sack of food apiece, and a rifle filched from one of the lodges. He was sure they would join their people in time, to boast of the white man's cure. A story of this sort, however garbled, would stand him in good stead later.

On the eighth day, the casebook recorded fever cases by the dozens—enough to keep John furiously busy in an effort to reduce the discomfort of patients of all ages. A precise diagnosis was of course impossible under these conditions. He could not even be sure if the fevers sprang from an entirely different cause—or if they were, indeed, an overture to a genuine case of smallpox, induced by the inoculation itself. As he brooded on these imponderables, he was glad that the two Creeks had taken themselves elsewhere. Their gaunt, near-naked frames, deep-pitted as some lunar landscape, had been a hideous reminder of what might happen to the others if his gamble failed—and to Faith in particular.

Faith, he discovered, exemplified the direction of this strange course of smallpox much more definitely than the others. The pustules on her arm were larger, the inflammation that ringed them more pronounced. So far, she had failed to develop a fever—and he could only pray that his suspicions would prove unjustified. He could not yet know if he had erred in permitting her to continue nursing, when she was herself a walking reservoir of the very disease she had defeated in the lazarette.

On the ninth night, he remained with the worst of his patients until dawn, dosing them with Peruvian bark and waiting fearfully for the first telltale eruption that would spell out an answer to his doubts. The sun had already risen above the live oaks on the bank when he stumbled to his own lodge. Faith was tossing restlessly in her sleep, and he felt sure that she murmured his name as he parted the grass matting across the door. The pustule around each of the two wounds, he noted, was now larger than a good-sized pea. The adjacent skin was a deep, taut red for a circular area of some two inches, and the swelling was marked on the whole upper arm.

He touched her forehead gently, finding it hot and dry with fever. When he took his hand away, he saw that her eyes were open. Her lips shaped his name, but she did not smile.

"Did you have a good night, my dear?"

"I think so, John. But I have a headache—and I feel a bit chilly——"

Her tone was strangely light, the words slurred. John pretended to sort the contents of his medical kit, so that she would not see the fear in his eyes.

"So you've caught up with the others at last," he said. "I've been hoping for that."

"What does it mean? That I'll be feverish later?"

"Yes, Faith. It's what we've been waiting for."

"Couldn't it also mean I'm getting smallpox?"

He forced himself to look into her face as he spoke: lies would be wasted on Faith. "It could, of course. But there are others in camp with fever. And there's been no eruption so far, beyond the point of entry."

"How is Stella?"

The abruptness of the query startled him. "Stella's fever broke yesterday," he said. "She's up and around again. So are more than half the others."

"Then the treatment was a success, John."

"Not until you're well too."

"No doctor can win every case. You mustn't be too downcast if you've guessed wrong with me."

"You're going to get well," he said. "I'll see to that."

"Will it matter too much if I don't? You can still take these people to Talassee. Eventually, I suppose, you can marry Stella —if marriage is what she wants from you now."

He stared at her without speaking. There had been no accusation in her tone, and no hint of tears. Faith had merely stated a fact that admitted no argument. He felt that he could do no less than match her honesty, however he might bungle the effort.

"You asked me that same question in Natchez—remember?"

"Can you answer it today?"

Her voice was still dead calm, for all the lightness of her tongue. Knowing the depths of her feeling, he could draw but one conclusion: Faith Gordon was facing death this morning—and settling her account with life, while she held the adversary at bay.

"She wants me to go on to East Florida," he said. "To set up a practice there with Dr. Wright——"

"Will you go with them?"

"Would you hate me, if I did?"

"I've no right to hate you, John—when you've done so much for me."

"You must hate me a little," he said. "How can you help yourself? It's thanks to me you're here. I've let you risk your life to save mine——"

"Never mind that now," she whispered. "It was a—labor of love."

He sensed that her mind had already begun to spin down the long vortex to delirium. Taking her in his arms, rocking her there as he might rock a child, he knew there was little he could say to comfort her, though he made the effort.

"Do you think I'd let you die—after what you've done for me?"

"Some of us must die—on every journey." Her whisper was so faint he could hardly catch the words.

"Not on this one, Faith. We've a special providence that decrees otherwise."

"Don't ask too much of providence, John. It isn't fair." She seemed to be reasoning aloud now, as though she were only half conscious of his presence. "Some of us must die—that others may live. That's my last lesson. I can't teach you another——"

Stella, he remembered, had cried out for death as an escape from a dilemma she was powerless to solve. Faith, like a true philosopher, was accepting the fact of death, as the end product of all men's strivings. Not that she welcomed it; she would fight that ancient enemy to her last anguished breath. It was her resignation that moved him most of all. She would go beyond the brink—if she were indeed fated to make that journey—as bravely as she had lived.

"You're much too young to talk of death," he said. "I'll pull you through this business. Rely on that."

"Perhaps you will." Her eyes could tease him even now, clouded though they were with fever. "You've always had your way."

"Promise you won't stop fighting. This fever may be worse before it's better."

"I want to live, John. Have I ever stopped fighting—for what I want?"

"We're both in this battle," he said. "Don't think we'll lose it. We've come too far together."

"Much too far," she said drowsily. "Even if I had no right to intrude on the journey."

Her voice trailed off on that, though she cried out now and again, from the fog in which her mind wandered. All that morning, while she slept, he remained at her side—though he knew he was urgently needed elsewhere. She had saved his life more than once. Her resourcefulness and her example had kept these migrants on the trail. Had he repaid her devotion to them all by dooming her to extinction—or, perhaps, to a mutilation worse than death itself?

All through that day, and the one that followed, he carried that agonizing question in his mind, without daring to frame an answer. When twelve full days had passed since the fugitives' first exposure to smallpox, he risked recording his first faint hope of success in his casebook. Elsewhere in camp, most of the severe fevers had broken. Nor was there the faintest trace of rash, save at the point of inoculation.

On the dawn of the thirteenth day, Faith gave a great cry in her sleep, and half started from her brushwood bed. He took her in his arms to restrain her—and tears of joy blurred his eyes when he found that her body, like the others', was bathed in sweat. The worst of her delirium, he knew now, was behind her.

Fourteen days from the first exposure, he told himself with a kind of fierce pride, was the maximum for the development of smallpox. On the fourteenth morning, he noted that the pustules on his patients' arms, without exception, had begun to shrivel away. Fever was nonexistent in every lodge, and there was still no trace of rash. True, the whole cycle of preventive treatment had been unusual. But he was sure that his hundred-odd charges were out of danger.

Faith, who had suffered the most violent reaction, smiled up at him faintly as he bathed her one more time, wrapped her tired, blessedly unmarked body in a fresh blanket, and poured out her medicine.

"Sleep, my dear," he advised her. "Sleep the clock around, if you can. I've given you a double potion of laudanum."

"I—almost disgraced you, didn't I, John?"

"You couldn't if you tried."

"Suppose I'd died—and spoiled your record?"

"Don't mention that word again."

"Was I terribly sick?"

"You had a high fever. But it's gone now."

"I won't get smallpox?"

He laughed aloud, for the first time in weeks. "No, Faith. That's one thing we can be sure of."

Her hand closed on his, and her eyes searched his face anxiously. "Tell me one thing more. Was I—out of my head?"

"For a day or so."

"I can't remember what I said, John. Was it too foolish?"

He kissed her eyelids shut without speaking; though her head seemed clear enough today, she was not quite in command of her tongue. Still, he could understand this urge to think aloud, now that the dread weight of her sickness had lifted.

"Of course you'll never tell me," she said. "A doctor must have some secrets from his patient."

"I'll be honest," he told her. "You talked a great deal—but I couldn't understand a word."

As white lies go, he thought, *yours has a large grain of truth.* The Faith who had bowed her head to death, however briefly, was not the Faith he knew. That Faith would never surrender him willingly to Stella Wright—even on the edge of doom.

Talassee

Though he was positive his ex-patients were sound enough to travel, John held the cavalcade two precautionary days beside the Tascaloosa, while stores were replenished. It proved a lucky halt. On the second day, a trader rode into camp from upriver, with an eight-mule pack train and a store of gossip from the Creeks' Upper Towns.

The story Jeff Cowert told was vastly reassuring. There had been no smallpox along the higher reaches of the stream—and though Jeff himself was an avowed Whig, the Indians had been receptive enough. Rumors were afoot among the Creeks that the war on the Atlantic seaboard would soon be ending and they had been eager for the trader's report. The only real hostility he had encountered had come from certain sachems who suspected him to be an advance scout for invasion.

"You folks are safe here, if you're really King's men," Cowert assured them. "Specially if the doc's a friend of McGillivray's."

"Any idea of Colonel McGillivray's whereabouts at the moment?" asked John.

"He's generally at the Long House in Talassee until harvest-time," said Cowert. "And Talassee's only a few miles from the Hickory Ground. If you want my advice, gentlemen, I'd head straight for there, and ask his help."

"Would you care to guide us?"

So far, the talk with Cowert had been conducted at the river's edge, with Obadiah the only listener. Dr. Wright had been resting at the chief's hut, and John had his own reasons for keeping this part of their conversation secret. The trader's news about the war might be only unfounded rumor: he had no desire to depress the old doctor needlessly.

"You won't need a guide, Doc," said Cowert. "Once you clear the valley on the Tascaloosa, the Indian trail's plain as a road. You'll cross two little rivers, the Cabo and the Ampohla, but they'll make no trouble for you. With any push at all, you should be at the Koosah in ten days' time."

"We'd make it even sooner, with those pack mules," said Obadiah. "What's your idea of a fair price?"

In the end, after the usual amenities of barter, it developed that the peddler was glad to part with his mules for a reasonable sum—along with what trade goods remained in his packs. Convinced that the war's end was imminent, he intended to strike south to Mobile, to be on time for the jubilation.

At John's request, he had kept these reasons to himself when he was presented to Evan Wright, and the agreed-on sum paid out of the doctor's saddlebags. Even if Cowert's beliefs were verified, there would still be a water route open to East Florida and St. Augustine—and an asylum of sorts for the Wrights, during the inevitable *pourparlers* abroad that must precede a formal peace. These rumors from the outside world (to which the cavalcade had so long remained strangers) seemed unimportant indeed when measured against the fact that they could finish their march to Talassee without hardship.

Thanks to Cowert's mules, it was now possible to relieve some fifty human porters of the load of pelts they had transported intact from Natchez. The packs of trade goods (calicos, knives and gewgaws, for the most part, with a few packs of salt and a jug or two of mountain whiskey) were taken as added insurance, if the migrants should need proof of good intentions before reaching McGillivray.

Their rest beside the falls, the medical legerdemain that had preserved them from the scourge of smallpox, and this final stroke of good fortune were enough to send the fugitives on trail again in the best of spirits. Heading the marchers one more time, watching the cavalcade fall into position like a seasoned army that has survived most hazards of the field, John could cross his fingers in silent hope.

Luck (or was it the grace of the Almighty?) had brought them this far, without a single grave to mark their progress. Now that a hard-packed trail had opened beside the riverbank, now that they had food and mounts in plenty, it seemed that they would finish this wilderness march precisely as they had planned. Yet John did not unlatch his fingers until the last migrant had quitted the village beside the Tascaloosa. He could not let down his guard until he stood in the Long House at Talassee, face to face with the king of the Creeks.

2

Jeff Cowert had given them precise directions to the Hickory Ground, along with the opinion that they would arrive there at the time of the late summer powwow. As John had hoped, the Romans map he had used (which had proved so accurate during their long pilgrimage) confirmed the trader's estimates, almost to the mile. Nine days after they left the village, they stood on the banks of the Koosah—or the Alabahma, as it was also called on the chart—secure in the knowledge that the great council ground of the nation was only a short march to the northeast.

Another day was needed to build rafts to ferry the cavalcade across the Koosah. This time, the crossing was made without mishap; the river was broad and placid at this point, with gentle banks; the meadow on its eastern shore proved an adequate campsite. John ordered the tents raised at once, though hours of daylight remained. If Cowert's guess was accurate, and the Indians were assembled in force, he had no intention of bringing a hundred white marchers to the Hickory Ground without warning.

His map informed him that a large Creek town (called Tukabatchee) adjoined the actual place of powwow; McGillivray's own Long House at Talassee was only a few miles distant from the Hickory Ground. Common prudence dictated that he approach Tukabatchee openly, with Cowert's trade goods and a mule, and ask there for the Creek leader. Yulee would accompany him as interpreter; the campers, with Obadiah in charge, would await word beside the Koosah.

At the last moment, Faith insisted on joining him. Remembering her knowledge of Indians and their ways, John assented with only a token argument. He could not believe that his visit at Tukabatchee would be dangerous; even if it were, he knew it was a danger she wished to share.

"Shouldn't we invite the Wrights?" he asked.

"Maybe yes—logically," she agreed. "But there are times when Indians don't respond to logic. This might be one of them."

"Meaning, I take it, that there's no point in more than three of us getting scalped?"

"Precisely, John," she smiled. "If we must lose our hair, let's lose it together."

He found he could respond to her teasing mood, though he sensed the note of concern beneath. "Surely there's nothing hostile about us."

"A hundred strange whites, deep in Creek country—and war on all sides? Naturally, they'll be suspicious. More than ever, now their side is losing."

"The nation has remained practically neutral, Faith."

"No Indian is ever really neutral. Colonel McGillivray's sentiments are well known to his people; I'm sure they take his view. You'll have to convince them that we're Loyalist down to the last babe-in-arms."

It seemed like old times to follow another riverbank with Faith and Yulee—the former scouting the trail ahead, the latter marching beside him with her graceful, tireless stride. Once the forest had closed in on them, he could pretend that time had performed a neat back-somersault—and that they were foraging for supper beside the Mississippi, with the enigma of Natchez still ahead. . . . The enigma remained, he thought, though he had put Natchez itself behind him. But the solution was imminent now.

"Can you believe our troubles may be over tomorrow?" he asked.

Faith kept her eyes on the path. "For a veteran of the Trace," she said, "that remark hardly does you credit. We're still on the march. There are still rivers to cross, horses to purchase, Creek guides to engage, and peace pipes to smoke. In a word, Dr. Powers, you're still captain. Keep your mind on that."

"I'll accept the rebuke," he said, with the meekest grin he could manage. "But you needn't pretend to misunderstand me."

"I understand perfectly," she said, with her eyes still hard on the path. "If you must know, that's why I insisted on joining you today."

Ever since their battle with death in the village, and the quiet victory they had shared, he had felt no need to stress the future, so far as Faith was concerned. Whatever fate might bring at Talassee, he knew she would abide by the issue.

"It's like you to keep busy to the end," he said.

"Talassee isn't an end—only a beginning."

"For us both, my dear."

"Only for you," she corrected. "I've known who I am from the start."

"So you have, Faith. I envy you for that."

"At Trail's End, I'll admit, I tried to be someone I wasn't. Now I'm back where I belong. I wish I could say as much for you."

His mind returned to their argument in Natchez, when she had held up the mirror to his divided nature. He remembered that she had used almost the same words then, to drive home her point. He could see now why she had refused to remain in camp today. With a logic only women use, she had preferred to make this march—in the hope she could be with him to the end.

"Perhaps I'll never belong anywhere," he said. "Perhaps this whole journey—for me, at least—has been both a search and a flight."

"I told you as much in New Orleans," she said quietly.

"These others will make homes again, now *their* flight is ending. Even you are back where you belong——" He broke off, a little ashamed of his bluntness.

"At least I've come full circle," she said. "I can always go down the Koosah to Mobile, and return to the Perdido. Isn't that better than standing outside looking in?"

"Much better," he confessed.

"That's why you must take sides at Talassee, John."

"Curiously enough, McGillivray himself told me the same thing, the day I left Pensacola."

"Just before you met me." Faith smiled, a little crookedly. "I've led you a merry chase ever since."

"Don't think I haven't enjoyed it."

"If it hadn't been for me, you'd have escaped long ago. Instead, I made you stay—and lead these people to safety; but at least you've seen what men can endure, and still survive. Wasn't the lesson worthwhile?"

"Worth all that's gone before, Faith."

"I've learned my lesson too," she admitted. "Not that it's much comfort today. I learned it at the Tascaloosa, when I thought I was dying."

"That's behind us now, thank God."

"The lesson remained, John. I'll never try to change another person's destiny again—including yours."

"Thank you for that much, my dear."

"My wisdom's of the earth—so I'll survive," she told him gravely. "You must still learn to live with others, to choose your own world. The choice itself isn't important, so long as it comes from within you. Not even if it's East Florida and the Wrights."

He found he could accept her challenge quite calmly. "It's the first real home I've been offered," he said. "Can you deny that I've earned it?"

"Not for a moment, John."

"You could come to East Florida too, you know."

"Can't you see that would be impossible? Even if it weren't for Stella?"

"I can't see it too clearly, Faith."

"The Wrights are *English*. They'll be English till they die. I'm all Whig—as much as Obadiah or Yulee. Such differences haven't mattered on the trail. With God's help, we'll all learn to be friends again in time. But it's wiser if we separate now. There'll be too much bitterness left over—once this war is really lost."

So his choice would go deeper than self, deeper even than love. Incredible as it was, he had not yet dug to the roots of his being, to learn his real name—or the name of the nation that would have his ultimate loyalty. Again, he remembered Alexander Mc-Gillivray, and his solemn warning. No man could play the masquerader forever, with no allegiance outside himself.

"You've saved my life before, Faith," he said. "Can't you help me now?"

"Only you can choose, John," she said. "I don't really have to remind you of that."

She avoided his eyes thereafter, pretending a deep interest in the articles that filled her saddlebags, which hung beside his own on the pack mule. From time to time, Yulee came back to make his report: Indian sign, he told them, was everywhere. Twice he had watched hunting parties go by, but he had been careful not to advertise his presence. The fact that they were marching boldly down the path to the Hickory Ground, with no attempt at conceal-ment, should be evidence enough of their good intentions.

John heard these reports as from a great distance. Trudging beside Faith in stony silence, he fumbled in vain for the com-radeship that had just been so real. Instead, the loneliness that enveloped him now was deeper than any he had ever known. . . . A new nation, he told himself, had just held out a hand in friendship—and he had ignored the gesture. Could he have done otherwise as a King's man, and an ally of the Wrights?

One fact was constant, though, and he faced it grimly. Faith had spoken her last word today; she had taken his implied rejection with her usual courage. Try as he might, he could not avoid the conviction that his wilderness sojourn was ending. All roads seemed to lead to Florida now—and, eventually, to fulfillment with Stella Wright.

3

For the last lap of their march, the trail had turned northward, to skirt one of the many tributaries of the Koosah. Tukabatchee stood near that feeder stream—a typically Creek town, from its steep-roofed permanent lodges to the row of hothouses along the little river, where fires smoldered day and night for the purification rites of youths about to assume the warrior's scalp lock. Before each lodge, tall willow poles were tufted with white crane feathers to signify that the nation was at peace; a circle of red just below warned that each lodge was armed for instant retaliation, in event of war.

With something akin to shock, John saw that the women and children of the town had scuttled to the haven of their lodges as they caught sight of the newcomers' approach to the outer palisade. Only the men remained—seated cross-legged in their doorways, or waiting in tight groups on the wide council ground.

The Creeks (and he recalled this with a tardy flush of guilt) were still a primitive people, despite their adoption of many white customs. Far less tamed than such neighbors as the Cherokees, they were considered more amenable than the Choctaws; still, they retained many of the totems of their savage counterparts to the north, including a distrust of strangers that is a constant hallmark of the Indian. Intensely loyal to friends, they could be outrageously cruel to intruders they considered enemies. . . . Noting the scowls that followed them as they marched into the council ground, ignoring the prickles of fear in his scalp as he saw knives and hatchets flash in the sun, John could feel that his progress, so far, was no better than a living nightmare. And one part of that nightmare was the strange urge to shout to these impassive, savage faces that they came as friends.

As if he had been reading John's thoughts, Yulee spoke in a tight-lipped whisper. "First, we must walk to the council fire, *jefe*." Pipe and tobacco were already cupped in his hand, a gesture which John had duplicated. "We cannot speak sooner; we would seem lacking in courage."

"What if they try to stop us?"

"They will give us a path. Already, they have cut off our retreat."

What the half-breed had said was ominously true. By now, perhaps three hundred braves were assembled on all sides of the council ground, armed to the last man, and staring at the visitors without a murmur. It was as though the savages were daring the newcomers to dispute their right to mistrust strangers.

John smiled at Faith, and spoke in the same taut whisper. "Keep your eyes ahead. Yulee will explain who we are."

They had reached the council fire now, only to find themselves completely circled by near-naked bodies. So far, the braves had kept a fair distance, but their hostility seemed a tangible thing. Had a ring of steel been drawn about the hardpan clay on which they stood, John could not have felt more tightly penned.

Taking care to move slowly, he sat down tailor-fashion in a place of honor before the deeply banked fire. Yulee (as suited his role of sense-bearer) stood behind him with folded arms, and stared at the nearest of the Creeks with cold-lidded eyes. At a sign from John, Faith unstrapped the saddlebags on the pack mule, and spread a random sampling of their trade goods on a mat at John's feet—a few trinkets such as children prize, a gaudy string of wampum beads, a work knife from Jeff Cowert's special stores.

John weighed the knife on his palm, then tossed it into the air. The blade, making three lazy turns, landed point down in the soil at his feet. For the first time, a low ripple of interest went round the circle. With each breath he drew, John was certain that the ring was narrowing. At least the braves had permitted curiosity to conquer prudence, as heads craned over neighbors' shoulders for a better view.

"Tamp your pipe, Doctor," whispered the half-breed. "Mrs. Powers will light it."

John calmly blew a smoke ring in the windless air when Faith stepped back with the burning twig she had plucked from the fire. Though he continued to puff leisurely, there was no similar move among the braves. He could count calumets by the dozens in the scalp belts, but no hand moved to lift these primitive pipes to their owners' lips. Instead, the hands of those same owners remained firmly attached to musket and knife handle.

"Shall I speak first, Yulee?"

"Now is the time, Doctor. They show us no welcome."

"Tell them we come in peace, seeking our great and good friend Colonel McGillivray."

Yulee lifted his hand palm outward and spoke in measured tones. But the arms of the silently staring braves remained obstinately folded. A low murmur rose and subsided when he paused. In the ground swell of this hostility, a young subchief stepped forward and shouted a quick, incisive question.

"He asks why we come here. To settle or to trade?"

"To visit with his king, who is my friend. The trade goods in our packs are presents for his brothers and their squaws."

The young warrior came forward when this was translated. Still puffing tranquilly, John drew the knife from the ground, and offered it on his open palm. The Creek snatched the blade from his hand, examined it with minute care, then began an excited discussion with several of his fellows. As though taking this for a signal, the entire group drew closer about the fire—so close that the pack horse stirred restlessly. Faith gentled it with a practiced hand on the bridle.

As the talk among the braves grew more heated, Yulee translated swiftly. "They have seen other knives like this—forged in Virginia."

"Do they think we're Whigs?"

"So it seems, *jefe*."

"Explain that we bought these goods from a trader."

Yulee spoke at some length, as calmly as before. But the explanation was rejected before he could finish his harangue. This time, the young subchief capered as he spoke, a ritualistic, chest-arching measure that sent spurts of dust across the council fire. The frenetic, strutting patter was, as yet, only the outline of a full-dress war dance, though the pattern was unmistakable.

"He says you carry long-knives made in Virginia. You are a Virginian, and his enemy."

"Tell him we come from Natchez. We are travelers fleeing from the Spanish and loyal to the King."

The words brought another shout of disbelief. "He says we are Whig spies," Yulee translated. "Natchez is more than sixty sleeps away, on the Big River. No white men could march that far, in such numbers."

John felt his heart skip a beat. "Have they discovered the main group?"

Yulee nodded soberly. "They watched us cross the Koosah and make camp. But they held their hands, until we showed our intentions. Now they call us liars as well as spies. They will kill us all, unless we can prove otherwise."

From the Indian point of view, John reflected, this reasoning was entirely logical. Pressed on all sides by potential enemies, loyal to the English who had befriended them, the Creeks had no doubt been violently stirred by rumors from the seaboard— where the Whigs seemed about to score their final victory. Stories retailed by such travelers as Jeff Cowert had evidently been magnified; now, when a hundred armed men had marched into the region, they had naturally been labeled the vanguard of an invasion.

"They saw that we came from the west, if they scouted us," said John. "Surely that proves us fugitives from the Spanish."

Yulee translated rapidly. His face was impassive as ever as he listened to the shouted reply, but there was a new gleam of hope in his eyes when he faced John again.

"They ask that you make the paper talk, *jefe*—and prove we are what you say."

"Make the *paper* talk?"

"They think that we should have some record of our journey, if we have traveled from the Mississippi. A ledger or a journal, with writing in it."

Too late now, John realized the depths of his oversight. A methodical man as well as a just one, Alexander McGillivray had kept a daily history of the growth and doings of his people; all of West Florida knew it was his custom to read from this account by the hour, while the Creeks sat at his feet in the council ground. Evan Wright had kept his own diary of their migration, but there was no time to send for that precious, leather-bound volume.

While one part of John's mind worked with frantic haste, trying to devise some way out of this dilemma, another part noted that Faith had turned to the saddlebags and was opening the leather flap that closed one of them. He dared not hope that she had somehow found an answer, for he knew, with equal certainty, that there had been no paper in the stores they had purchased from Jeff Cowert. Rigidly, he controlled a start of surprise when he saw her lift a battered ledger from its depths. With hands extended palm upward, she offered him this travel-stained volume—her face expressionless, her eyes modestly lowered as befits a squaw.

"The talking paper," she said.

"What is it?"

"My travel diary. Tell them our story from the beginning. But *read* it, if you value your hair."

John opened the book—and kept down another start of surprise as he saw the pages were blank. Glancing cautiously above the half-open covers, he noted that the village had now turned out en masse, to the last toddling papoose, the last starveling dog. With a great effort he squared his shoulders and rose from the mat to his full height, pretending to pore over the journal as he did so.

Like a sigh from the earth itself, he felt the low, swelling murmur that rose from that coppery mass of bodies. The mood of the Creeks was hair-triggered: the fact that the squaws had appeared was ominous proof that Tukabatchee was prepared to make sport of three white captives. . . . And yet, for all their instinct toward cruelty, the braves of the Creek nation were just. If the white man could prove that his story was truth, this concerted hostility could change in a twinkling. Already, John could read doubt in more than one frowning visage: here and there, he could catch a current of low-voiced argument that seemed to run counter to the prevailing mistrust.

"Hear me, warriors and sachems," he said. "Is this an English voice, or a Whig's?"

He had spoken in his best barracks manner, clipping his words with a precision that would have graced an Oxford don. The question seemed to quiet the listeners. He guessed that many of these braves had had contact with the English in Pensacola. Enough, at any rate, to assure him of a hearing.

"Would an enemy come into your midst, with his rifle in his saddle, and his squaw beside him? Would he pitch his camp in the heart of your hunting ground—knowing that you could destroy him at will—if he did not come as your friend?"

This time, the crosscurrent of talk in the tight-packed circle threatened to drown his queries. John raised his hand in a plea for silence—and, when silence was not forthcoming, lifted his voice to a parade-ground bellow.

"Move back, men of the Creeks—that your visitor may draw breath! The talking paper will tell his story from the beginning."

He waited with lifted chin, looking hard at each subchief in turn until the Indians gave ground—enough to suggest the illusion of freedom. Turning the blank pages of the ledger slowly, he pretended to read with great deliberation as he began the story of their travels. He told it fairly, fully—but with no attempts at rhetoric. From the first words, he sensed that this tale could stand on its own merits, with no need of literary flourish.

His reading was a sonorous one, as usage demanded—and Yulee matched him word for word as he rolled out the translation. Yet not for a moment did John depart from the informal simplicity of the teller of tales before the campfire: instinct told him that his story would have a decisive impact if it was cast in a style his readers understood.

He remembered in time that Creek and Choctaw were in a state of armed truce, and held back no details of Red Shoes' treacherous attempt at massacre, or the steps he had taken to save the cavalcade. He spoke of the day-by-day sufferings during the long drive through canebrake and savanna—of the battle with forest fire in the ravine and of their near-disaster on the Tombigbee. Long before he had reached the episode of the Tascaloosa crossing, he could sense that his audience was intent on every word, wrapped in the tranced silence that is the raconteur's best tribute.

The battered ledger in his hands had become a symbol of his integrity; the ring of truth in his voice made the pattern complete. Like children at a storyteller's feet, the Creeks were reliving his account with all their senses. They, too, had fought fire and prairie drought; they had hunted and fished on swollen riverbanks, and tracked game in swamp and pine barren. No man who had not viewed this wilderness with his own eyes, or submitted his own body to its hardships, could have painted such a re-creation.

When John reached the point in his narrative that dealt with smallpox-haunted villages on the Tascaloosa, one of the subchiefs broke in excitedly. This time, even with his rudimentary knowledge of the language, John could see that the interruption was friendly.

"They know of the smallpox among the Upper Towns," said Yulee. "Those people wanted to join the powwow at Hickory Ground, but were driven off until the disease ran its course."

"Do they believe now that we come from the west?"

"So it seems. But you must tell our story to the end."

John turned the last page in the ledger. He spoke of his long friendship with Alexander McGillivray, of the rewards that Evan Wright was prepared to offer the Creek nation for horses and guides to Augusta. Stressing the fact that they were but peaceable transients, he ordered his sense-bearer and his squaw to spread the trade goods on the council mat as a payment on account. Daring to look up from the book at last, he saw that a dozen pipes were lighted in the circle now. Even the children, held high in their mothers' arms for a glimpse of the visitors, were crowing with joy as they caught the change in mood.

When he saw Charley Emathla shoulder his way into the crowd, John felt he could drop his guard. The arrival of McGillivray's own sense-bearer could not have been more opportune—for there were still grumblers in the circle. The silence that clamped down on the council ground, as Charley came forward to offer him a brother's armclasp, put the final seal of verity on his account.

Charley, he learned, had been sent for by special courier when John had first confronted the subchiefs. He accepted the sense-bearer's grandiloquent introduction with the proper aplomb; when these same subchiefs filed by the council fire to offer him a solemn handclasp, he accepted their welcome as his due. He could even afford to withdraw a little, and puff on a freshly prepared calabash, while Faith and Yulee distributed the trade goods. His recital had proclaimed him a chief—and Charley Emathla had endorsed the proclamation when he had announced that horses and an escort of sachems were already on the trail to escort him to Talassee. As befitted his rank, he would address the nation no more, until he stood beside the king himself.

There was still time for a whispered word with Faith, before John rode off to that long-awaited meeting. Tucking the empty ledger carefully from sight in the saddlebags, he covered her hand with his.

"You've saved me one more time," he said. "It seems I'll never even the score."

"*You* were the savior today," she said. "All I supplied was the shield you worked behind."

"You said it was your diary," he told her reproachfully. "Why are the pages empty?"

"I bought it in New Orleans," she said—and her lashes were still lowered like a model squaw's. "Somehow, I've been too busy to write a line."

"Will you write your own story later, Faith?"

"Perhaps, John. When I'm certain of the ending."

4

Alexander McGillivray, taking his ease on the platform of the Long House at Talassee, looked hard at John as the latter made yet another turn on that wattled eminence. Below them, a handsome stand of oak and yellow pine dropped by easy stages to yet another placid tributary of the Koosah: the grove had made a perfect shelter for the cavalcade's latest bivouac. Beyond, in a corral beside the stream itself, a score of red *vaqueros* worked busily to rope the last of the pack train that would transport the migrants to Augusta.

On each restless turn of the platform, John paused at its edge to stare down at these preparations. After a two days' rest at the Creek king's headquarters, the Natchez refugees were eager to be up and away. Now that the last cinch had been tightened, the last saddlebag loaded, it would be impossible to delay their departure beyond the morrow.

"For a man whose troubles are behind him," said McGillivray, "you seem troubled enough, Doctor."

"Just give me time, sir. I'll learn to sit and think again."

"Is it really so difficult to arrive at a decision?"

John pulled up sharp, with a contrite grin. "Your offer is most generous," he said. "I'd accept it, if I could."

McGillivray sighed. "I could have brought you here months ago, and made you an overnight success as doctor to my people. Now that you've worked your miracle on the Tascaloosa, your success has preceded you. Believe me, Dr. Powers, you could call yourself a rich man in a few years, if you'd cast your lot with us."

"I'm afraid I'm committed elsewhere, sir."

"Surely your wanderings are behind you."

"In Natchez, I agreed to help the Wright party reach Augusta. I must fulfill that promise."

"Only this morning, Dr. Wright told me that you'd discharged that bargain, ten times over. I've guides and outriders in plenty to take his people to the Savannah. You can rest here on your laurels."

John found that he could settle beside the other man now— though it was impossible to join in the Creek leader's wooden-idol repose. "I'll never thank you properly for the help you've given us——"

"Save your thanks. Dr. Wright has paid well for our help. It is I who should thank you for bringing us together."

"I'm glad you liked each other so well," said John. It was quite true that the Indian half-caste and the London aristocrat had turned out to be kindred spirits, though their origins were poles apart.

"Dr. Evan Wright is a person one cannot help but admire," said McGillivray. "Had your colonial governments been placed in such hands, the revolution would never have been fought."

"That sentiment I endorse," said John.

"Unfortunately, his is a brand of idealism that seems out of place today—like my own wish to keep a forest screen between my people and tomorrow. I'm afraid your mentor will soon be facing a rude awakening, Doctor." The Creek's eyes brushed John, with a gleam of urbanity strangely out of place in that mahogany-brown visage. "My days are numbered too, of course. Still, I look forward to a few years of kingship here. What does Dr. Wright expect to find—once Lord Cornwallis gives up at Yorktown?"

"For the present, he plans to settle in East Florida."

"St. Augustine may be a temporary asylum. But all Florida will go to Spain once the peace is official. The Wrights will face the same heartbreak that drove them out of Natchez."

"I'm sure they'll find a way to survive."

"Not in this country, Doctor. Others in their party will learn to accept the new regime. *They'll* have no choice but a second flight—to the Bahamas, Canada, or England. Will you continue to flee with them?"

So far, John reflected, McGillivray's words had been almost an echo of Faith's. "Your sachems will tell you I spoke like an Englishman, when I told the story of our journey."

"A man can assume strange disguises when his life's at stake," said the Creek king dryly. "Will yours sit as well in a year's time? Will you hang out your shingle in London—or take up your army career again?"

"Aren't you forgetting my court-martial?"

"On the contrary. I'm commending myself for voting your acquittal. Should you wish to claim it, your commission as surgeon captain awaits you in St. Augustine."

"If you're jesting, sir——"

"I was saving that bit of news, Dr. Powers. Only this morning, dispatches arrived here from East Florida—including your regimental gazette. It seems that young Innes left a confession after all—a letter to an uncle in London, admitting that he was an embezzler. The uncle happens to be a peer of the realm, with a permanent footing at the War Office; he insisted you be cleared at once. The mills of the army grind slowly—but they've ground out your innocence at last. You have only to report to Colonel Montfort to receive a handsome apology—and your epaulettes."

John continued to stare into space with a vast leaden weight on his brain. He had already heard that Montfort's troops had been allowed to march out of Pensacola with honor when the town surrendered—and that they were now billeted at the *castillo* in St. Augustine, along with other units of General Campbell's defeated forces. Try as he might, he could not even summon a token satisfaction at McGillivray's news. It was good to know his name was cleared; yet he had all the sensation of a man on the brink of some strange, new adventure, who has just heard a gate slam between him and freedom.

"What about Fanning?"

The Creek leader laughed. "I'm afraid there's no blot on *his* record; the court-martial dossier was merely destroyed as incompetent, being based on false evidence. And you'll have to travel quite a distance if you intend to challenge him; he put in for transfer some time ago. At this moment, he's en route to Bengal, to join the Indian Army."

It was John's turn to echo McGillivray's sardonic chuckle. Fanning was hardly a man to champion lost causes. He would never cool his heels on the outskirts of a war whose outcome was already conceded.

"Well, Doctor? Will you reconsider my offer? Or is it still East Florida, and another scarlet tunic?"

"In Natchez," said John, "my plan was to enter practice with Dr. Wright. I've as yet made no official change in that plan—even if it takes me eventually to London."

"By all means stay with the good doctor, if it's what you really want. You have my best wishes, no matter what you decide." McGillivray gave John a quick, shrewd glance. "But what of Mrs. Powers?"

John had braced himself for that question—knowing in advance that frankness was the only answer. "The lady is my wife in name only, sir."

The Creek leader nodded, unsmiling. "I suspected as much."

"Some time ago it was—necessary to protect her good name. I took it upon myself to offer that protection. The need no longer exists, so we'll go our separate ways."

"That seems fair enough."

"Dr. Wright has made a generous gift to each member of our

party. I'm adding my share to Faith's; she'll have more than enough to buy back her people's homestead on the Perdido."

"Have you already made this bequest?"

John could not quite meet McGillivray's eyes. "I'm afraid I've been too busy to—complete all the details. But Obadiah and Yulee are bound for New Orleans by canoe. They've promised to escort her to Mobile."

"May I ask when you arranged the lady's travel plans?"

"Yesterday. The moment the shares were given out."

"Apparently they have anticipated your instructions a little. An hour ago, they loaded their gear in two canoes and started downstream. By now, they should be on the Koosah."

"Yulee, Obadiah—and *Faith*?"

"It was she who paid Charley Emathla for the transport."

With no conscious sense of motion, John leaped from platform to ground. Just in time, he remembered that no man takes leave of a king without permission, and turned to offer McGillivray his best salute.

"I must look into this matter, sir. It seems that my orders have been disobeyed."

"I'm afraid you're correct in that assumption, Doctor."

"Will you excuse me while I set things right?"

"By all means," said the king of the Creeks. "I hope you aren't too late."

5

Only that morning, Faith's bedroll had stood beside his own in the canvas shelter they had shared between Natchez and Talassee; her poncho had hung with his on a tent peg, along with the slouch hat that had served her so well on that sun-wearied trail. There was just one sign of her presence this morning—the battered ledger that had saved their lives, lying face down on his blanket.

Even before he could snatch it up, John guessed that its pages would still be blank—though a note was thrust between the leaves like a bookmark.

I've persuaded Obadiah and Yulee to leave early. They'll take me as far as Mobile. I can find my way from there.

Forgive me for going like this. But I've never cared for good-byes.

F.

I'm leaving the book for a souvenir. God bless you.

At the Tascaloosa, he had told himself that Faith Gordon would never surrender. Today, she had left the field of battle without awaiting the final blow. As he sank down on the blanket and buried his face in his hands, he knew that even in farewell she had done her best to spare him.

He understood her clearly, now that he had lost her. From that night in New Orleans, she had considered herself his wife in fact as well as name; if their marriage had never reached completion, it had been his fault, not hers. Loving him, she had stayed at his side to the end. She had saved him from folly in Natchez, and from death on the trail. Now, when he had made his final choice, she had written her own bill of divorcement.

It seemed a long time later when he stepped into the open air again. To his surprise, he saw that it was only noon. He could not believe that the sun was in the zenith, and children happy in their games beside the river; it seemed unfair that life should flow on as before, now that Faith had left the camp.

The ledger was still in his hands when he turned toward the great council oak in search of Stella Wright. He found her alone in her tent, in the act of brushing her hair before a scrap of mirror. It was a ritual she had performed daily on the trail, no matter how wretched their campsite. For a moment, he paused just inside the tent flap, unwilling to announce his presence; as always, her beauty took his breath away.

Today she was wearing a sprigged muslin gown and a shawl to match. With the gloves and bonnet that awaited her on the traveling trunk, she might almost be dressed for a round of calls on the Natchez bluff. He remembered now that McGillivray had invited the Wrights and the Powers to dine with him—for a final discussion of traveling plans to Augusta. A king's invitation was not to be accepted lightly, even in the heart of the wilderness—certainly not by a fellow Loyalist.

Standing there in silence, watching Stella wind her hair into a coronet braid, he had an absurd feeling that he was reliving a scene from the past. So his mother might have looked, when he had come to her room as a boy, and watched her last-minute preparations before a *soirée* in Philadelphia. With a start, he realized that Martha Powers and Stella Wright were much alike. Here, once again, was the same blond beauty, the same near-regal manner—the same quiet certainty of purpose, no matter what the situation. Stella had seemed a Valkyrie on the trail, serene and unconquerable. Today, she was the epitome of all his yesterdays.

What was he doing here? The question answered itself as part of him continued to stand aside, to study the tall man in buckskins just inside the tent flap. It was true that he had always belonged to the world that Stella represented, the world to which she would return when the pack train left Talassee. But he had renounced that world in Natchez. His flight was ending at last—and the sundering was deeper than he knew.

Perhaps the break had begun long ago. Perhaps Captain Thaddeus Fanning's orderly had really booted him from the security of the past, on the parade ground at Pensacola. Or had he glimpsed the path to the future when he looked into a strange girl's eyes, behind a cocked pistol in Mobile? It made no difference now, and he could feel a vast sense of relief flood his soul at the thought. The silver cord that ties each man to his past was broken. He was free at last—with all the exciting things that freedom meant.

Stella turned quickly, and crossed the tent to take his hands in hers. He had the strange conviction that she had guessed his presence, and had been reluctant to acknowledge it.

"Evan is at the corral, with the *vaqueros.*"

"He should be resting, if he means to ride tomorrow."

"He insists he hasn't felt sounder in months, John. Could it be true?"

"Of course. Phthisis is a strange disease. Recovery, even in advanced cases, sometimes occurs rapidly and for no visible reason."

It was, he reflected, hardly the speech of a lover. A family physician, hoary with years and wisdom, could not have spoken more formally. For the first time, he realized that Stella's voice, like her manner, had been quite as coolly poised.

"Perhaps there's a reason, John," she said slowly—as though she were measuring each word.

"Can you name it?"

"Men will fight to the death for a woman they love. Could they fight disease as bravely?"

"What are you trying to tell me?"

Her eyes wavered at his directness, but only for a moment. When they met his again, her clear blue gaze had never been calmer.

"Do you remember that night beside the falls?"

"All too well. You weren't yourself then, Stella. No more was I."

"I prayed for death that night," she said. "For death and expiation."

"For a sin you hadn't committed—a wrong you'd never inflict."

"Even then, I desired you," she said quietly. "I wanted to die, if it meant losing our love. I begged you to be strong for us both. Do you remember that too?"

"Of course I remember. I gave you my promise, didn't I?"

"Will you fulfil that promise, John? Will you let me ride out of Talassee alone?"

He just escaped laughing aloud as he felt an invisible pressure loosen within his brain. There were no words to describe to Stella the decision that had crystallized as he stood beneath the tent flap. Now, thanks to her own decision, there was no need to make the effort.

"Is this your way of saying goodbye?" he asked.

"We said our goodbye, John. At the falls of the Tascaloosa."

"You're sure it's what you want?"

"No, John. It's *you* I want. I'll go on wanting you with my last breath. But I can call duty by its right name today, if you'll help me."

"I'll do my best, Stella——"

"You'll stay here tomorrow, then? Even if I change my mind —and beg you to join us?"

"We needn't take that risk," he said, with a rueful smile. "I'll go downriver now. The moment I've wished your husband Godspeed."

"This isn't goodbye," she told him softly. "We'll meet again."

"I think we're through deceiving each other," he said—and took her gently in his arms. The final kiss she gave him was both his reward and his absolution.

Ten minutes in the past, he would not have believed that he could walk from her presence, and all it stood for, without a backward glance. Now, following the riverbank to say his farewell to Evan Wright, he could feel his heart bound with each step. There would be times (how could he doubt it) when he would regret the memory of Stella Wright—and the fulfillment that had eluded them; no man's fortitude lasts forever. And yet, he had never felt more free since his boyhood—when he had first ventured into this same wild land, and found there the answer to his doubting.

6

Charley Emathla had given him the lightest canoe in Talassee, and he had paddled hard from noon to sunset. But the last light was fading on the Koosah when he picked out the two drifting specks on that tan-colored flood. He had no real assurance, even now, that he had not mistaken a pair of drifting logs for the dugouts he was seeking.

He identified them beyond question when the river widened at the next bend. The two canoes seemed to hug the western bank with no visible motion; the reason was soon apparent. The freight canoe (which contained the packs of the three *voyageurs*) was managed by Yulee, who braked constantly on his paddle to avoid ramming the lighter vessel that preceded him. Here sat Faith and Obadiah, the latter leaning on his blade no less firmly than the half-breed, the former huddled in the bow with her paddle across her knees and her head buried in her arms. Had he not known better, John would have sworn that she had fallen asleep, with no real desire to awaken.

Yulee gave him a silent salute when he came abreast and cut the painter joining the two dugouts; Obadiah offered a welcoming grin and steadied the meeting of the two craft, so gently that he was able to change places with John in a twinkling. There was no need for words as the lead dugout swam into the current unimpeded. No need to glance back to make sure that Yulee and the Kentuckian had dropped discreetly behind.

Faith lifted her head just before he spoke. Even before she could dip her paddle to match his own vigorous stroke, he knew she had been aware of the change of steersmen.

"Thanks for the map," he said. "And the timetable. I might have lost you without them."

"Obadiah thought you'd catch up by sundown," she told him. "Yulee was afraid you'd take a little longer."

"And when did *you* think I'd find you?"

Faith's paddle, already deep in the Koosah, raised an eddy iridescent with the sunset that filled the world. "Does it matter, if you've come home? If you've realized that Stella was forever England?"

"What are we, Faith?"

"Americans," she said. "I'll translate that tomorrow."

AUTHOR'S NOTE

I first found the amazing story of the Natchez refugees in Pickett's *History of Alabama,* a fascinating treasure chest of early Americana. That more than a hundred Loyalists—men, women and children, masters and slaves—should travel nearly five hundred miles to the haven of Colonel Alexander McGillivray's plantation at Talassee, traversing the territories of hostile Indians and ardent Revolutionists, enduring hunger, thirst, and the fury of raging streams without losing a single life, would have been startling enough in any story of adventure, were it not also completely true. But that their final fate should have hinged upon such a thing as the "talking paper" could only have been true from the start; no novelist would dare to invent such a fantastic happening to avert peril from his principal characters. It is no truism, but a law of the writing trade brought home more and more forcibly as I study history, that truth is, indeed, "stranger than fiction."

Frank G. Slaughter

KASAWS

CHEROKEE OR TENNESSEE

UPPER TOWNS

ARKANSAS R.

CREE

TOMBIGBEE R.

MISSISSIPPI RIVER

YAZOO R.

THE TRACE

TASCALOOSA R.

CHOCTAWS

Deserted Village

MIDDLE TOWNS

Cahaba

PEARL R.

Tumbiebe

KOOSAH R.

Fort
Panmure

Natchez

PLVS VLTRA

WEST FLORI

Mobile

Baton Rouge

Biloxi

Pensacola

Manchac

New Orleans

Belize

MILES
0   20   40   60   100

Gulf